# LINGUISTICS AND PSYCHOANALYSIS

This groundbreaking, provocative book presents an overview of research at the disciplinary intersection of psychoanalysis and linguistics.

Understanding that linguistic activity, to a great extent, takes place in unconscious cognition, Thomas Paul Bonfiglio systematically demonstrates how fundamental psychoanalytic mechanisms—such as displacement, condensation, overdetermination, and repetition—have been absent in the history of linguistic inquiry, and explains how these mechanisms can illuminate the understanding of the grammatical structure, evolution, acquisition, and processing of language. Reexamining popular misunderstandings of psychoanalysis along the way, Bonfiglio further proposes a new theoretical configuration of language and expertly sets the future agenda on this subject with new conceptual paradigms for research and teaching.

This will be an invaluable, fascinating resource for advanced students and scholars of theoretical and applied linguistics, the cognitive-behavioral sciences, metaphor studies, humor studies and play theory, anthropology, and beyond.

**Thomas Paul Bonfiglio** is Professor of Literature and Linguistics, William Judson Gaines Chair in Modern Foreign Languages, and Coordinator of the Linguistics program at the University of Richmond, USA. He has written a number of books, including *The Psychopathology of American Capitalism*; *Why is English Literature?: Language and Letters for the Twenty-First Century*; *Mother Tongues and Nations: The Invention of the Native Speaker*; and *Race and the Rise of Standard American*.

# LINGUISTICS AND PSYCHOANALYSIS

## A New Perspective on Language Processing and Evolution

*Thomas Paul Bonfiglio*

NEW YORK AND LONDON

Designed cover image: © Getty Images | heckepics

First published 2023
by Routledge
605 Third Avenue, New York, NY 10158

and by Routledge
4 Park Square, Milton Park, Abingdon, Oxon, OX14 4RN

*Routledge is an imprint of the Taylor & Francis Group, an informa business*

© 2023 Thomas Paul Bonfiglio

The right of Thomas Paul Bonfiglio to be identified as author of this work has been asserted in accordance with sections 77 and 78 of the Copyright, Designs and Patents Act 1988.

All rights reserved. No part of this book may be reprinted or reproduced or utilised in any form or by any electronic, mechanical, or other means, now known or hereafter invented, including photocopying and recording, or in any information storage or retrieval system, without permission in writing from the publishers.

*Trademark notice*: Product or corporate names may be trademarks or registered trademarks, and are used only for identification and explanation without intent to infringe.

*Library of Congress Cataloging-in-Publication Data*
Names: Bonfiglio, Thomas Paul, 1948- author.
Title: Linguistics and psychoanalysis : a new perspective on language processing and evolution / Thomas Paul Bonfiglio.
Description: New York, NY : Routledge, 2023. | Includes bibliographical references and index. |
Identifiers: LCCN 2022044049 (print) | LCCN 2022044050 (ebook) | ISBN 9781032018188 (hardback) | ISBN 9781032018171 (paperback) | ISBN 9781003180197 (ebook)
Subjects: LCSH: Psycholinguistics. | Psychoanalysis.
Classification: LCC P37 .B66 2023 (print) | LCC P37 (ebook) | DDC 401/.9—dc23/eng/20220917
LC record available at https://lccn.loc.gov/2022044049
LC ebook record available at https://lccn.loc.gov/2022044050

ISBN: 978-1-032-01818-8 (hbk)
ISBN: 978-1-032-01817-1 (pbk)
ISBN: 978-1-003-18019-7 (ebk)

DOI: 10.4324/9781003180197

Typeset in Bembo
by codeMantra

# CONTENTS

*Acknowledgments*   vii

   Introduction: Toward a new transformational model of language   1

1  The contributions of Michel Bréal and Julia Kristeva to a psychoanalytic science of language   9

2  Recursion and metacognition   21

3  The psychoanalytic linguistics of Jean Piaget   40

4  Dreamwork: The precognitive formation of language   52

5  Speech errors and humor: *In principio non erat verbum*   68

6  Language, consciousness, and identity   92

7  Neuro-psychoanalysis   108

8  Language and mimesis   126

9  Language and mirror neurons   136

10  What is grammar?   147

11  The evolution of language in a psychoanalytic perspective    161

12  Metaphor and psychoanalysis    174

13  Psychoanalysis and linguistic relativity    188

　　Conclusion    197

*Glossary of relevant psychoanalytic terms*    209
*Index*    213

# ACKNOWLEDGMENTS

The research for this project was supported by a sabbatical leave from the University of Richmond and greatly facilitated by the generous services of the Boatwright Interlibrary Loan Department. I am also grateful to the Bibliothèque nationale de France, the Columbia University Library, and the New York Public Library for the use of their collections.

# INTRODUCTION

## Toward a new transformational model of language

### Theoretical outline

The postwar American quantitative/empirical turn in the social sciences largely marginalized psychoanalytic theory from the field of linguistic research. This study demonstrates the value of psychoanalysis for the science of language. It shows how psychoanalysis can illuminate the evolution, acquisition, and processing of language—especially as concerns the transition from ideation to spoken language—and reveals the primacy of parapraxes (speech errors) in that transition. It shows how the master mechanisms of psychoanalytic theory—displacement, condensation, overdetermination, secondary revision, inversion, repression, projection, and parapraxes—can illuminate the development of language and its cognitive aspects in its phonetic, morphological, syntactic, and semantic manifestations (among others), as well as the critical period for language acquisition.

Psychoanalysis is largely misunderstood in American scholarship, and in the popular sphere, as well. And for this study, there is one fundamental aspect of psychoanalysis that is little known: that it presents a linguistic configuration of consciousness and the unconscious, especially as concerns the transition from the latter to the former. For Freud, becoming conscious involves putting thought impressions into language; indeed, consciousness itself is constituted in and through language; we are fully conscious of something when we speak of it. Most of our mental functioning, however, takes place on either an unconscious or preconscious level, and these levels are transitional—there is no clear distinction among them. So it is with the evolution and processing of language—it is transitional and transformational.

## 2  Introduction

One of the most influential works by Freud is *Die Traumdeutung* (1900) (*The Interpretation of Dreams*), which he considered to be his most important work. It has had wide-ranging influence in hermeneutics and semiotics in general. The work is arguably most foundational for the development of his theories. It explains the generation and interpretation of images in dreams, especially as these relate to their mediation in and through language. The structure informing dream generation and interpretation is fundamentally transformational—there is a transition from infrastructure to superstructure, which Freud characterizes as one from the latent to the manifest. This is fundamentally a transformation from unconscious to conscious processes upon a fluid continuum with no sharp boundaries. At the conscious end of the process lies the interpretation of the dream itself, where the subject attempts to understand the dream and to describe it. At the other end lie the unconscious processes that construct the dream and slowly progress along the continuum of unconscious–preconscious–conscious processes (Freud, 1923). And the preconscious, a transitory state between the unconscious and the conscious, is where language becomes first formulated.

The transformations along the continuum of unconscious–preconscious–conscious are presented as "the same subject matter in two different languages" (Freud, 1900, p. 311). The transformation is one of words and images into rebuses (picture puzzles), much as one sees in children's games, where, e.g., the image of an eye stands for the first-person pronoun "I". The transformations take place in a multivalent interconnectivity of word and image and are constructed by two master mechanisms: condensation (*Verdichtung*) and displacement (*Verschiebung*), which correspond to the mechanisms of metaphor and metonymy, respectively. Images and words in dreams undergo considerable combination and compression into nodal points that allude to the structure as a whole. At the same time, the dream becomes differently centered—displaced into another narrative. It will be shown in the course of this study that these mechanisms—condensation (metaphor) and displacement (metonymy)—constitute the foundation of language and thought. Freud emphasizes, however, that "we are dealing with an unconscious process of thought, which may easily be different from what we perceive during purposive reflection accompanied by consciousness" (315).

Roman Jakobson emphasized the polarity and tension between the metaphoric and the metonymic, between the symbolic and the contiguous. Referring to Freud's theories, he saw symbolism as metaphoric, and displacement and condensation as metonymic:

> A competition between both devices, metonymic and metaphoric, is manifest in any symbolic process, either intrapersonal or social, thus in an inquiry into the structure of dreams, the decisive question is whether

the symbols and the temporal sequences used are based on contiguity (Freud's metonymic 'displacement' and synecdochic 'condensation') or on similarity (Freud's 'identification and symbolism').

*(Jakobson & Halle, 1956, pp. 80–81)*

And on discussing aphasia, he held that "metaphor is alien to the similarity disorder, and metonymy to the contiguity disorder" (76). He notes:

From the two polar figures of speech, metaphor and metonymy, the latter, based on contiguity, is widely employed by aphasics whose selective capacities have been affected. Fork is substituted for knife, table for lamp, smoke for pipe, eat for toaster…phrases like 'knife and fork', 'table lamp', 'to smoke a pipe', induced the metonymies.

*(69)*

It should be noted that such substitutions, in their non-pathological form, are common in adult speech, thus demonstrating an intrusion of unconscious precognitive structures into adult language.

These observations by Jakobson tie together many fundamental questions pertaining to the phenomenon of language and its relation to psychoanalytic theory, especially dream theory. Research on these interconnections became gradually sidelined in the decades since Jakobson outlined them. This study will explain and revisit these interconnections.

Language is generated unconsciously—we know that. And its final formulation in structured conscious articulation occurs at the end of a gradual transition that begins in unconscious processes. It is important to emphasize that consciousness itself is a transitory phenomenon. In *Das Ich und das Es* (1923) (*The Ego and the Id*), Freud held that

being conscious is in the first place a purely descriptive term connected to the most immediate and most certain perceptions. Experience shows us that a psychical element—a representation (*Vorstellung*), for example—, is not, in normal circumstances, continuously conscious. A major characteristic of the state of consciousness is that it passes quickly. The now conscious representation is not there a moment later.

*(Freud, 1923, pp. 3–4)*

Thus it is with language. We start developing language at an infantile state, in which we are as yet conscious of very little.

This model of the psyche is non-modular. This study does not see the unfolding of language as an automatic assembly of discrete entities hierarchically arranged, nor as a sequence of algorithms. It is not at all unconscious in that sense. It is a collage of interconnected multivalent processes. And most importantly, the generation of language is never separate from the psychological moment.

In his investigation of the two principles of mental functioning, Freud said,

> Thinking was probably unconscious in origin, which is to say that it went beyond mere representation, became directed to the relations between impressions of objects, and acquired further qualities perceptible to consciousness only when it became connected to verbal residues.
>
> *(Freud, 1911, pp. 233–234)*

Thus consciousness rests upon the recall of linguistic elements. It is important to note that the notion of a relation between impressions of objects and verbal residues is structurally similar to Saussure's view of the relation between a concept and a sound image, and not between the word and the thing in itself. Freud, however, takes this several steps further in relating it to the emergence of conscious awareness.

Wilson and Weinstein revisit the work of Lev Vygotsky (1896–1934) in their article "Language, Thought, and Interiorization. A Vygotskian and Psychoanalytic Perspective". They observe that, for Vygotsky, "thought is not expressed but completed in the word…before a thought can reach its fully formulated state, a person must go back and forth between thought and word searching for the proper articulation" (Wilson & Weinstein, 1992, p. 26). And in this process, the utterance traverses networks of associations on its way to expression. The authors claim that this goes on "outside of awareness" (26). The sense of a word "is the aggregate of all the psychological facts emerging in our consciousness because of this word. Therefore, the sense of a word always turns out to be a dynamic, flowing, complex formation which has several zones of differential stability" (31). Language is thus processed here in a multivalent way via chains of associations. This can be compared with Freud's placement of language processing along the continuum from the unconscious to consciousness as linguistic. The authors note that Vygotsky also surpassed the old binary distinction of thought vs. language, which got stuck in a chicken or egg debate, when he proposed that "meaning is created by the unification of speech and thought" (28).

The authors also observe that for Freud, when the word gets attached to a visual representation of an object, this constitutes the transition from the unconscious to consciousness, and that the separation of the representation of the word from its object is what constitutes repression and the resultant neurosis. In other words, consciousness is eclipsed by the corresponding repression of language.

Unconscious processes are illogical, contradictory, and often absurd, but they, nonetheless, constitute the bulk of mental activity. The mechanisms of displacement and condensation are subject to repetition and overdetermination, a term that Freud used to describe their interrelations with diverse mental functions. This derives from his profession as a neurologist and his view of the plasticity of the brain. This study will demonstrate the presence of displacement, condensation, and overdetermination in linguistic and cognitive processes.

The unconscious is a collection of things that are not part of consciousness. They are repressed, blotted out, and excluded by the defense mechanisms of denial, displacement, inversion, projection, transference, and so on. But the repressed eventually passes into wakefulness; this causes us to slip, to blunder, to misspeak, to misperceive: These are the famous "Freudian slips". They also appear in jokes, which often pretend to be innocent. The repressed is always present in varying degrees of partial and often total eclipse, but there nonetheless, and its emergence into observable behavior is determined by psychoanalytic mechanisms (condensation, displacement, overdetermination, etc.).

It is common knowledge that evolutionary theory has met with much public resistance in the United States. In *Ever Since Darwin*, Steven J. Gould asks, "Why has Darwin been so hard to grasp"?, to which he adds: "The basis of natural selection is simplicity itself". He summarizes:

> Organisms vary, and these variations are inherited (at least in part) by their offspring.
>
> Organisms produce far more offspring than can possibly survive.
>
> On average, offspring that vary most strongly in directions favored by the environment will survive and propagate. Favorable variation will therefor accumulate in populations by natural selection.
>
> *(Gould, 1977, p. 11)*

Perhaps the resistance to Darwin may lie in the fact that he insisted that humans are animals.

One may ask a similar question of Freud. He invokes Darwin as the greatest single influence on the development of his theories, and he also views humans as animals. Repressed animals. It is also common knowledge that Freudian theory has met with much resistance in the United States, as well. Why do his theories continually meet with denial? His view is also quite simple:

- humans are animals
- animals do not repress their instincts
- humans need to repress their instincts in order to construct civilization
- this repression causes the instincts to become expressed in deformed modes of behavior

Language is the articulation of those repressions. In *Early Social Interaction*, Michael Forrester holds that "when you learn how to talk, you learn how to repress" (Forrester, 2015, p. 65).

Freud's theories have received their widest reception in English translations that were done in the first half of the twentieth century. As such, the translations are frequently antiquated. They have also been occasionally altered in the transition into the grammar of English. One major example concerns the English phrase "the unconscious", which gives an erroneous impression of a location or container. This misprision is explained in Chapter 7. For the sake of more current and accurate versions, all translations from French, German, Italian, and Latin are my own.

## Chapter summaries

Chapter 1 studies the contributions of Michel Bréal in his *Essaie de sémantique* (1897). A contemporary of Freud, Bréal offers what could have contributed to a psychoanalytic science of language, one that configures language in opposition to a system of formal logic. It also studies the views of Julia Kristeva on the possibilities of combining psychoanalysis and the linguistic science of the second half of the twentieth century.

Chapter 2 examines the concept of recursion as formulated by the theory of universal grammar. It shows how recursion, and the related concept of merge, are insufficient models for an understanding of language; recursive reflection is limited to four or maximum five levels of embedding in the acquisition, production, and processing of speech. The chapter also demonstrates that recursion and metacognition are homologous constructs.

Chapter 3 studies the work of the Swiss linguist Jean Piaget and his understanding of language development in children. It shows the similarity between Piaget's stages of language development, especially as these concern the transition from the preoperational to the fully operational, and Freud's model of the progression from unconscious, to preconscious, to conscious instantiations of language. It is demonstrated that these transitions are fluid and not clearly demarcated, and that earlier precognitive modes remain present in adult language and thought.

Chapter 4 studies the mechanisms of dreamwork—the construction of dreams—and how these mechanisms can account for the emergence of language, consciousness, and cognition. It continues the discussion of precognitive and preoperational modes in the development of the child's conception of language and thought and relates these to the mechanisms of dreamwork, as these are present in adult narration of dreams.

Chapter 5 studies adult speech errors and shows how these are constructed by the mechanisms of dreamwork. It also studies parapraxes in general—bungled actions—in this context. It shows, as well, the structural similarities between speech errors and wit/humor along the sequence conscious—preconscious—consciousness.

Chapter 6 situates the production of language within the dynamics of ego formation, i.e., of the articulation of identity. It is demonstrated that speech is co-articulated by images of self, especially in the context of self vs. other, and that this co-articulation functions in the transition from preconscious to consciousness.

Chapter 7 examines the tripartite structure of language, consciousness, and identity formation within current research on neuro-psychoanalysis. It shows how the primacy of the auditory function is more involved in the development of self-consciousness than is the visual function, and that self-consciousness develops in dialog with the vocalizations of authority and prestige figures. It also describes the emergence of syntax from the psychoanalytic process of secondary revision, and the emergence of lexica from visual, auditory, kinesthetic, and motor networks.

Chapter 8 discusses language and gestural mimesis as a symbiotic unity, and as the original point for the symbolic function. Here, self/nonself mirroring and role-reversal imitation are seen as the original point for meta-discourse. The chapter argues for a human mimetic instinct, not a language instinct. In the embodiment of gesturing in language and cognition, it is shown how gesturing is continually present, even in displaced form, i.e., from one part of the body to another. The phenomenon of conversion disorder is discussed in this context.

Chapter 9 discusses the mimetic role of mirror neurons in the embodiment of the matrix of language and thought. The subjects studied include vowel production, facial expression, the bodily self, the activation of muscle stimulation in the processes of reading and listening, the involvement of basal ganglia in the processing of syntax in a distributed (non-modular) rather than hierarchical system, and the activation of corresponding neural circuits in the brain when thinking of concepts associated with a word.

Chapter 10 discusses the theories of universal grammar, merge, and the minimalist program as improbable models for explaining the production and processing of language. It offers instead a psychoanalytic perspective in combination with current theories of cognitive grammar. Language emerges in a continual and preconscious processing via perceptions, anticipations, and perseverations involving condensation, displacement, repetition, and overdetermination. It is argued that syntax is a product of repetition and, ergo, habit.

Chapter 11 places elements of the evolution of language in a psychoanalytic perspective. It posits the development of intonation and gesture as the initial point for language and demonstrates correspondences with the psychoanalytic account of verbal parapraxes. It revisits the theories of the primal horde put forth by Darwin and Freud and coordinates these with research in linguistic anthropology that places the origin of syntax within primate male bonding and reciprocal altruism in resistance to single male dominance.

Chapter 12 places the work of Lakoff and Johnson (1980) within a psychoanalytic account of language and makes use of their notion of the cognitive unconscious. It shows how condensation and displacement function as ubiquitous cognitive and linguistic modes of apprehension. It includes research on embodied cognition to show how thought and language become manifested in metaphors that extend from the body, and how these aid in the consolidation of identity.

Chapter 13 introduces psychoanalytic perspectives into the discourse on linguistic relativity. It examines how words shift meaning in acts of displacement and condensation that perform the defense mechanisms of repression, sublimation, inversion, and denial. It is argued that a linguistic relativizing of the semantic shifts is strongly resisted, because it problematizes the configuration of national identity. The semantic shifts act to restrict meaning and cognition.

The glossary following the conclusion contains working definitions of the key terms: condensation, displacement, overdetermination, dreamwork, libido, id, ego, superego, repetition compulsion, unconscious, preconscious, repression, primary process, secondary process, secondary revision, parapraxis, projection, conversion disorder, and transference.

## References

Forrester, M. (2015). *Early social interaction.* Cambridge University Press.
Freud, S. (1900). *Die Traumdeutung. Gesammelte Werke* (Vols. 2–3, pp. 1–724). Imago. [English edition: Freud, S. (1953–1974). *The interpretation of dreams. The standard edition of the complete psychological works of Sigmund Freud* (Vols. 4–5, pp. 9–686). Hogarth].
Freud, S. (1911). *Formulierungen über die zwei Prinzipien des psychischen Geschehens. Gesammelte Werke* (Vol. 8, pp. 230–238). Imago. [English edition: Freud, S. (1953–1974). *Formulations on the two principles of mental functioning. The standard edition of the complete psychological works of Sigmund Freud* (Vol. 12, pp. 218–226). Hogarth].
Freud, S. (1923). *Das Ich und das Es. Gesammelte Werke* (Vol. 13, pp. 235–289) Imago. [English edition: Freud, S. (1953–1974). *The ego and the id. The standard edition of the complete psychological works of Sigmund Freud* (Vol. 19, pp. 1–66). Hogarth].
Gould, S. (1977). *Ever since Darwin.* W. W. Norton.
Jakobson, R. & Halle, M. (1956). *Fundamentals of language.* De Gruyter.
Lakoff, G. & Johnson, M. (1980). *Metaphors we live by.* University of Chicago Press.
Wilson, A., & Weinstein, L. (1992). Language and the psychoanalytic process: Psychoanalysis and Vygotskian psychology. II. *Journal of the American Psychoanalytic Association 40*(3), 725–759.

# 1
# THE CONTRIBUTIONS OF MICHEL BRÉAL AND JULIA KRISTEVA TO A PSYCHOANALYTIC SCIENCE OF LANGUAGE

Linguistics as we know it—as the scientific study of language—begins with the European philologists of the nineteenth century and was largely motivated by the encounter with Sanskrit during the British colonization of India. At that time, philology (literally, the "love of the word") did not separate the study of language from the study of its instantiations. The major nineteenth-century philologists, such as Wilhelm von Humboldt (1767–1835), considered to be one of the founders of modern linguistic science, viewed language as *the* central human science, inseparable from culture and thought.

The status of philology as one of the premier sciences of the nineteenth century was quite strongly stated by Humboldt. He held that "the study of the languages of the earth is thus the world history of the thoughts and sensations of humankind. It represents humankind in all aspects and all stages of its culture" (*unter allen Zonen und in allen Stufen seiner Kultur*) (Humboldt, 1908, pp. 602–603). Language came to be viewed as epistemology itself. The idea that ideas could be separated from language would have seemed quite strange to the philologists of that era. The term "philology" gradually gave way to the term "linguistics" as the science of language.

Walter Rüegg notes that nineteenth-century philology included subjects "from the philosophy of language, hermeneutics, and criticism to geography, history, chronology, numismatics, and archaeology" (Rüegg, 2004, p. 422). This contrasts sharply with the insular turn taken by the science of language in the second half of the twentieth century, especially in the United States, when it attempted to transform itself into an autonomous discipline. Since then, the science of language, especially in the field of cognitive linguistics, has been rediscovering its interdisciplinarity.

DOI: 10.4324/9781003180197-2

Strongly influence by Darwin and the nascent evolutionary science of the nineteenth century, philologists came to see language as an organic entity that "unfolded" into a superstructural expression generated by an infrastructural nuclear form, as in a plant emerging from a seed (Bonfiglio, 2010). John Forrester, in *Language and the Origins of Psychoanalysis*, observes: "The idea of laws that act forever below the surface of what is spoken, determining what can be spoken without recourse to what can be represented, was the goal of the new philologists" (Forrester, 1980, p. 169). This would be proto-Indo-European producing "branches", e.g., Italic, Germanic, Celtic, etc., via regular sound shifts, in a transformation from infrastructure to superstructure. He sees this as the source of the transformational dynamic of unconscious → preconscious → conscious: "The activity of the unconscious would seem to have been borrowed as much from the creative and archaic activity of language as from a conception of biological forces overflowing in to the psyche" (179). This is interesting, as Freud was a contemporary of the new philologists.

The nineteenth-century philologists situated language firmly within the field of epistemology and of human cognition, but there is a very important aspect of their understanding of language that has become less and less visible over time. They configured language in a framework that was fundamentally psychoanalytic: Language is generated by myriad parapraxes that ignore the principles and categories of formal logic. One of the major contributors to this understanding of language was Michel Bréal (1832–1915), who was a professor of comparative grammar at the École pratique des hautes études and at the Collège de France from 1866 to 1905. He is considered to be one of the founders of the study of semiotics. Ferdinand de Saussure was one of his students.

His most recognized work is *Essaie de sémantique*, first published in 1897. Bréal views language not as a system of formal logic, but, on the contrary, as a system that resists logical categorization, one where overdetermination rules. He notes, for instance, that the same term can be employed variously in a literal or metaphoric sense, a restricted or extended one, or a concrete or abstract one (Bréal, 2005, p. 111). Terms can carry contradictory meanings that do not bother the speaker at all. We do not even need to repress different, even contradictory meanings of the same word when we employ it. It is possible for the other meanings not to even enter into consciousness (112). A good example is the English "hull", which can mean "to cover something in a hull", but also "to remove the hull from it". What is true of the speaker is equally true of the listener, who "speaks internally at the same time we do", and who "is no more inclined than we are to be troubled by allied meanings (*des significations collatérales*) that sleep at the most profound levels of the mind" (112–113). In addition, terms that are orthographically identical can appear to be different, as long as the meanings are distant enough. Bréal notes as an example a rhyme from Corneille using the word *point*.

Les accommodements ne font rien en ce point
Les affronts à l'honneur ne se réparent point.

*(113)*

Accommodations do nothing at this point
Affronts to honor do not mend themselves at all.

The French term *point* means the same as the English "point", but when combined with the negative particle *ne*, as in *ne...point*, as used in the strings cited here, it means "not at all". Here, we have an example of semantics overriding phonetics and orthography. Bréal also has an interesting discussion of the semantic drift of the Latin *matures*, an adjective meaning "morning". *Lux matura* meant "early light", i.e., "daybreak". *Aetas matura* meant "adolescence" ("early age"). When applied to products of nature, it took on the meaning "to ripen", and thus to indicate an advanced state or age. This yielded *maturum consilium*, "a mature plan/project". Thus, opposite meanings of early and late exist in the same word in different contexts (114–115). Why is the mind not troubled by this? He adds an observation that, as we will see subsequently, fits well into the psychoanalytic paradigm: "The dictionary that juxtaposes the two meanings could lend credence to the opinion held by a scholar only a few years ago that language began by an identity of opposites" (115). (Bréal does not identify this scholar.) This corresponds to the psychoanalytic observation that negation arose from an identity.

Bréal holds that the word, in its isolated state, "does not exist very clearly in popular understanding (*dans la conscience populaire*)...it can meld with that which precedes it or follows it" (128). He offers as an example the semantic difficulties in the telegraph communications of his era, where the recording of words one by one, and in a minimal context, caused interpretive difficulties.

One of the key misprisions that determine language change and, indeed, the structure of language itself, is a phenomenon referred to as *cum hoc ergo proper hoc*, Latin for "with this, therefore because of this". It describes the tendency to misinterpret correlation as causality. Words that do not stand in immediate rapport with the rest of the phrase can progressively take on an adverbial function and then appear to alter the phrase itself (135). In consequence, they can then turn into prepositions. This is what happened with the Latin adverbs *ab, ex, in, ad*: they were adverbs of place, used to modify a word in the ablative or accusative case. Eventually, they were misperceived as causing the change in case itself and consequently took on prepositional value, moving, in popular misprision, from accompaniment to causality. Another instance can be found in the Latin *cum*, which originated as an adverbial suffix of manner, e.g., *vobiscum* ("with you"). The misattribution of causality detached *cum* from its accompanied pronoun and generated *cum vobis, cum nobis* ("with us"), etc.; thus meaning became highjacked by prepositions.

This is language in the service of the psyche, a psyche that is predisposed to view correlation as causality, which is an action anathema to the principles of science. A similar misprision causes sequentiality to be misperceived as causality. The term for this is *post hoc ergo propter hoc*, or "after this, therefore because of this". If event B follows event A, it must have been caused by event A.

He notes a similar misprision with the German use of the proto-Germanic *\*hwilo*, which has rendered the English "while" and the German *Weile* "while", and *weil* "because". In German, the initial idea of time changed into one of causality, i.e., "while you did this" became "because you did this". He notes a similar process with the Latin *quoniam*, which moved from expressing simultaneity to expressing causality (138). For Bréal, misprisions override lexical categories: language is "a work superior to human reason" (*une œuvre supérieure à la raison humaine* (137)).

He also posits that intransitive verbs are also primordial; transitives would have come later. One can readily imagine prehistoric humans expressing action in and of itself, before the entry into syntax (140). Certain initial intransitives came to be used with words that properly accompanied the action of the verb, as linguistic accessories in the same semantic field. The association between word and accompaniment became, in time, habitual, and perceived as obligatory, in the same manner as the evolution of prepositions from adverbs. Eventually, the accompanying element came to be seen as a causal result of the action of the verb, and thus a causative relation was born between verb and complement. He sees this as an example of our intelligence attributing sense to words that was only the product of our own habits (141). One result of this was that the value of case endings weakened (*la valeur significative des désinences casuelles a été affaiblie* (141)). This can account for the general analytic tendency in Indo-European languages, especially in English, which now has but a few pronouns inflected for case.

Another result was that the verb began to appear incomplete without its accompaniment, much as in the inverse of the way in which the verb "to disappoint" has recently acquired intransitivity. A film, for example, can "disappoint". Some decades ago, such a usage would have been marked as incorrect by an English teacher, who would have insisted that the verb take a direct object. The film must disappoint *someone*.

He also sees the primacy of the pronoun. It precedes the noun, "because it requires less invention, because it is more instinctive, more easily commented on by gesture...pronouns are...the oldest part of language. How would the self (*le moi*) ever have lacked an expression for designating itself"? And he also holds that "it is probably via the pronoun, having differentiated itself from other kinds of words, that grammatical categories began" (139). Thus, grammatical categories begin in the separation of self from non-self.

Another very important suggestion made by Bréal concerns the origin of the relative pronoun, clearly one of the pillars of the theory of universal grammar. He demonstrates that it is more recent than one normally assumes, and that it originates in a modification of the interrogative pronoun. He cites the Latin phrases:

| quod | aetas | vitium | posuit, | id | aetas | auferet |
|------|-------|--------|---------|-----|-------|---------|
| what | time | fault | posited, | it | time | will remove |

"What time has set up as a fault, time will remove it".

"The fault that time has set up, time will take away".

| Qui | pro | innocente | dicit | is | satis | est | eloquens |
|-----|-----|-----------|-------|-----|-------|-----|----------|
| Who | for | innocents | speaks | he | enough | is | eloquent |

"He who speaks for the innocent is eloquent enough".

He asks what the reason would be for placing the relative proposition before the primary one. He posits that an interrogation must first be established, so that the two propositions form a question and an answer, and concludes that this is the reason why many Indo-European languages use the same pronoun for the relative and the interrogative (152). This seems a more likely explanation that the idea of a relative pronoun transformation that begins with two discrete sentences, such as in the classic UG formula:

Structural Description:
X–NP–Y    S2:    W–NP–Z
1  2  3           4  5  6
Condition: 2 = 5
Structural Change: 1–2 + which/who/that + 4 + 6 – 3
Example: Input: The student graduated. I liked the student.
Output: The student that I liked graduated.

This ignores the question that underlies the process. For example, in the phrase "France is the team that won the world cup in 2018", the question as to which team won the world cup underlies the use of the relative clause. This usage is common in English in such phrases as, "What you say is nonsense". Also, in a recent survey in England, the majority of the subjects accepted the use of "what" as a relative pronoun, as in "the man what I saw" (Armstrong & Mackenzie, 2013).

Concerning language and formal logic, Bréal says,

> Language has its logic, but it is of a special kind. Formal logic forbids uniting contradictory terms into one proposition, such as to say that a square is long, but language is not at all averse to this. It permits, if you will, saying that a circle is square.

*(158)*

He amplifies this:

> One has often tried to find a kind of logical structure beneath the rules of grammar, but language is too rich and insufficiently rectilinear to fit into this kind of configuration. It overflows the banks of logic on all sides. In addition, its categories do not coincide with those of reason. Behaving in a way that suits itself, it winds up grouping things together in ways that cannot be reduced to any abstract concept.
>
> *(158)*

To illustrate this special kind of logic, Bréal offers numerous examples of case endings on nouns and pronouns in Latin when there is no verb modifying them. He cites this engraving on a Roman milestone indicating distances to cities along the Appian Way:

| HINCE | SVNT | NOVCERIAM | MEILIA | L | CAPVAM | XXCIII |
|---|---|---|---|---|---|---|
| From here | are | Nuceria | miles | 50 | Capua | 83 |

"From here, it is 50 miles to Nuceria, 83 to Capua".

| MVRANVM | LXXIIII | COSENTIAM | CXXIII | VALENTIAM | CLXXX |
|---|---|---|---|---|---|
| Muranum | 74 | Cosentia | 123 | Valentia | 153 |

"74 to Muranum, 123 to Cosentia, 153 to Valentia".

In Latin, a noun took on accusative endings (referred to as the accusative of direction) to express direction in and of itself, here indicated by the inflectional endings um/am. The nominative (subject) form of, e.g., Capua in Latin is *capua*. The inflected form *capuam* indicates direction and distance. There is no verb used. Bréal says of this, "The accusative is employed in its proper sense and with its original value" as "the case of place to which one directs oneself" (160).

Now it was only natural for expressions of distance to be used with verbs of motion. This gave the impression that the case ending was caused by the verb, another example of *cum hoc ergo propter hoc*. The accusative of distance was extended to indicate the accusative of duration, in other words, "a length of time". Bréal cites the example of a phrase conveying the idea of staying two nights outside of the city: *noctem unam extra urbem* (162). He observes that space and time are, "for the logic of language, two quite similar things" (162). And here, one sees the transgressive power of analogy, one that does not observe the conventions of logic. He holds that analogy is the manner of reasoning of children and of the masses (*la façon de raisonner des enfants et de la foule*) (163). Since language is the work of the people, one must, in order to understand it, "strip the logician and, along with him, become one with the people" (*dépouiller le logicien et se faire peuple avec lui*) (163). These words have an air of unpretentiousness about them, as if Bréal were saying that we are all equal before language; we are spoken by it, as we speak and analyze it.

Bréal holds that language begins and began in subjectivity: "To express a desire, to make a demand, to mark the taking possession of persons or things—these were the first usages of language. For many people, they are more or less the only ones" (169). He adds:

> Humans are so far away from viewing the world as disinterested observers, that one could hold, on the contrary, that the part they have appropriated for themselves in language is completely disproportionate. Of the three persons of the verb, there is one that they reserve absolutely for themselves (that which is conventionally called *the first*). In this way, they already oppose themselves to the universe.
>
> *(169)*

Some of Bréal's observations are supported by a recent study on syntactic variability in Greek. In 2000, Devine and Stephens published *Discontinuous Syntax: Hyperbaton in Greek*. Hyperbaton is a term designating an inversion of the normal order of words. The authors discuss configurational versus non-configurational word order, the former designating relatively fixed, hierarchically determined syntactic structure, and the latter a freer one, in which word order is pragmatically determined by what elements one wants to emphasize. This is characteristic of highly inflected languages, where case endings free up syntactic order. Ancient Greek, a highly inflected language, permits variable syntax. The authors say,

> However syntactically free Greek word order may be, it is semantically fixed in grammatically determined configurations. In this regard—to put it in the most mischievous and provocative way possible—the Greeks spoke in Greek but they thought in English...if Greek semantics is configurational...it does not follow that Greek syntax is grammatically configurational too.
>
> *(Devine & Stephens, 2000, p. 289)*

In other words, habits will fix idiomatic word order, but that does not indicate a fixed infrastructural syntax. I would say it the other way around. They thought in Greek but spoke in English, in the sense that the thinking is freer, but the phrases are lexicalized and fixed.

One of the first linguists to argue for a psychoanalytic linguistics was Charles Hockett, who, in 1967, noted that in the *Psychopathology*, Freud suggested that studying slips of the tongue may shed light on the generation of speech. He emphasizes: "I propose here to take Freud's suggestion seriously" (Hockett, 1973, p. 93). Unfortunately, he was among the few who did so. His work is studied in Chapter 5.

One of the most intelligent assessments of the relation between psychoanalysis and linguistics has been offered by Julia Kristeva in *Language: The Unknown: An Initiation into Linguistics* (1981). Kristeva operates within the distinction among *langage* (the capacity for language), *langue* (a language), and *parole* (speech). She sets up an initial mutual exclusivity between the psychoanalytic model of language and that of formal linguistics, an exclusivity, for which she eventually offers a proposal for reconciliation. In the psychoanalytic model, the relation between analyst and analysand is a solely linguistic one; there is only language: "The psychoanalyst has no other means within his reach, no other reality with which to explore the unconscious functioning of the subject, than speech (*parole*) and its laws and structures" (Kristeva, 1981, p. 266). At the same time, however, "psychoanalysis considers every symptom as language (*langage*)", including the images in dreamwork. This renders "psychoanalysis inseparable from the linguistic universe" (266). And one must include body language here, the analyst's attention to the analysand's revelatory body movements: "For psychoanalytic psychopathology, the body itself speaks. Remember that Freud founded psychoanalysis starting with hysterical symptoms which he sees as 'talking bodies'. The corporal system is overdetermined by a complex symbolic network" (272). This would be a neural network in a mind–body unity, with no mind–body dichotomy. Kristeva refers to Lacan's assertion that the unconscious and the symptom are structured as a language (*structuré comme un langage*) (Lacan, 1966, p. 269). And this is language as in the faculty of language, not in a specific language (*une langue*).

Kristeva holds that "psychoanalytic principles…have profoundly modified the classical notion of language (*langage*)" (Kristeva, 1981, p. 266). Subjects are no longer seen as masters of their own discourses—language speaks for them and expresses their anterior motivations, those that the modern subject is unaware of. Whatever "truth" emerges here, emerges in dialog, in communication with the analyst, and, in general, in communication with the interlocutor, "in and through a discursive, horizontal position" (267).

Kristeva agrees with Freud that "the unconscious is the true psychical reality" (267). The ego, according to Lacan and Kristeva, is *frustration dans son essence* (250). She quotes Lacan, who says that the construction of identity undermines the certitude that the self seeks, because the self seeks to constitute and reconstitute itself *for* another, and that other can dispossess the self of the self. (*Car dans ce travail qu'il fait de la reconstruire pour une autre, il retrouve l'aliénation fondamentale qui la lui a fait construire comme une autre, et qui l'a toujours destinée à lui être dérobée par un autre* (Lacan, 1966, p. 313)). Loosely rendered: The subject winds up realizing that the construction of self is insufficient and uncertain, because the subject, in dialogue with the other, constructed the self *for another*, and in doing so *like another*, with the result that the self can be taken away by the other. This corresponds to Tomasello's idea that language arises by imitating the other, by imagining oneself as this other (see the discussion in Chapter 9). This also fits into Freud's model of the oral incorporation of the other. Kristeva adds that the self

> ends up by recognizing that this being has never been anything more than his construct in the imaginary and that this construct disappoints in him all certainty. For in this labor which he undertakes to reconstruct *for another*, he rediscovers the fundamental alienation that made him construct it *like another*, and which has always destined it to be taken from him *by another*.
>
> *(Kristeva, 1981, p. 267)*

Kristeva believes that

> the language studied by psychoanalysis can in no way be confused with the formal object-system that la langue represents for modern linguistics. For psychoanalysis, language is, as it were, a secondary signifying system, which relies upon la langue and has an obvious relation to its categories, but which superimposes its own organization and specific logic.
>
> *(268)*

She also proposes that the signifying system of the unconscious is in this sense supralinguistic (268), the argument being that the condensations in dream would not be found in formal language. Here, I have to differ. They are neither superimposed nor supralinguistic, because they are found at the fundamental level of the generation of language. They are the processes that interrupt formal language, which is seldom formal, because of hesitations, slips of the tongue, and the general irregularity of conversation. Formality is mostly found in the sphere of written language. If one puts the unconscious first, which is what she recommends, then the generation of speech begins to look quite different. This theme is taken up below in the discussion of the relation between morpheme and allomorph in Chapter 5. In this sense, formal language is an abstraction from applied language.

Kristeva adds:

> We can easily see that for Freud a dream could not be reduced to symbolism; it was truly a language [*langage*], that is, a system of signs, even a structure with its own syntax and logic. The syntactic character of Freud's vision of language must be emphasized.
>
> *(271)*

This is because the symbolism depends on the context—the dream makes use of symbols as it will. She observes that "this language [*langage*] is not identical to *la langue* studied by linguistics; it is, however, made in this *langue*...at once ultralinguistic and supralinguistic, or *translinguistic*, the signifying system studied by Freud has a universality that 'traverses' constituted national languages" (272). She then goes on to reference Freud's hypothesis, stated in *The Ego and the Id*, that dream symbolism was probably united in prehistoric times by a conceptual and linguistic identity. This is the symbolism found in myth, folklore, and verbal idiom.

She does, however, note the presence of psychoanalytic mechanisms in jokes, where one finds "concision (or ellipsis), compression (condensation with the formation of substitutes), inversion, double meaning, etc." (274). Jokes are, however, obviously located in the specific language. The presence of psychoanalytic mechanisms in jokes seems to be an exception to the division of language as studied by psychoanalysis and language as studied by linguistics. She asserts:

> It is hard to imagine how the formalizations of American structuralism and generative grammar, for example, could possibly be reconciled with the laws of linguistic functioning such as they have been formulated by modern psychoanalysis after Freud. It is clear that these approaches constitute two contradictory or at least divergent tendencies in the conception of language.
>
> *(274)*

The problem is that generative grammar forgets "that language does not exist outside the *discourse of a subject*" (274). And also the discourse of a subject with an other.

Here, the signifier floats independently and becomes bound to the signified by the subjectivity of the subject:

> The principle of the supremacy of the signifier has instituted a syntax in analyzed language that explodes the linear meaning of the spoken chain, and reconnects the signifying units located in various morphemes of the text by following a combinatory logic.
>
> *(276)*

The location of signifying units in the morphology of the text is important, because morphemes function as nodal points of the dreamwork text and interrelate, as will be illustrated in the subsequent chapters. Similarly, Lacan shows that overdetermination is an instantiation of syntax. And its effects are not imposed upon the text, but instead come from the sense of the text itself.

(*Car ces effets s'exercent du texte au sens, loin d'imposer leur sens au texte*) (Lacan, 1966, p. 468).

Writing initially in 1969, with a revision in 1981, Kristeva concludes her discussion of psychoanalysis and language with the following prediction. (By "the analytic conception of language", she means the psychoanalytic one):

> The schematic summary of the fundamental principles of the analytic conception of language, and their radical novelty with respect to the modern linguistic vision, inevitably raises the question of whether they can be introduced into linguistic knowledge. We are not able today so foresee the possibility, much less the result, of such a penetration. But it is obvious that an analytic attitude toward language will not spare the neutral systematicity of scientific language, and that it will force formal linguistics to change its discourse. What seems even more probable is that an analytical attitude will invade the field of study of signifying systems in general, the semiology that Saussure dreamed of, and that, from that angle, it will modify the Cartesian conception of language and enable science to grasp the multiplicity of signifying systems elaborated in and from *la langue*.
>
> *(Kristeva, 1981, pp. 276–277)*

Over a century ago, Bréal cautioned us not to view language as a product of formal logic, not to attempt "to find a kind of logical structure beneath the rules of grammar" (Bréal, 2005, p. 158). Much of the twentieth-century science of language has not heeded that advice and has instead attempted to view language within the structures of propositional symbolic logic and information science. This study will offer an alternative configuration of language, a psychoanalytic one.

As stated above, Freud wrote in the same era as Bréal. He viewed human behavior as motivated by unconscious forces and configured language itself as a transitional phenomenon between unconscious and conscious modes of thought. His view of consciousness itself was fundamentally linguistic. In the *Psychopathology of Everyday Life* (Freud, 1901), he proposed that slips of the tongue could shed light on the generation of speech itself. This study will gradually configure language within the science of the unconscious.

Before reconfiguring the genesis and processing of language in a psychoanalytic context, it is necessary to properly contextualize and problematize the foundational tenet of universal grammar, which is the model of recursion. For it is here that the psychoanalytic view of language clashes head-on with the generative one, especially as concerns the relationship between language and consciousness. Also, psychoanalysis sees language as associative and rhizomic (horizontal); generative linguistics sees it as arborescent, hierarchical, and modular. The insufficiency of recursion as a model for language is demonstrated in the following chapter.

## References

Armstrong, N., & Mackenzie, I. (2013). *Standardization, ideology, and linguistics.* Macmillan.
Bonfiglio, T. (2010). *Mother tongues and nations: The invention of the native speaker.* De Gruyter.
Bréal, M. (2005). *Essaie de sémantique.* Lambert-Lucas.
Devine, A. & Stephens, L. (2000). *Discontinuous syntax: Hyperbaton in Greek.* Oxford University Press.
Forrester, J. (1980). *Language and the origins of psychoanalysis.* Columbia University Press.
Freud, S. (1901). Zur Psychopathologie des Alltagslebens. Über Vergessen, Versprechen, Vergreifen, Aberglaube und Irrtum. *Gesammelte Werke* (Vol. 4, pp. 5–321). Imago. [English edition: Freud, S. (1953–1974). The psychopathology of everyday life. *The standard edition of the complete psychological works of Sigmund Freud* (Vol. 6, pp. 1–279). Hogarth].
Hockett, C. (1973). Where the tongue slips, there slip I. In V. Fromkin (Ed.), *Speech errors as linguistic evidence* (pp. 93–119). De Gruyter.
Humboldt, Wilhelm von. (1908). Fragmente der Monographie über die Basken. *Wilhelm von Humboldts Gesammelte Schriften. Herausgegeben von der Königlich Preussischen Akademie der Wissenschaften* (Vol. VII/2, pp. 593–608). B. Behr's Verlag.
Kristeva, J. (1981). *Le langage, cet inconnu.* Editions du Seuil. [English edition: Kristeva, J. (1989). *Language: The unknown: An initiation into linguistics.* Harvester Wheatsheaf].
Lacan, J. (1966). *Ecrits.* Editions du Seuil. [English edition: Lacan, J. (2006). *Ecrits.* W.W. Norton].
Rüegg, W. (2004). *A history of the university in Europe. Vol. III: Universities in the nineteenth and early twentieth centuries.* Cambridge University Press.

# 2
# RECURSION AND METACOGNITION

One of the central concepts in the attempt to define human language pivots around the concept of recursion. In linguistics, recursion refers to the phenomenon of imbedding syntactic parts within other syntactic parts, as in the case of relative clauses, e.g.: "The cat that ate the bird that ate the worm that ate...", which, in theory, could continue indefinitely. In the minimalist program of universal grammar, recursion is seen as the nuclear faculty that generates the universe of linguistic possibilities, an atomic algorithm of infinite potential.

In 2002, Hauser, Chomsky, and Fitch published "The Faculty of Language: What Is It, Who Has It, and How Did It Evolve"?, in which they reduce human language to a "narrow language faculty" that "only includes recursion and is the only uniquely human component of the faculty of language" (Hauser et al., 2002, p. 1569). Pinker and Jackendoff offer a succinct definition of recursion along with a comment on the article by Hauser et al.: "Recursion refers to a procedure that calls itself, or to a constituent that contains a constituent of the same kind. In the article itself, the starkness of this hypothesis is mitigated only slightly" (Pinker & Jackendoff, 2005, p. 203). Hauser et al. also simply assume this narrow language faculty a priori and say that it is independent of other cognitive systems. One begins to sense here echoes of the ghost in the machine.

In *The Recursive Mind: The Origins of Human Language, Thought, and Civilization*, Michael Corballis brilliantly contextualizes the issue of recursion. Corballis begins in a recursive manner by commenting on the satirist Ambrose Bierce's ironic comment on Descartes: "Cogito cogito ergo cogito sum—'I think I think, therefore I think I am.'" He then concocts "a not-too-serious dictionary definition: 'Recursion (rĭ-kûr'-zhən) noun. See recursion'" (Corballis, 2011, p. 1). This is followed by an observation on the sign "Post no bills":

DOI: 10.4324/9781003180197-3

There is a paradox here in that the sign was itself a bill, thereby contravening its own presence. Perhaps there needed to be another sign that said *Post no 'Post no bills' bills*. But of course this is itself in violation of its own message, so we might envisage another sign that reads *Post no 'Post "Post no bills" bills' bills*. There is no end to this process.

(5)

These ironic examples are quite to the point. The comic dictionary definition above is not, however, a real recursion, but a simple tautology. Corballis proposes that recursion "takes its own output as the next input, a loop that can be extended indefinitely to create sequences or structures of unbounded length or complexity" (5–6). Thus simple repetition is not recursion, because no operation is performed on the preceding element; one needs to recoup the preceding element and subsume it into the next operation for recursion to occur.

Similarly, Fitch, in "Three Meanings of 'Recursion': Key Distinctions for Biolinguistics", says that "recursive functions take their own past output as their net input and potentially allow...indefinitely complex output" (Fitch, 2011, p. 75). In computer science, recursion occurs "where a command to run function x appears within the definition of function x itself" (76). The computer science definition derives from mathematics, naturally, and is most clear in a geometric progression, where one multiplies a term by a fixed number, called the common ratio, and then multiplies the result by the same number. A good example is found in the diagramming of family trees, where the fixed ratio is 2. One begins with oneself and multiplies each quantity of ancestors by two. We have two parents, four grandparents, eight great-grandparents, sixteen great-great-grandparents, and so on. Fitch adds that in linguistics, "a recursive rule is one which has the property of self-embedding, that is, in which the same phrase type appears on both sides of a phrase structure rewrite rule" (79), i.e., $S \rightarrow ASB$. Compound interest is also a good example of recursion. Interest is calculated upon the principal and the interest accrued since the last calculation.

Earlier formulations of universal grammar held that all languages have recursion, until we documented some that do not. For instance, Pirahã (Brazil) and Riau (Indonesia) do not have relative clauses or hierarchical grammar. Daniel Everett, in *How Language Began*, says that their grammars "are little more than words arranged like beads on a string rather than structures as chunks within chunks" (Everett, 2017, p. 105). So instead of saying, e.g., "I know the guy who found it", they say something like, "I know the guy. He found it". And they understand each other perfectly well.

But Fitch has an odd qualification of Everett's claims about Pirahã. He is skeptical, because "all Pirahã are monolingual, and none of them are linguists— so we currently lack any reports from a native speaker about their grammar" (88). This is perplexing, as linguists commonly judge grammaticality by inquiring among native speaker informants who are not linguists. And in doing so, we are quite careful. For instance, instead of asking if a sentence is grammatical, we might ask, "Does this sentence sound ok to you"? He does admit, however, that "Pirahã speakers can construct and communicate recursive thought structures like any other human group, and thus they must have self-embedding of conceptual constructions" (89). True, otherwise they would be idiots. And here one arrives at an important observation. Pinker and Jackendoff believe, and with reason, that "the only reason language needs to be recursive is because its function is to express recursive thoughts. If there were not any recursive thoughts, the means of expression would not need recursion either" (Pinker & Jackendoff, 2005, p. 230).

Recursion is primarily a cognitive function applied to language. In the current era that uses the discourse of information science as the episteme for understanding the brain, one could say that recursion is a cognitive function "downloaded" into language. But why would the cognitive function of recursion have arisen in the first place, and why would it have been advantageous for our hominin (modern human) ancestors? I propose here that recursion is the state of consciousness itself. It is metacognition, the capacity for self-reflection and for thinking about thinking about something.

In graduate school, I attended a seminar on second language teaching. The presenter began by highlighting the basic extrapolation from the initial level of teaching language to the level of teaching people how to teach language. Then she extrapolated one step up to the problem of designing a course for such a purpose, i.e., how one would design a course that designs a course that teaches people how to teach. I am also reminded, in this context, of the song *Montage,* from the film *How Sweet It Is,* which contains an eightfold recursion of the phrase "I knew that you knew". The reader/listener gets lost along the way; the written model continues, having left cognition far behind (Webb, 1968).

Robin Dunbar, in "On the Origin of the Human Mind", makes some excellent observations that help put all of this in focus. Dunbar's work shows that anything above fourth-order intentionality (A believes that B supposes that C thinks that D wants) is extremely difficult to process and remember (Dunbar, 2000, p. 241). I discussed this with a colleague who responded that even little children are capable of this kind of "nesting". They can say, e.g., "the cat that ate the rat that ate the bat that ate the gnat that ate the hat", and so on. But if we examine this, we see that there is no transcendent awareness of all the embedded clauses here. While these seem to be hierarchies of relative clauses, they are in reality mere conjunctions of repetitive phrases, because by the end of the sequence, the speaker has most likely forgotten the beginning. This can be compared to an arithmetic progression in mathematics, as opposed to the truly recursive geometric one. That is the true nature of the putative merge function as posited in the minimalist paradigm, where the master structure can subsume an infinite number of substructures. This is not how conversational speech works. The multi-level hierarchical plan of any highly centralized system is not speech.

In reflecting on how this all came about, i.e. how and why humans developed the talent of embedding, Dunbar invokes the growth in human brain size, which increased in proportion to the increase in social group size (Dunbar, 2000, p. 247). He posits that "the need to evolve alliances to provide access to limited ecological resources (almost certainly permanent water) was most likely to have been the key pressure selecting for increased brain size" in ancestral hominins (249). Now this would have been the necessity for alliance within the clan, over and against another clan. Thus he invokes the possibility that brain size increased with the increasing competition among human groups, which would have favored greater cognitive skills: "Fighting a mind-reader is a very different proposition to fighting a predator (which will typically only have first-order intentionality)" (250).

This is a very valuable observation that, however, underestimates the strategic thinking of the predator. For simpler organisms, the simple structure of stimulus and response seems to be applicable. Predator approaches: Run. Or, see predator: Run. Or, anything approaches: The insect flees. Whether or not the predator sees you is not relevant. For more advanced organisms, and clearly in most mammals, there is an exchange of seeing and being seen that constructs the chase. In hunting prey, lions are aware of whether or not the prey can see them. This elementary state of knowing that someone sees you is clearly a nascent form of consciousness.

Let us take as an example a predatory situation in nature involving mammals with a frontal lobe, the part of the brain dedicated to planning, memory, reasoning, etc. This would not be a simple situation of instinctive automated response, but instead one that would necessitate awareness of self. In other words, the animal would know that it is in a vulnerable situation:

- I see myself as vulnerable
- I see the animal seeing me and think that it wants to eat me
- the other animal sees that I see it and think that it wants to eat me
- I see the other animal and see that it sees that I see it and think that it wants to eat me

The first stage, simple perception, would be a kind of zero-grade. The other stages seem to multiply like a hall of mirrors, but with the exception that the images in mirrors that face each appear to regress infinitely. This would be the premise of recursion in universal grammar, but, as we have seen, the number of reflections is limited.

Dunbar's findings informed the work of Lisa Zunshine in the excellent study "Theory of Mind and Experimental Representations of Fictional

Consciousness", where she applies Dunbar's observations to the use of levels of recursion and embedding in the reading process. She discusses "a series of recent experiments exploring our capacity for imagining serially embedded representations of mental states (that is, 'representations of representations of representations' of mental states)" (Zunshine, 2003, p. 271). She begins within the framework of theory of mind (ToM), an unfortunate term for an invaluable concept, one that was self-evident until radical proponents of universal grammar proposed that language is not for communication. ToM is based on the premise that humans intuit the emotional and cognitive states of others, i.e., they represent to themselves what they think the other is thinking and experiencing. This is the essence of the communicative model of language, of exchanges between interlocutors. "Theory of mind" is now lexicalized, and one would wish that a clearer phrase could emerge and do justice to the imperative faculty of intuiting the thoughts and feelings of others, a faculty that is radically impaired in cases of autism. Alternative terms include "mind reading", which is also problematic, and "second-order intentionality", a nice term that has yet to take hold.

She discusses how we evidently know what gestures mean (276). The example that she cites concerns a student raising their hand in class. We implicitly know that the student has a question or comment, and not that the student would be, for instance, pointing at a spider on the ceiling. (At times, however, I find it ambiguous when students stretch their arms in class.) This is all quite clear, as we know that different gestures mean different things in different contexts and different cultures.

Zunshine observes that the autistic cannot "see bodies as animated by minds" (272). Those working in theory of mind believe that this adaptation must have developed during the Pleistocene epoch, when human brain size tripled. She reminds us that in autism,

> a glaring failure in mind-reading would be a person's not even knowing that the water coursing down her friend's face is supposed to be somehow indicative of his feelings at that moment. If you find the latter possibility absurd, recall that this is how (many) people with autism experience the world.
> 
> *(274)*

Zunshine notes that "the levels of intentionality can 'recurse'" further back, for example, to the fourth level, as in a statement like "I believe that you think that she believes that he thinks that X" (278). Now according to the notion of recursivity proposed by radical universal grammarians, this could go on indefinitely. But Zunshine refers the reader to the work done by Dunbar and his colleagues showing that we have great difficulty keeping multiple levels of intentionality in our mind at once, especially at and above the fourth level.

In reading character interaction in Virginia Woolf's *Mrs. Dalloway*, Zunshine claims that Woolf inserts additional levels of intentionality into the text, e.g., Woolf wants the reader to think: that A knows that B knows that C thinks that D believes, etc. And this presents a challenge to the reader. Zunshine says that, in reading Woolf,

> We first have to process several sequences that embed at least five levels of intentionality. Moreover, we have to do it on the spot, unaided by pen and paper and not forewarned that the number of levels of intentionality that we are about to encounter is considered by cognitive scientists to create 'a very significant load on most people's cognitive abilities'.
> 
> *(281–282)*

(One wonders if Zunshine intended the multiple levels of reflection in this sentence.) Of course, Woolf is by no means the master of this embedding; it is found in many British crime novels, or "whodunnits", and also in frame stories, such as:

> Fred sat me down on the hood of his car and said, let me tell you a story. Once upon a time there was a watchmaker who had been told a story about a blacksmith who had heard that Austria had invaded Serbia.

In the article "Negotiating with Other Minds: The Role of Recursive Theory of Mind in Negotiation with Incomplete Information", De Weerd et al. emphasize the imperative importance of the faculty to intuit the experiences of others:

> Without this theory of mind, an individual is limited to reasoning only about behavior, such as in the sentence "Mary is looking in the drawer". Such individuals are said to have a zero-order theory of mind. First-order theory of mind allows agents to reason about unobservable mental content of others as well, and understand sentences like "Mary is looking in the drawer because she believes that there is chocolate in the drawer". People are also capable of taking this theory of mind ability a step further, and reason about way others are using theory of mind. Using second-order theory of mind, people understand sentences such as "Alice believes that Bob knows that Carol is throwing him a surprise party", and reason about the way Alice is reasoning about Bob's knowledge.
> 
> *(De Weerd et al., 2017, p. 251)*

In these models, it is not always clear where one begins counting. Such inconsistencies are common and occur, for instance, in planning ahead. If today is Monday, and one wants to plan something for next Monday, one would say, in English, "a week from today", or "seven days from now". In German, however, one says "today in eight days" (*heute in acht Tagen*). Nonetheless, the argument about reflection and scaffolding is clear.

The idea that theory of mind arose because complex social structures necessitated it seems to exclude pre-social or individual strategies for survival, similar to the example above of animal hunting. And it is here that one can make use of some of the work done by Julian Jaynes in *The Origins of Consciousness in the Breakdown of the Bicameral Mind*. Jaynes makes some very important observations for this study. His conception of consciousness is fundamentally lingua-centric. In our discourse, consciousness "does something", which he sees as "a metaphor. It is saying that consciousness is a person behaving in physical space who does things" (Jaynes, 1976, p. 53). And he asks, "In what 'space' is the metaphorical 'doing' being done"? (53). Clearly in a metaphorical one that is an analog of behaviors and perceptions: "Subjective conscious mind is an analog of what is called the real world. It is built up with a vocabulary or subjective field whose terms are all metaphors or analogs of behavior in the physical world" (55), and he adds: "An analog is at every point generated by the thing it is an analog of. A map is a good example" (53).

When we are "seeing" what somebody means, we operate in "a metaphor of actual space...and the adjectives to describe physical behavior in real space are analogically taken over to describe mental behavior in mind-space" (55); More precisely: "Conscious mind is a spatial analog of the world and mental acts are analogs of bodily acts" (66). He claims that spatialization is the *sine qua non* of consciousness:

> Time is an obvious example. If I ask you to think of the last hundred years, you may have a tendency to excerpt the matter in such a way that the succession of years is spread out, probably from left to right. But of course there is no left or right in time. There is only before and after, and these do not have any spatial properties whatever — except by analog. You cannot, absolutely cannot think of time except by spatializing it. Consciousness is always a spatialization in which the diachronic is turned into the synchronic, in which what has happened in time is excerpted and seen in side-by-sideness. This spatialization is characteristic of all conscious thought.
>
> *(60)*

This corresponds to Freud's assertion (Freud, 1940, p. 67) that mental life (*Seelenleben*) is the functioning of an apparatus to which we attribute spatial extension and composition from numerous pieces.

And consciousness is always fragmentary: "We are never conscious of things in their true nature, only of the excerpts we make of them" (Jaynes, 1976, p. 61). One of the most important features of consciousness is "the metaphor we have of ourselves, the analog 'I,' which can 'move about' vicariously in our 'imagination', 'doing' things that we are not actually doing" (62–63). Thus the analog is the mental image we have of a scenario, as in a map, which is an analog diagram of the geographical space. Consciousness "operates by way of analogy, by way of constructing an analog space with an analog 'I' that can observe that space, and move metaphorically in it" (65).

The "I" that sees is itself that analog, creating the mental representation. This is an excellent description of consciousness as the act of imagining oneself in a situation, the capacity to see ourselves, for "I" to see "me". And this would not be limited to humans, but instead limited perhaps to mammals with a frontal lobe. And self-recognition in a mirror is the litmus test: "When presented with mirrors, most fish, birds, or mammals react with complete disinterest or else engage in social or aggressive displays or attack their mirror images" (459). I recall that our dog thought that her reflection in the mirror was just another dog. Curious at first, she soon realized that the image had nothing to do with her, and she soon simply ignored it. This may be due, as well, to the absence of all non-visual sense input, especially smell. (Recent experiments have shown, however, instances of self-awareness in non-human primates.) Human children recognize their own image at a young age and thus begin slowly building the bridge to consciousness.

One thing that Jaynes is unclear on is where the sensation of being aware comes from. And here, he is as baffled as we are. He claims that "understanding a thing is to arrive at a metaphor for that thing by substituting something more familiar to us. And the feeling of familiarity is the feeling of understanding" (52). But this is not the experience of awareness; it still leaves consciousness itself unexplained. We are aware that there is an analogy or homology between x and y, but that awareness—the transcendental light that illuminates what we are thinking and sensing—will always be one step beyond (53–54). And that is the nature of metacognition. It is not infinite, as we have seen, but limited to four or perhaps five levels.

He does opt for a materialist element to consciousness: "The general rule is: There is no operation in consciousness that did not occur in behavior first" (449), but he also speculates in the idealist direction:

> The analog 'I' is contentless, related I think to Kant's transcendental ego. As the bodily I can move about in its environment looking at this or that, so the analog 'I' learns to 'move about' in mind-space, 'attending to' or concentrating on one thing or another.
>
> *(450)*

Here, the ghost in the machine haunts the discourse of consciousness and recursion.

One of the most striking things about Jaynes's view of consciousness is the belief that consciousness is a linguistic construct. It is an "invention of an analog world on the basis of language" (66). He posits that "if consciousness is based on language, then it follows that it is of a much more recent origin than has heretofore been supposed. Consciousness came after language"! (66). He concludes that "consciousness is the work of lexical metaphor" (58).

This needs a bit of modification in order to coincide with the psychoanalytic view of language and consciousness, in which one becomes *fully* conscious of an idea in and through language. Which came first is a kind of chicken-or-egg question. They emerge in symbiosis. Analogy, however, seems to reside first in the symbolic, and is then expressed in verbal language. For example, if I were to think that my neighbor looks like Fred Flintstone, I would be making an analogy, but I may not even be *fully* conscious of the analogy until I say it.

Another important contribution made by Jaynes lies in the idea that consciousness involves doubling oneself, i.e., being capable of imagining oneself in a situation, reflecting on that, and acting accordingly. And again, this is not limited to humans, as is seen in the predatory situation described above. Mammals with a developed frontal lobe would not be limited to instinctive automated responses, but instead would be capable of knowing that they are in vulnerable or opportune situations and acting and planning accordingly. The adaptive advantage of such a faculty is clearly indisputable. Recursion may have arisen in the faculty to see yourself as eatable.

Jaynes's view corresponds to that of William James, in *Psychology. Briefer Course*:

> Whatever I may be thinking of, I am always at the same time more or less aware of myself, of my personal existence. At the same time it is I who am aware; so that the total self of me, being as it were duplex, partly known and partly knower, partly object and partly subject, must have two aspects discriminated in it, of which for shortness we may call one the Me and the other the I. I call these 'discriminated aspects,' and not separate things, because the identity of I with me, even in the very act of their discrimination, is perhaps the most ineradicable dictum of common-sense, and must not be undermined by our terminology here at the outset, whatever we may come to think of its validity at our inquiry's end. I shall therefore treat successively of A) the self as known, or the me, the 'empirical ego' as it is sometimes called; and of B) the self as knower, or the I, the 'pure ego' of certain authors.
>
> *(James, 1985, p. 176)*

Here, the "pure ego" would correspond to the transcendental ego posited by Kant. Carruthers, in "The Evolution of Consciousness", proposes that consciousness evolved in the nexus of social organization:

> Our mind-reading faculty is set up so as to represent, process, and generate structured representations of the mental states of ourselves and other people...to work out and remember who perceives what, who thinks what, who wants what, and how different people are likely to reason and respond in a wide variety of circumstances.
>
> *(Carruthers, 2000, p. 273)*

This places the discussion in the theater of ToM. And it is most important to emphasize that, in this perspective, language and consciousness would have slowly emerged in a long and incremental evolutionary process, and not in a "saltation", i.e. a sudden recent mutation.

Saltation comes from the Latin *saltare*, "to jump", indicating a rapid change from one situation to another. Evolutionists, however, prefer the slogan *natura non facit saltum* ("nature does not make jumps"), a phrase that Darwin used repeatedly in *On the Origin of Species* (1859). Saltation is also called "evolution by jerks" (which has an interesting double meaning). But has there been anything catastrophic in human history and prehistory that changed all of us suddenly? The Latin *saltare* also means "to dance" or "portray in pantomime". And here, an inadvertent connection to mirror theory appears (see the discussion of mimesis in Chapter 8).

Paul M. Bingham, in "On the Evolution of Language: Implications of a New and General Theory of Human Origins, Properties, and History", states the case most forcefully against the language gene saltation theory:

> The evolutionary logic of animal and human communication and of its underlying neurobiology...plainly suggest that human language involves no qualitatively new elements or features. Rather, human language apparently looks precisely as it should if it was produced by merely enhancing and redeploying universal animal devices and properties...there is no reason whatever to suppose that any qualitatively new neural/cognitive capability was necessary to initiate the evolution of human language (or communication more generally). Indeed, such proposals are arbitrary and gratuitous.
>
> *(Bingham, 2010, p. 223)*

And Corballis holds that

> language does not appear fully formed in different cultures as a product of universal grammar, but comes about gradually as a product of

culture and accumulated experience, and a practical concern to make communication more efficient. That is, it grammaticalizes itself.

*(Corballis, 2011, p. 33)*

The saltation theory of the sudden appearance of human language is proposed by Chomsky and other adherents of the minimalist program for language. This is forcefully stated by Chomsky and Berwick in *Why Only Us. Language and Evolution*. The case, as (over)stated by the authors, is that language is so complex that it could not be evolvable. (Ergo: High complexity is not evolvable?) They hold that all "human language syntax is hierarchical, and is blind to considerations of linear order, with linear ordering constraints reserved for externalization" (Berwick & Chomsky 2016, p. 8). Externalization here refers to "superficial" things like meaning and sound. The assertion that "syntax is blind to considerations of linear order" may be one of the most untenable of Chomsky's assertions. It stands in antithesis to the present inquiry.

The authors then try to illustrate this with examples, but unconvincingly so. They discuss the string "instinctively birds that fly swim" (8) and say that it is less ambiguous than "birds that fly instinctively swim", which could mean either that they fly instinctively or swim instinctively, whereas in "instinctively birds that fly swim", "instinctively" can only modify "swim", because of a hierarchical order that they impose upon the sentence: Instinctively [birds that fly] swim. Here, "birds that fly" is imbedded in "instinctively swim".

This is quite curious. If someone were to say to me, "Instinctively birds that fly swim", I might not know what they meant, as the word "instinctively" floats around more ambiguities than those that the authors discuss. Do you instinctively know that birds can swim? Furthermore, the string would most likely never drop out of the blue. It would be clearer contextualized in a conversation, e.g.:

> Birds can swim instinctively.
> – Right, like ducks? They all have a swimming instinct?
>   Right, birds that fly instinctively swim.
> – But what about Penguins? They can't fly, but they swim like champions.
>   Good question. I guess once they became flightless, they were left with just swimming.
> – But Osprey can't swim. They just dive bomb into the water and hook the fish and then take off.

And so on. When a student once asked me what I teach, I responded, "Languages and linguistics". The student then asked, "What's languages and linguistics"?, clearly seeing the two nouns as a unit. With that in mind, we can imagine another possible interpretation, especially if we put the conversation in the current scenario of two people conversing while manipulating their smartphones, and not paying full attention:

> Instinctively, birds that fly swim.
> – They fly swim? You mean like flying fish?
> No, I mean if birds can fly, then they can swim.
> – Oh, ok. That makes sense. Birds that fly instinctively swim.

The authors neglect to discuss that the strings they analyze are examples of written language, which is an imposition on language itself. Moreover, the strings themselves would not be pronounced in a monotone fashion, as in synthetic speech, but with ample intonation and pauses, which would add clarity, e.g.: "Birds that fly (pause) instinctively swim". But in the UG model, intonation is an "externalization" that forms no part of the minimalist faculty of language.

In "How Hierarchical Is Language Use"?, Frank et al. state: "It is beyond dispute that hierarchical structure plays a key role in most descriptions of language. The question we pose here is: How relevant is hierarchy for the use of language"? This politely skirts the issue, ostensibly valorizing hierarchical structure, but on closer reflection, it actually separates the description of language from its essence. If it does not explain how language is used, then what is its real referent? They add:

> Indeed, cross-species comparisons and genetic evidence indicate that humans have evolved sophisticated sequencing skills that were subsequently recruited for language. If this evolutionary scenario is correct, then the mechanisms employed for language learning and use are likely to be fundamentally sequential in nature, rather than hierarchical.
> *(Frank et al., 2012, p. 4523)*

It is this sequential nature that fits in best to the psychoanalytic configuration of language as unfolding in a multivalent, associative, and allusive network of displacement, condensation, and overdetermination:

> A sentence's meaning is also derived from extra-sentential and extra-linguistic factors, such as the prior discourse, pragmatic constraints, the current setting, general world knowledge, and knowledge of the speaker's intention and the listener's state of mind. All these (and possibly more) sources of information directly affect the comprehension process thereby reducing the importance of sentence structure.
> *(4526)*

And it seems safe to say that the post facto imposition of orthography upon the generation of language creates the impression of what one understands conventionally as "structure".

And the authors extend this to syntax: "Hence, insofar as the same neural substrates appear to be involved in both the processing of linear sequences and language, it would seem plausible that syntactic processing is fundamentally sequential in nature, rather than hierarchical" (4523). And of hierarchy, they add:

> Evidence for hierarchical operations will only be found when the language user is particularly attentive, when it is important for the task at hand (e.g., in meta-linguistic tasks) and when there is little relevant information from extra-sentential/linguistic context…even if some hierarchical grouping occurs in particular cases or circumstances, this does not imply that the operation can be applied recursively, yielding hierarchies of theoretically unbounded depth, as is traditionally assumed in theoretical linguistics. It is very likely that hierarchical combination is cognitively too demanding to be applied recursively. Moreover, it may rarely be required in normal language use.
>
> *(4528)*

One sees here that infinite recursion (which is really never infinite; it may be best to say that it is multi-hierarchical) is a product of structures *imposed upon language*. They discuss the comprehension of the sentence: "The spider that the bullfrog that the turtle followed chased ate the fly" (4524). It took me 47 seconds of intense concentration to understand this sentence. Such a high degree of embedding is an example of an abstract game played with language; it would be nearly impossible to find it in normal language generation.

Corballis sees Chomsky's genesis of human speech as "a somewhat miraculous view of how language evolved" (Corballis, 2011, p. 56). This would be a kind of Edenic concept, in that Adam had no one to learn language from, thus he was born with language; *Genesis* tells us that he had the power to name things. Eve, who, in *Genesis*, was created from Adam's rib, may have been born with language, as well, or perhaps she had tutorial sessions with Adam. If one accepts the saltationist view, one would most likely hold that the mutation must have emerged in a single individual, as in the case of Adam, and possibly, but highly unlikely, in two people, as in Adam and Eve. Dante posed a similar question, in his *De vulgari eloquentia*, where he asserts that we learn language from our mothers (a kind of renaissance version of motherese), and then asks where Adam learned his language, since he was a *vir sine matre, vir sine lacte* ("man without mother or milk") (Dante Alighieri, 1896, Lib. I, Cap. 6, 1).

Chomsky elaborates upon this idea in his article "Some Simple Evo Devo Theses: How True Might They Be for Language"? "Evo-devo" is an abbreviation for evolutionary developmental biology (although it does evoke images of the 1980s punk rock). Kind of out of the blue, Chomsky simply asserts:

> First, why are there any languages at all? Second, why are there so many languages?…Roughly 100,000+ years ago, the first question did not arise, because there were no languages. By about 50,000 years ago, the answers to both questions had been settled. By then our ancestors began to leave Africa.
>
> *(Chomsky, 2010, p. 58)*

This was the window of opportunity, or rather accidence, for language, which Chomsky puts in the framework of the simultaneous "emergence of creative imagination, language, and symbolism generally, mathematics, interpretation and recording of natural phenomena, intricate social practices", along with the human "intellectual and moral nature" (58). This is a sudden grand opening of a prehistoric software store where all of these faculties just happened to lie. And this store opened within a window of about 50,000 years. He concludes that this must have been due to a sudden genetic mutation, otherwise it would not have happened that quickly. But how would this compare qualitatively with the window of about 200 years that took us from horse and carriage to interplanetary space probes? From news traveling by horse or boat (the news of American independence took over a month to get to London) to instantaneous communication? Was this, too, the result of a sudden genetic mutation in humans 200 years ago?

It is interesting to note that Chomsky formerly rejected the study of language evolution in one of his grouchier statements, saying that it was all "pop-Darwinian fairy tales" (Chomsky & Place, 2000, p. 7). But this was before he found a safe space for his theories within the model of saltation and genetic mutation. Language evolution quickly evolved from pop culture to "good natural science", as McGilvray would put it (see Chapter 10).

And the language gene mutation, the recursion mutation, is supposedly the catalyst for this creative explosion. He says, "Within some small group from which we are all descended, a rewiring of the brain took place in some individual, call him *Prometheus*, yielding the operation of unbounded Merge" (Chomsky, 2010, p. 59). The use of Prometheus is an apt metaphor here. He was a Greek god who is credited with the creation of humans by blowing into clay, inspiring them, literally and symbolically. He was also punished by the gods for stealing fire and giving it to humans. Now fire was clearly a major advancement in human evolution, as it enabled our ancestors to cook, keep warm, and defend themselves against animals, most of whom are quite scared of fire. But the domestication of fire is dated at about 800,000 years ago.

In this context, Ian Tattersall discusses the phenomenon of exaptation, which refers to the evolution of a function from a previous one that served a different purpose. The evolution of limbs from fish fins would be a good example; initially developed for swimming, they became exapted for terrestrial locomotion. He reminds us that

> there is a strong argument to be made that any novelty must arise as an 'exaptation', a new variant arising independently of any novel function for which it might later be co-opted…the neural substrate for our remarkable symbolic cognitive abilities initially arose as a byproduct, or at least a co-product, of the extensive physical reorganization that we see so clearly reflected today in our unique osteology.
>
> *(Tattersall, 2010, p. 197)*

(Osteology refers to skeletal structure.) Otherwise, if exaptation did not precede adaptation, then one might conclude that evolution is teleological instead of haphazard.

Tattersall is a paleontologist, and he posits language as an exaptation from already existing cognitive capacities:

> Importantly, by the time demonstrably symbolic behaviors began to be expressed, the structures that permit speech had already been in place for a considerable time—certainly since the emergence prior to 150,000 years ago of homo sapiens as an anatomical entity—having initially been acquired in some other context entirely.
>
> *(198)*

He reminds us that "birds had feathers for many millions of years before they co-opted them for flight, and homo sapiens very plausibly possessed a symbol ready brain well before symbolic cognition was adopted" (198). He sees language as coterminous with symbolic cognition and asserts that "this substrate must have lain unexploited for some considerable lapse of time until it was 'discovered' by its possessors" (197). And he posits that it was the engagement of language that enabled the great cultural advances of homo sapiens beginning about 100,000 years ago. It was the medium of engagement, the communication center for a host of cultural factors: "The most plausible candidate for this cultural stimulus is the invention of language" (197). And the word "invention" is crucial here. The invention of the wheel can serve as a good example. It is dated to about 6,000 years ago. Clearly, the human cognitive capacities for wheel invention had already been in place. There was no sudden genetic mutation at work here. While language is the stuff of symbolic cognition, its emergence would have been precipitated by a host of codeterminative factors, and in a gradual manner.

Corballis holds that

> there is no reason to suppose that the recursive mind evolved in some single, miraculous step, or even that it was confined to our species. Instead, it was shaped by natural selection, probably largely during the last two million years.
>
> *(Corballis, 2011, p. 226)*

He adds: "Animals have memory, but our forebears added a recursive principle that allowed them to insert past episodes into present consciousness, and generate potential future episodes" (222). This opens up a wide area for the inclusion of psychoanalytic theories of ego formation, namely, the connection between memory and identity. The perception and construction of self is based upon memories; they are the constitution of the ego. And these memories are subject to processing by defense mechanisms. Similarly, Corballis observes:

> The importance of episodic memory, then, lies not in providing a detailed record of the past, which it does very poorly, but rather in its role in constructing future scenarios…episodic memory itself is essentially a construction…it is a process whereby we establish our own identities, often in defiance of the facts. This leads to fiction itself. The same constructive process that allows us to reconstruct the past and construct possible futures also about time allows us to invent stories. We humans are addicted to folktales, legends, novels, movies, plays, soap operas, and everyday gossip. It is the power of recursion that makes these things possible.
>
> *(110–111)*

This configuration of memory and recursion corresponds well with the notion that consciousness of self necessitates the capacity to imagine oneself in a situation, to create the "analog I", as Jaynes posited.

Corballis also holds that

> one of the functions of language, especially in the form of speech, is to create impenetrable social fortresses. The bonding of peoples within those fortresses, and the separation of fortresses from each other, creates further diversity. People in different areas of the world also develop different habits and skills. Culture is as much a mechanism for bonding as a mechanism for intercultural divergence.
>
> *(218)*

This describes the impetus for the formation of individual and clan identity vis-à-vis an other, *in and through language*. He adds:

> The extension of recursive principles to manufacture and technology was made possible largely through changes in the way we communicate. Language evolved initially for the sharing of social and episodic information, and depended at first on mime, using bodily movements to convey meaning. Through conventionalization, communication became less mimetic and more abstract. In the course of time it retreated into the face, and eventually into the mouth, as late Homo gained voluntary control over voicing and the vocal tract, and the recursive ability to create infinite meaning through combinations of articulate sounds.
>
> *(223–224)*

And here, one is left with a mimetic configuration of language, born in self/non-self interaction, emergent and transitional, moving from unconscious to conscious articulation, and subject, along the way, to the principal psychodynamic mechanisms described in psychoanalytic theory. The relation of language to the establishment of identity will be discussed in Chapter 6.

Bernard Baars, in *A Cognitive Theory of Consciousness* (1988), says that "Freud's work *presupposed* a cognitive theory of conscious and unconscious processes… Freud tended to take the existence of conscious experience for granted. He treated it as equivalent to perception, and did not discuss it in much detail" (Baars, 1988, p. 113). This is certainly not the case, however, as psychoanalysis illuminates the many defense mechanisms that constitute the transition from the unconscious to consciousness, especially in the genesis of dreams, parapraxes (slips), and humor/wit, but also in human cognition in general. Baars does, however, emphasize that

> Freud's insights have achieved extraordinary cultural influence. Indeed the art, literature, and philosophy of our time are utterly incomprehensible without his ideas…but Freud had curiously little impact on scientific psychology, in part because his demonstrations of unconscious influence could not be brought easily into the laboratory—his evidence was too complex, too rich, too idiosyncratic and evanescent for the infant science of psychology to digest.
>
> *(6–7)*

And this is a spot-on assessment of the marginalization of psychoanalysis.

Fred Karlsson notes that languages have hierarchy (embedding) but not recursion, the difference being that recursion is infinite embedding. He also holds that there are no genuine instances on record of quadruple embeddings, as in w said that x said that y said that z said that…with four subordinate clauses. In saying that these instances are genuine, he means that they are not fabricated in theoretical discussions. The problem here is the definition of recursion as infinite. On paper yes, providing one has enough paper. But in spoken language, it cannot be infinite. He observes: "A linear grammar with symbols, intonation, and gestures" is a minimal requirement for language (Karlsson, 2009, p. 222). Recursion would be infinite hierarchy, but "the fact remains that no language has been documented in which any sentence is endless" (224). He says that in conversations, "The meanings are composed by speakers from disconnected sentences, partial sentences and so on. This supports the idea that the ability to compose the larger meanings of conversations from their parts (or 'constituents') is mediated by culture" (224).

If humans were capable of conscious infinite recursion, then civilization would not have needed to wait for the development of a writing system in order to organize itself. We would have been able to keep everything in our heads. The first organized civilizations arose in Sumer in southern Mesopotamia around 5,000 years ago, after the development of a complex writing system in the Sumerian language. This was Sumer's early dynastic phase, which saw the appearance of the first cities and states. Why does the absurdly obvious need to be stated here? They had to write everything down first, to produce a written schematic, in order to structure a hierarchically organized civilization. But they clearly had full-blown language. Even the most radical advocates of the minimalist paradigm do not date the appearance of human language to more recently than 40,000 years ago. The implementation of apparently infinite recursion awaited the discovery of writing. As said, recursion is theoretically infinite on paper (if you have an infinite supply of paper) but neither in language, nor in thought.

Thus the model of recursion, downloaded from information science and imposed upon language, has only a minimal application to the genesis, production, and processing of language. A rhizomic model of associative connections needs to be implemented, one that proceeds along the principal psychoanalytic mechanisms (displacement, condensation, overdetermination, repetition, inversion, repression, and secondary revision).

Language and consciousness emerge gradually, incrementally, and in reciprocal codetermination. The following chapter will examine that emergence, relying considerably on Jean Piaget's account of the development of language and consciousness from childhood to early adulthood. His work is most helpful for a psychoanalytic understanding of language.

## References

Alighieri, D. (1896). *Il Trattato De vulgari eloquentia*. Ed. Pio Rajna. Firenze: Le Monnier. [English edition: Alighieri, D. (1996). *De vulgari eloquentia*. Cambridge University Press].

Baars, B. (1988). *A cognitive theory of consciousness*. Cambridge University Press.

Berwick, R. & Chomsky, N. (2016). *Why only us? Language and evolution*. MIT Press.

Bingham, P. (2010). On the evolution of language: Implications of a new and general theory of human origins, properties, and history. In R. Larson et al. (Eds.),

*The evolution of human language: Biolinguistic perspectives* (pp. 211–224). Cambridge University Press.

Carruthers, P. (2000). The evolution of consciousness. In P. Carruthers & A. Chamberlain (Eds.), *Evolution and the human mind: Modularity, language, and metacognition* (pp. 254–275). Cambridge University Press.

Chomsky, N. (2010). Some simple evo devo theses: How true might they be for language? In R. Larson et al. (Eds.), *The evolution of human language: Biolinguistic perspectives* (pp. 45–62). Cambridge University Press.

Chomsky, N., & Place, U. (2000). The Chomsky-Place correspondence 1993–1994. *The Analysis of Verbal Behavior* 17, 7–38.

Corballis, M. (2011). *The recursive mind: The origins of human language, thought, and civilization*. Princeton University Press.

De Weerd, H. et al. (2017). Negotiating with other minds: The role of recursive theory of mind in negotiation with incomplete information. *Autonomous Agents and Multi-Agent Systems* 31, 250–287.

Dunbar, R. (2000). On the origin of the human mind. In P. Carruthers & A. Chamberlain (Eds.), *Evolution and the human mind: Modularity, language and metacognition* (pp. 238–253). Cambridge University Press.

Everett, D. (2017). *How language began*. Liveright.

Fitch, W. (2011). Three meanings of "recursion": Key distinctions for biolinguistics. In R. Larson et al. (Eds.), *The evolution of human language: Biolinguistic perspectives* (pp. 73–90). Cambridge University Press.

Frank, S. et al. (2012). How hierarchical is language use? *Proceedings of the Royal Society B. Biological Sciences* 279, 4522–4531.

Freud, S. (1940). *Abriss der Psychoanalyse. Gesammelte Werke* (Vol. 17, pp. 63–140). [English edition: Freud, S. (1953–1974). *An outline of psychoanalysis. The standard edition of the complete psychological works of Sigmund Freud* (Vol. 23, pp. 144–207). Hogarth].

Hauser, M. et al. (2002). The faculty of language: What is it, who has it, and how did it evolve? *Science* 298(5598), 1569–1579.

James, W. (1985). *Psychology: The briefer course*. University of Notre Dame Press.

Jaynes, J. (1976). *The origins of consciousness in the breakdown of the bicameral mind*. Houghton Mifflin.

Karlsson, F. (2009). Origin and maintenance of clausal embedding complexity. In G. Sampson et al. (Eds.), *Language complexity as an evolving variable* (pp. 192–202). Oxford University Press.

Pinker, S., & Jackendoff, R. (2005). The faculty of language: what's special about it? *Cognition* 95, 201–236.

Tattersall, I. (2010). A putative role for language in the origin of human consciousness. In R. Larson et al. (Eds.), *The evolution of human language: Biolinguistic perspectives* (pp. 193–198). Cambridge University Press.

Webb, J. (1968). *Montage* [Recorded by The Love Generation]. ABC Records.

Zunshine, L. (2003). Theory of mind and experimental representations of fictional consciousness. *Narrative* 11(3), 270–291.

# 3
# THE PSYCHOANALYTIC LINGUISTICS OF JEAN PIAGET

Humans begin to acquire language during a stage of minimal consciousness, especially a minimal consciousness of self, if at all. Indeed, they become operational in language production before full consciousness is attained. The development of consciousness and of operationality in language are interdependent. Moreover, the stages of the infant production of language must be foundational in its acquisition.

The work of the Swiss developmental psychologist Jean Piaget (1896–1980) is most important for placing the origin and development of language in a psychoanalytic context. A Swiss Francophone, Piaget did extensive research on the development of language and consciousness in children, especially as they transition to early adulthood. His work can be easily situated in a psychoanalytic context. It parallels extensively that of Freud, but the two of them differ on the persistence of childhood modes of thought and language into adulthood. Whereas Freud sees a continuum, in which the child remains in the adult— i.e., egocentric, precognitive, and prerational behavioral characteristics remain active in the adult psyche—Piaget prefers to see distinct stages that become jettisoned and left behind—as in rocket launches—as the child develops, although he is never completely clear on this.

In *La représentation du monde chez l'enfant* (1947), Piaget examines the child's conception of causality, and says that, because thought has not yet attained consciousness of self (*conscience du moi*) then thought is exposed to continual confusions between the objective and the subjective. This is the state of adualism. The term *conscience du moi* could also be translated as "consciousness of the ego", *le moi* (literally: "the me") being the French equivalent for the German *das Ich*, (literally: "the I"), which is regularly translated as "the ego". The permutations of this term can become confusing, but the most important

DOI: 10.4324/9781003180197-4

aspect of this concept is that it characterizes the point at which the child realizes that "I am me", i.e. consciousness of self.

Piaget's stages of development are as follows:

- the sensory-motor stage from 0 to 2 years
- the preoperational stage from 2 to 7 years
- the concrete operational stage from 7 to 11 years
- the formal operational stage from 11 to 19 years (approximately)

The first stage is one of adualism, which is "a primitive state in which images are simply presented to consciousness, without their being a distinction between self and non-self" (Piaget, 1947, p. 32). In the psychoanalytic context, adult projection can be seen as a regression to this stage of non-differentiation, although with a psychological motivation. In projection, one denies one's own thought or emotion and attributes it to another. Adualism would be the beginning, the basis of projection. It is set off by the regression to an infantile state, which is made possible by the persistence of unconscious and preconscious processes in the adult state.

Piaget found that at the age of six, "the notion of thought is confused with the notion of the voice, meaning the words that one is pronouncing or hearing" (36). Children concretize and embody thought within language and say that one thinks with the mouth; one thinks as one speaks, and one stops thinking when the mouth is closed (36). There is also a concretization of words and names—they are seen to exist within the things themselves: At the age of five to six, "the child considers names to be a property of objects themselves, ones that emanate directly from the objects" (56). The child believes that, with the name for something, it can "penetrate into the essence of the thing and discover a real explanation" (55). At the age of seven to eight, the child believes that names have been invented "by the creators of things" (56), and that the thing did not exist before there was a name for it. It is important to note that the perception of the provenance and ownership of oral and auditory speech, of "the words that one is pronouncing or hearing", do not yet reside in the awareness of self. They can be seen as external to the self, external to the sense of the "me".

Up to age seven, there is no distinction seen between the signifier and the signified, in the child's mind. After age seven, children understand that words and things are not of the same nature, but they cannot resolve the problem until age 10–11, when they begin to distinguish words from things, and "the notion of thought separates itself from the notion of physical matter" (53).

At the age of seven to eight, the child says that one thinks with the head— with a little voice inside the head—and that words are "written into the flesh" (*écrites sur la chair*) (42), an early indication of embodied language.

The realization of a separation of word and thing is also bound up with literacy and orthography, with learning to read and write. Until then, the child has a fluid and approximate notion of a word that remains in the realm of an indefinite mental image, a space where language and thought coincide, a realm of thinking in pictures. And, in the mind of the child, both are embodied. As stated above, thought is not separate from matter.

It is important to note that the persistence of primary, prelogical processes in the child's conception of thought and language coincides with the critical period for language acquisition, both for *langage* and *langue,* for the engagement of the faculty of language and for the acquisition of what is popularly termed "native fluency" in a given language. Does this not indicate that the forces that construct language are not those of formal logic?

The concept of syncretism is important here. In the French definitions employed by Piaget, syncretism refers to the combination of initially incompatible doctrines and systems, as well as to a global and undifferentiated apprehension of objects that are clearly distinct from one another. The term is also used in linguistics to signify the fusion of several grammatical traits into one element. Syncretism is a characteristic of narcissistic and egocentric modes of thought. Piaget describes the perceptions of the child as such, in that, again, it sees no difference between self and non-self. All perceptions can be connected to the self, thus the propensity to relate unrelated things to one another. This is a consequence of the lack of self-consciousness, or, for that matter, consciousness itself. This stage corresponds to Freud's notion of primary narcissism. One becomes conscious of self through difference, through seeing that there are other selves out there. And seeing that one is being seen.

This stage is also characterized by the dominance of animism, the belief that life and spirit reside in all objects. Thus the child believes that everything has an intention. (One may relate this to the adult need to find/create causes—there must be a motivator.) Until about the age of eight, the child says that it is being followed by the sun. Around the age of 10–11, the child says that the sun appears to follow it, but that it really does not—this is the stage at which the child begins to comprehend the notion of artificiality. Interestingly, the infantile confusion between the signifier and the signified (i.e., the word is the thing in itself) begins to decline before the decline of the distinction between self and non-self and the distinction between the psychical and the physical (211). Thus the concept of representation precedes the decline of egocentrism and pan-animism.

Until the age of around eight years, the child takes all metaphors and personifications literally and concretizes them (209). For instance, for the setting sun, one says in French that the sun goes to bed (*le soleil se couche*), and the child takes this literally.

In *Le langage et la pensée chez l'enfant* (1923), Piaget notes that up to the age of six years, language is not used to communicate thought (Piaget, 1923a, p. 15). It is egocentric language with no interlocutor. (Interestingly, this corresponds to Chomsky's assertion that language did not evolve for purposes of communication.) It begins with echolalia, the repetition of sounds heard by the child, proceeds to the monologue (without awareness of an interlocutor), and then to the collective monologue, where the child is aware that there are listeners, but dialog is not yet a concern (18). Echolalia occurs in an egocentric form, it is the pleasure involved in the repetition of sounds.

In discussing the child's conception of language, especially of the word, Piaget makes comparisons with similar conceptions among illiterate adult populations. He cites studies showing that nonreading adults among the Gola culture in Liberia do not see their language as consisting of words; the effective segment for them is the phrase or sentence. He calls this *la véritable unité de conscience*, the unit of consciousness (of language). This would be where consciousness of language begins, the metalinguistic moment. For them, it is the phrase that they perceive as a unity; they do not perceive the significance of individual words. He compares this to the orthographic errors made by children and adults with minimal literacy who have difficulty segmenting phrases into their lexical constituents. Phrases such as, e.g., *Le courrier va passer ma chère amie* (The mail will arrive, my dear friend (fem.).) become written as: *Le courier vapasé ma cherami*.

These examples indicate the absence of lexical awareness. But Piaget notes that this does not, however, prevent them from speaking good French! He concludes that "the phrase-word precedes the word" (135) in the development of language. But one must add that this persists into adulthood, and that "correct" lexical segmentation appears later in language development and is a product of orthography, of learning to read.

He notes that for children, once the word is removed from its context, it no longer has an evocative function. The semantic function of the word derives from the whole of its context, and is, most importantly, the result of "a syncretic liaison of all the terms in the context and of the pseudo-logical justifications always ready to surface" in the mind of the child (135). Thus one sees that the meaning that infuses the word is multi-valent and, in psychoanalytic terms, overdetermined by the associations that crisscross among the syntactic elements in the phrase, with no respect paid to part of speech. Moreover, meaning is subject to other psychological elements that weigh upon the context, and that are below the surface, i.e., unconscious or preconscious. This corresponds well to the presence of speech in dreamwork, as described by Freud (see Chapter 5).

He also discusses similar syncretism in drawings made by children:

> Similarly, in infant drawings, the salient details and the whole of the figure are united (*solidaires*). This is why the child, when expressing the figure of a person, is satisfied in juxtaposing a few insignificant or essential details (a head, a button, legs, a navel, etc., randomly) that we would

have chosen in a completely different way, for our perception is no longer syncretic to the same degree.

*(150–151)*

Thus the child perceives via fragmentary condensations and displacements, with the whole being represented in a collage of some of its parts. Thus the child is already processing metonymically (via displacements). This is not, however, entirely absent in the adult. He notes that "egocentric thought, which produces these syncretic phenomena, is closer to autistic thought and to dream than to logical thought". These aspects are aligned "to dream or daydream: to verbal approximations or word-plays" (151). And here, one sees a valuable bridge to psychoanalytic theory:

> Everything moves us to consider the mechanism of syncretic thought as an intermediary between that of logical thought and that which the psychoanalysts have characterized by the ambitious term dream "symbolism"...Freud has demonstrated...on the one hand, condensation, which makes several disparate images melt into one (like several persons into one), and on the other, displacement, which transposes, from one object to another, the characteristics belonging to the former...syncretism... as does the dream, "condenses", into one, elements that are objectively disparate. Like the dream, it "displaces", according to the associations of ideas, completely extraneous resemblances, or word-play assonances (*habit, habitude*).
>
> *(152)*

Here, syncretism is a valuable concept, as it indicates the unity and simultaneity of condensation and displacement in the initial stages of thinking and speaking. As an example of displacement via word-play associations, he offers partial homonymities that have different meanings: French *habit* (costume) and *habitude* (habit, custom). A similar displacement pun in English would be "custom" and "costume". He also notes, however, that these condensations and displacements "are not as absurd as in dreams...or in the autistic imagination... they are close to logical comparison itself. One could posit that they form the transition between prelogical and logical mechanisms of thought" (152). Thus one sees here a fluid continuum from unconscious and preconscious to conscious modes of thought and language. He adds that

> for psychoanalysts, the word was originally connected to the action and consequently expanded in concrete meaning to the point where, even separated from the action, the act of pronouncing the word was taken to be the implementation of the action itself.
>
> *(21)*

One notes here that, at the bottom, the word and the thing are coterminous. In human development, decentering, along with becoming aware of other selves, becomes the vehicle to the logical separation of sign and referent. Moreover, one notes here the origins of magical incantations, the powerful effects of curses, verbal insults, etc.

Piaget illustrates the persistence of unconscious and preconscious motivation in the adult (motivations that he would term preoperational or autistic) with the example of ritualistic uses of water:

> Viewed intelligently, water is a natural substance, of explicable origin, or at least of empirically observable formation. But in autism, on the other hand, water is only interesting in its relationship with organic satisfaction…it has become a motif for purely organic representations for all the phantasies of the people, of children, and of the unconscious of the adult. It has become assimilated, in effect, to liquids issued from the human body, and, because of this, it has come to symbolize birth itself, as attested to by numerous myths (the birth of Aphrodite, etc.), and rituals (baptism, symbol of a new birth).
>
> *(42–43)*

He underscores this in the article "La pensée symbolique et la pensée de l'enfant", where he says that one of the most fruitful principles of psychoanalysis is that adults are always regressive, which is to say that they remain influenced by the memory of infantile thought much more than by consciousness (Piaget, 1923b, p. 302).

In *La formation du symbole chez l'enfant*, he notes that, during the sensory motor period, the signifier and the signified remain undifferentiated (Piaget, 1945, p. 293). Symbol formation begins in the transition between the sensory motor and preoperational stages, at about the age of 1.5–2 years, when the child becomes capable of representing an absent object (the signified) by means of a symbol (the signifier), e.g., it uses a stick or its finger to mime a pistol. Piaget sees this as the debut of interior thought and imaginary production and notes that symbolic play in children is fundamentally compensatory. In its imagination, the child realizes its unsatisfied desires without having to yield to reality. For example, it "feeds" its doll by dipping a spoon into a hollow bowl. It is important to emphasize that, in symbol formation, the image is not an alien element (*élément étranger*) that just appears during development, but an "integral part of the process of imitative accommodation…it marks the point of juncture of the sensory-motor and the representational" (294).

But symbolic play is fundamentally syncretic; it is "the assimilation of whatever object to whatever other one, mediated by imitative images" (295). This is done via vague correspondences, and exists for "the sole pleasure of combination" (301). This corresponds to the synthesizing of objects in dream, and also to Freud's analysis of bungled actions (*Das Vergriefen*), illustrated in the *Psychopathology of Everyday Life* (1901). And it is important to note that the child imitates in its most egocentric stages (308), brought about by its as yet undifferentiated perceptions. For Piaget, the transition from assimilation to accommodation, from making the input correspond to established cognitive structure to the opposite—modifying the cognitive structure to accommodate the new input—characterizes intelligence itself. Intelligence constitutes itself in the process of decentering.

There are several recent and crucially important studies on language processing independent of orthography. They involve studying how those who cannot read understand the concept of a word. This includes preliterate children and illiterate adults. In their study of metalinguistic awareness among adult illiterates, Kurvers et al. found a very concrete understanding of a word as a thing: "In talking about language, words like 'empty' or 'hole' confused them, because they could not understand how something could be a word, 'when there is nothing'" (Kurvers et al., 2006, p. 69). They also found a very poor understanding of word boundaries and cite research showing that "illiterate adults, like young children, perform poorly in segmenting words into phonemes" (70). However, "children who cannot read and write have difficulties in manipulating phonemes in words, while abilities like rhyming or manipulation of syllables are easier to handle" (71). Children have a sense of rhyme but a very limited sense of lexicon and morphology. Similarly, Kolinsky et al. (1987) and Gombert (1994) found significant differences between illiterate and literate adults in perceiving word boundaries.

Kolinsky et al. investigated abstract knowledge of language (metalinguistic knowledge), i.e., to what extent subjects are able to describe what a word is, or how many elements there are in compound nouns, such as, e.g., "roommate", and the influence of literacy on that knowledge. The subjects consisted of two groups: adult readers with about four years of primary school on the average, preliterate children, and illiterate adults. The second and third groups are also characterized as nonreaders.

The experiment focused primarily on awareness of what a word consists of. This is, of course, a tricky concept, as there are many languages with no word for "word". In polysynthetic languages, for instance, which fuse parts of speech into one long utterance, it is difficult to say where one element ends and another begins. One tends to take the concept of a word for granted, but when nonlinguists are asked for a definition of what a word is, they are invariably at a loss for words, and offer tangential responses, such as: "What's in a dictionary". The linguistic definition of a word as an unbound morpheme always comes as news to students in my introductory linguistics courses.

The authors arrived at a clever strategy: They asked subjects to break a sentence into "pieces" and to tell and demonstrate how many pieces were in the sentence. Some illiterate adults, unaccustomed to reflecting upon language, wondered why they were being asked questions about language in the first place, and referred the researchers instead to relatives who had been schooled. One interesting finding is that most illiterate adults had difficulty making rhymes. When asked to choose a word that rhymed with a given word (e.g., what rhymes with door?), they tended to respond by alliteration or with word meaning, i.e., they chose words based on semantic association. They could, indeed, judge if two words rhymed but had difficulties generating the rhyming word itself. Children, on the other hand, were quicker at generating rhyming words than all adults, both literate and illiterate.

Now this merits some reflection. Children, as has been noted, love playing with words, regardless of sense. Nonsense nursery rhymes provide the best example: "Hey diddle diddle, the cat and the fiddle", or "Eeny, meeny, miny, moe". (My adult spellcheck will not accept these spellings.) Such creativity with language comes naturally to children and engages preoperational (primary process) mechanisms of displacement, condensation, and repetition. As talking nonsense is generally frowned upon by both literate and illiterate adults, this faculty tends to lie dormant, reviving, however, in music and poetry, prestige forms of production that can sanction the transgression of the boundaries of sense. In his work on humor (wit) and its relation to the unconscious, Freud observed the connection between rhyming and wordplays. The child's innocent pleasure in rhyming is seen as the basis of humor:

> Playing with words and thoughts...would be the preliminary stage of humor. At a given moment, a critical or logical faculty puts an end to this playing. It is now rejected as nonsense or absurdity; criticism makes it impossible. It is now excluded...unless the maturing individual enters into a pleasurable mood that suspends the resistance, as it does in the joviality of the child.
>
> *(Freud, 1905, p. 144)*

The preliterate child operates freely in this rhyming and punning space, whereas the illiterate adult recognizes it, but no longer freely produces it. It lies dormant, there at the point of the generation of speech.

Similarly, in the experiment conducted by Kolinsky et al., most adults, literate and illiterate, resisted playing a game of inventing new words for common objects and animals. Children, however, played the game quite willingly, changing the names of animals and discussing their attributes afterward. Adults, on the other hand, wondered why one would do this, except for bilingual adults, who were well accustomed to the arbitrariness of names.

Most illiterates did not segment words into sub-lexical units at all. The researchers found that phonemic segmentation is only used by readers, otherwise the syllable is the preferred segmentation unit. Literate adults were better at judging word length than the nonreaders, while the latter tended to employ synesthesia in judging word length, saying, for instance, that a certain word "sounds longer". Some based their judgment on the length of the referent and judged "train" to be a longer word than "motorcycle". Multiple word utterances were judged as single words by most of the children and nonreaders.

The nonreaders offered various explanations for whether or not an utterance is a word, saying, for instance, that it is a word because its referent exists (e.g., car is a word because there are cars); it is not a word because it is too small (as in the case of prepositions and conjunctions); it is a word because it is the name of an animal (as in the case of monkey); or, conversely, it is not a word because monkey is an animal and a word is something spoken. The string: "The shop is closed" was perceived as two words. The nonreaders here seem to be grasping at straws. There seems to be no pattern here, because they have no concept of a word. The nonreaders hardly segmented any sentence into discrete words, tending instead to segment according to groups of words. Literate adults, however, did fine segmenting sentences into discrete words.

The authors decided to test the knowledge of syllogisms among the subject groups and found that the nonreaders had trouble with syllogistic propositions. For instance: "All stones on the moon are blue. A man goes to the moon and finds a stone. What color is it"? The nonreaders tended to base their answer on personal experience, which overrode the logic of the statement, saying, for instance, "I have to see it first", or, "Yellow, because the moon is yellow", or they simply referred to the colors that they know in their experience. The literates, however, used deductive reasoning. Concerning the syllogism, the authors refer to Walter Ong's explanation that a syllogism is an abstract problem treated in formal education. Illiterates rely on experience, in general. Thus the familiarity with syllogistic propositions must be due to schooling, not to the peculiar logic of language, nor to recursivity, nor to the ability to symbolize, since operational adults know the mobility of the sign. The authors conclude that "literacy brings a change in what people know about the language they already understand and speak fluently" (83). Nonreaders are "not aware of the phoneme as a linguistic unit" (83).

The authors posit that rhyming demands more analysis from adults than from children: "Most of the illiterates used kind of a holistic strategy. They judged word length on the basis of duration, they segmented sentences along conceptually or semantically meaningful units, or they mentioned speech acts as examples of words" (84). They tended to consider content words (substantives, verbs, adjectives) to be words, but to leave out function words (prepositions, conjunctions, etc.) from the category of word (84). They conclude: "Learning to read and write may attend, more than any other use of language, to discourse in which sentences or words only refer to each other and to nothing else" (84). Illiterates reacted to the content of the message, not to its constituent units.

Eve V. Clark, in the study "Awareness of Language: Some Evidence from What Children Say and Do", notes that by about the age of five, some children are capable of reflecting on their own language (Clark, 1978, p. 21). They can self-correct and correct others. They can segment with some success (identify words, morphemes, syllables, and sound segments) (27), but they cannot yet identify words well until the age of six or seven, nor can they define a word. Until that age, they offer answers such as: A word is "what you use to talk about something" (28).

Clark notes that children revel in puns, a pan-linguistic phenomenon (31). For example: "Why did the dog go out in the sun? He wanted to be a hot dog. What has an ear but cannot hear? Corn" (31). They also like homonyms and wide-ranging resemblances and associations. They are fascinated by illogical homonymies. She notes that children begin to use metaphors at age ten (32). Metalinguistic awareness also seems to begin here. It is important to note again the waning of these processes in adulthood.

Berthoud-Papandropoulou studied the linguistic knowledge of children aged five years and four months in Geneva. In her article, "An Experimental Study of Children's Ideas About Language", she noted, e.g., that children would explain that *chaise* (chair) is long because it has long legs, and *oeil* (eye) is short because it is little. *Train* is perceived as a long word because trains are long. These findings are interesting, in that they show the perception not of morpheme but of attributes. For a difficult word, they tend to offer a difficult task, with no focus on the unbound morpheme. A difficult word becomes a phrase about a difficult action, and they tend to offer phrases as examples of words (58). She claims that they are in a "semantic" mode. When children start learning to read and write, however, this affects the perception of a word. At age seven and above, they say that a long word has a lot of letters. But at the age of eight, they begin to retrofit grammar learned in school into the perception of language (Berthoud-Papandropoulou, 1978, p. 80).

The work of the Russian psychologist Lev Vygotsky (1896–1934) is important in this context, as he researched the relationship between language and thought, especially in children. His work can be best accessed, for the present purposes, in its reception by Wilson and Weinstein and their study "Language, Thought, and Interiorization. A Vygotskian and Psychoanalytic Perspective". The authors state,

> To Vygotsky, it is only through language that a child realizes his/her potential to supercede immediate sensory experience, because concept generalization is inherent to spoken thought; a word can refer to an entire class of objects, while a visual percept, for example, is singular.
> *(Wilson & Weinstein, 1990, p. 25)*

This is an excellent observation that inverts the common understanding of a word versus a visual image. In languages that have an isolating or analytic element in their grammars, a word is understood as referring to a thing, whereas a visual image is understood to offer a panoramic context. For Vygotsky, however, the semantic field of the word is multivalent, accessing a wide range of meanings.

Take for instance the utterance /raɪt/, which could indicate "write" or "right", the latter with diverse meanings of direction, correction, etc. But on the other hand, Vygotsky's claim leaves out the psychological moment of the visual perception, which can evoke a multitude of associations in a largely unconscious manner. The same is also true of the verbal utterance, be it the syllable, morpheme, or word.

Wilson and Weinstein point out

> an important distinction that Vygotsky draws between word sense and word meaning. Inner speech has as central semantic features a predominance of sense over meaning (sense being the entire context of a word, whereas meaning is the fixed and unchanging point which remains stable during all the changes of sense in various contexts).
>
> *(31)*

They cite Vygotsky directly:

> The sense of a word... is the aggregate of all the psychological facts emerging in our consciousness because of this word. Therefore, the sense of a word always turns out to be a dynamic, flowing, complex formation which has several zones of differential stability. Meaning is only one of the zones of the sense that a word acquires in the context of speaking. Furthermore, it is the most stable, unified, and precise zone.
>
> *(31)*

Again, one sees that language is processed here in a multivalent, associative way, in chains of associations.

Hans G. Furth, in "Symbol Formation: Where Freud and Piaget Meet" (1983), makes fascinating observations that join some of the ideas of the two theorists. He links the Eros drive to symbol formation. He sees symbol formation as the representation of a cathected (lost) object, an attempt to make the love object symbolically present:

> Symbol formation serves the function of social relation. Satisfying experiences of personal relations are symbolically reenacted—Freud spoke in this connection of primal experiences of satisfaction and of the finding again of a lost object—and in this manner the children construct their 'inner' world. It becomes the private protective context in which children's ego and their object relations develop further.
>
> *(Furth, 1983, p. 38)*

This would begin with the oral phase, when infants insert objects into the mouth. Nurslings then generalize the sucking function from nipple to any object insertable into the mouth, and that object then connects to the breast symbolically. This is the setting up of a lost object in the ego, as Freud described in *The Ego and the Id*. Identification is seen as a form of symbol formation.

This recalls Piaget's observations in *La formation du symbole chez l'enfant*, that, at about the age of 1.5–2 years, symbolic play in children is fundamentally compensatory. In its imagination, the child realizes its unsatisfied desires without having to yield to reality. As in the example stated earlier, it "feeds" its doll by dipping a spoon into a hollow bowl. Whether this stage is the origin of symbol formation, or an instantiation of it, remains to be seen.

The work of Piaget is invaluable for demonstrating how language emerges in preliterate and preoperational modes of thought, and how writing is an operation performed upon those modes. In Chapter 4, precognitive and preoperational manifestations of language are demonstrated in the mechanisms of dreamwork, in which the progression, in adult thought, along the syntagma of unconscious–preconscious–conscious cognition is readily visible, especially as concerns language processing.

## References

Clark, E. (1978). Awareness of language: Some evidence from what children say and do. In A. Sinclair et al. (Eds.), *The child's conception of language* (pp. 17–43). Springer.
Freud, S. (1901). *Zur Psychopathologie des Alltagslebens. Über Vergessen, Versprechen, Vergreifen, Aberglaube und Irrtum. Gesammelte Werke* (Vol. 4, pp. 5–321). Imago. [English edition: Freud, S. (1953–1974). *The Psychopathology of everyday life. The standard edition of the complete psychological works of Sigmund Freud* (Vol. 6, pp. 1–279). Hogarth].
Freud, S. (1905). *Der Witz und seine Beziehung zum Unbewussten. Gesammelte Werke* (Vol. 6, pp. 1–285). Imago. [English edition: Freud, S. (1953–1974). *Jokes and their relation to the unconscious. The standard edition of the complete psychological works of Sigmund Freud* (Vol. 8, pp. 1–236). Hogarth].
Furth, H. (1983). Symbol formation: Where Freud and Piaget meet. *Human Development* 26, 26–41.
Gombert, J. (1994). How do illiterate adults react to metalinguistic training? *Annals of Dyslexia* 44(1), 250–269.
Kolinsky, R. et al. (1987) Awareness of words as phonological entities: The role of literacy. *Applied Psycholinguistics* 8, 223–232.
Kurvers, J. et al. (2006). Discovering features of language: Metalinguistic awareness of adult illiterates. In E. van de Craats et al. (Eds.), *Low-educated second language and literacy acquisition: Proceedings of the inaugural symposium Tilburg 2005* (pp. 69–88). LOT.
Piaget, J. (1923a). *Le langage et la pensée chez l'enfant*. Delacheux & Niestlé.
Piaget, J. (1923b). La pensée symbolique et la pensée de l'enfant. *Archives de Psychologie* 18, 273–304.
Piaget, J. (1945). *La formation du symbole chez l'enfant*. Delacheux & Niestlé.
Piaget, J. (1947). *La représentation du monde chez l'enfant*. Presses Universitaires de France.
Wilson, A., & Weinstein, L. (1990). Language, thought, and interiorization. A Vygotskian and psychoanalytic perspective. *Contemporary Psychoanalysis* 26(1), 24–39.

# 4
# DREAMWORK
## The precognitive formation of language

In 1913, Freud published an essay on the value of psychoanalysis for the science of language (*Das sprachwissenschaftliche Interesse*). He begins by proposing a broad understanding of language that goes beyond just words: It includes gesture (*Gebärdensprache*). He states that the psychoanalytic interpretation of dreams is a translation from a foreign text into one we are familiar with. And he says of the language of dreams, "That it belongs, to a large degree, to an archaic system of expression" (*dass sie einem in hohem Grade archaischen Ausdruckssystem angehört*). He makes the crucial observation that negation is never marked especially in dreams, and thus in the unconscious, and that antitheses may replace each other and become represented by the same element. Concepts themselves are ambivalent and combine and recombine in contradictory meanings. The language of the unconscious is a symbolic one that operates as does a writing system, but here it operates as do rebuses. He is not speaking of established orthography, but instead of the generation of a rebus-like writing system:

> The interpretation of a dream is in fact fully analogous to the decipherment of an ancient pictograph, as in Egyptian hieroglyphics. Elements are present that are not there to be interpreted or read, but instead only function to help determine the meaning of another element.
> *(Freud, 1913, pp. 403–404)*

And here he resembles Saussure, in the notion that meaning is inter-symbolic, i.e., a relation among symbols, and not one of concept to referent.

Freud's *Traumdeutung* (*The Interpretation of Dreams*) serves as an excellent demonstration of the mechanisms of displacement, condensation, repetition, overdetermination, and repression, especially as these concern the generation

DOI: 10.4324/9781003180197-5

## Dreamwork: The precognitive formation of language 53

of language. Here, the rebus (picture puzzle) is at the basis of the formation of thought and language. The first dream studied is the "Dream of the Botanical Monograph". The dream content is simple and laconic:

> *I*ch habe eine Monographie über eine (unbestimmt gelassene) Pflanzenart geschrieben. Das Buch liegt vor mir, ich blättere eben eine eingeschlagene farbige Tafel um. Dem Exemplar ist ein getrocknetes Spezimen der Pflanze beigebunden.
> 
> *(Freud, 1900, pp. 287–288)*

> I wrote a monograph on an unspecified genus of plant. The book lies in front of me, and I am flipping over an inserted colored sheet. The copy contains a bound dried specimen of the plant.

Fortunately, the phonetic correspondences work in a similar fashion in both the German and English versions. Freud had seen that day a book on display on the botanical genus cyclamen. He was immediately reminded of his work on cocaine, which he shared with the physician Königstein. One notes the repetition of the phoneme /k/ in: botanical, cyclamen, cocaine, and Königstein, which enables the associative connections. He continues: "'Botanical' is connected to the person of Professor Gärtner, the blooming looks of his wife, to my patient Flora…Gärtner leads in turn to the laboratory and to my conversation with Königstein" (288).

The name "Gärtner" means "gardener" in English, and Freud comments on the looks of Gärtner's "blooming wife" *(seine blühende Frau)*. His patient "Flora" is associated here, as well. The narration of the dream reveals many other associations, but the ones listed here suffice for an interpretation of the images. The dream is motivated by two basic anxieties: professional and sexual. While cocaine was not illegal at that time, its indulgence was still subject to social censorship. In addition, his attraction to his colleague's wife, as well as his immediate mentioning of his patient Flora, while natural sexual responses, are not entirely unproblematic. The associations of these anxieties are enabled through phonetic and semantic correspondences, the semantic ones being a product of metaphorical extension.

One sees here a displacement and condensation of the problematic subtext: sex and drugs. These are displaced, sublimated, and neutralized into an allegorical narrative—a botanical monograph—and condensed into the floral images. This means that the semantic and phonetic associations were going on all the time, enabled by neural networks that connect associated sounds and meanings. These are unconscious and preconscious correspondences, precognitive in nature, that materialize in the formation of thought and language. This is the phenomenon of overdetermination *(Überdeterminierung)*, in which the phonetic and the semantic are "firing" along associative neural networks. One notes that the surface summary of the dream is at the tail end of this process. The subject here is articulating this experience in an act of avoidance. In other words, the linguistic end product is determined by defense mechanisms. This is the role of the secondary process and of secondary revision.

One important aspect involved in the act of becoming conscious of the dream concerns that which remains defended and hidden from introspection. The dream resists intelligibility, and there will be elements that the subject remains unaware of. An example can be found in the presence of the "dried specimen" (*ein getrocknetes Spezimen*), which partially alliterates with the word "semen" (*Samen*), and which can be related to the underlying sexual anxieties. Freud was approaching 50 at that time, an age that was considered to be much "older" than it is nowadays. Thus one can add another layer to the sexual anxiety: superannuation, a fear of "drying up".

Freud sees the words "botanical" and "monograph" here as repetitive nodal points for the condensations, because they have the most expansive interconnectivity for the dream thoughts. He specifies that "each element of the dream content manifests itself as 'overdetermined', as repeatedly represented in the dream thoughts" (289). And the overdetermination can access images that remain occulted from awareness.

There is another dream recounted by one of his patients that also sheds light on the phenomenon of overdetermination, where the word sits at the center of a network of phonetic and semantic correspondences. This is the *Käfertraum*, or "beetle dream" of one of his patients. The summary of the dream content is as follows:

> She remembers that she has two May-beetles in a box and has to give them their freedom, or they would suffocate. She opens the box, and the may-beetles are exhausted. One of them flies out of the open window; the other, however, gets crushed by the casement while she is shutting it at someone else's request (expressions of disgust).
>
> *(295)*

The casement here refers to casement windows (*Fensterflügel*), which open and close as do doors. The dream combines several elements. Her young daughter had begun collecting May-beetles during a beetle plague in their region. Her children were mad at the beetles and crushed them horribly. She herself was born, and also married, in May. Three days after her marriage, she had written home saying how happy she was. But this was not at all the case. She was continually worried about her absent husband and had waking phantasies that something bad would happen to him when away from home. They argued often about open and closed windows. She preferred to sleep with them open, and he with them closed. She often complained of exhaustion (296–298).

One sees here a nuclear anxiety that becomes articulated through condensations and displacements into the surface images of exhaustion, liberation, and two moths: one that escapes out of an open window and one that gets crushed at "someone else's request". She is "suffocating" in her marriage and feels "boxed in" (*eingeschachtelt*). She is also "plagued" by this. Her identity becomes split into two *Doppelgänger*: one who suffocates to death and one who flies off to freedom. The "someone" who requested that the window be shut is her husband, who prefers to keep them closed. The central condensation operates along the phonetic resonances of the morpheme "May", into which her identity is condensed: This is the month of her birth and marriage, and her predicament becomes transferred to the dilemma of the May beetles, with whom she shares an insignificant status. The dreamwork's indifference to contradictions should be noted: She dies, and she also escapes at the same time.

The dream content emerges along the chain unconscious…preconscious… consciousness, all the while dealing with "the antithesis between the coherent ego and the repressed which is split off from it" (Freud, 1923, p. 244). And here, the *Doppelgänger* reveals the incoherency that is at the seat of the anxiety of identity. Again, meaning and phonetics proceed together along the network of overdetermined correspondences.

Freud comments extensively on the presence of nonsense neologisms in dreams and says, "The work of condensation in dreams is best understood when it handles words and names. Words are frequently treated in dreams as though they were things and experience the same combinations as do representations of things" (Freud, 1900, pp. 301–302). This corresponds to the stage of nominal realism described by Piaget, where the child understands words and names in pre-symbolic form. It also fits well into the discussion of speech errors (see Chapter 5).

Freud gives the following example. He had read an article that overestimated the importance of a scientific discovery and dreamt of this sentence the following evening: "It is written in a positively *norekdal* style". He analyzes the dream as a parody of the words *kolossal* and *pyramidal*, and sees that it is a composition of the two names *Nora* and *Ekdal*—characters in two plays by Ibsen, about which he had read an article earlier. He was criticizing the author of the article in his dream (302). One sees here the expanse of the field of possible overdetermination. Beginning with the condensation centering on the author, the dream searches the "web" for morphophonemic correspondences. Such is the nature of language processing.

In another nonsense dream neologism, Freud discusses a dream reported to him, in which the dreamer saw the word *erzefilisch*. The segment *filisch* can be connected to the English affix "philic", meaning "fond of", as in, e.g., acidophilic, "fond of acid", i.e., growing well in acidic environments. The German derivational morpheme -*isch* is cognate with the English -ic, c.f., *philosophisch* / philosophic. So the blend *erzefilisch* would indicate "fond of erze". The blend evokes the compounds *erzieherisch* and *erzählerisch*, meaning "educative" and "narrative", respectively. The dreamer had been lecturing his governess on a medical topic and was being a bit too didactic (*erzieherisch*), as well as verbose (*erzählerisch*). The German word for governess is *Erzieherin,* literally "educator". The oneiric blend *erzefilisch* condensed the images of didacticism, verbosity, and governess into the root *erze*. The problem is that the lexical elements themselves are normally created by adding the productive morpheme *-er* to the stems of the verbs *ziehen* (*zieh-*) and *zählen* (*zähl-*). But the oneiric blend does not respect the conventional morpheme boundary, and instead of isolating *-er*, it isolates *-erze*. (The final vowel would be a schwa in the unstressed syllable.) This shows that the segmentation is not determined by morphological convention, but by the allusive properties of a sequence of phonemes. There is also a productive morpheme *-erz* in German, corresponding to the English "arch", as in Archangel (German *Erzengel*). Thus one can add that the dreamer was being arch-didactic and arch-verbose with his governess (308–309).

This would indicate that the solidification of agglutinative morphemes would be a secondary process imposed upon sequences of phonemes that, at bottom, can resonate and recombine randomly. More on this below.

In 1906, Emil Kraeplin published *Über Sprachstörungen im Traume*, a study of speech disturbances while dreaming, specifically psychologically motivated perseverations, anticipations, transpositions, and blends. His corpus foregrounds the psychoanalytic elements and uses the mechanisms of dreamwork in his analyses. His data is important for a psychoanalytic understanding of speech errors.

He notes the surfacing of contradictions in motivated slips, specifically a substitution of opposites within the same semantic field. In a dream of a physical examination, he reports a substitution of *lebensgefährliche Punkte* with *lebenslängliche Punkte* ("life threatening spots" with "lifelong spots"), thus indicating the wish that life be extended and not threatened (Kraeplin, 1906, p. 11).

A similar parapraxis is found in the string: *Ich spreche immer zufällig die Wahrheit* ("I always speak the truth randomly"), which substitutes *zuverlässig* ("reliably") with *zufällig* ("randomly"). The phonetic proximity is as such (the transcription presumes the vocalization of /r/):

[tsufɛᵊlɛsɪç]
[tsufɛlɪç]

The slip becomes facilitated by the phonetic identity of the first two syllables [tsu] and [fɛ] (11).

Kraeplin notes that such slips are found in wakeful speaking as well. The simultaneous representation of antitheses is also to be noted here.

In another example, the intended utterance *er hat noch mehrere Male eingeladen* ("he has invited a lot") (13) becomes blended into *im übrigen ist er noch mehrere Male erüberdernd warden*. The string is syntactically and semantically acceptable, with the exception of the neologism *erüberdernd*, without which the string would read "also he has been ____ several times". The dream inserts a corruption of the verb *erübrigen*, which carries the meaning of "left over, superfluous, excessive". This indicates invited/inviting to the point of excess. It is important to note that the blend carries the present participle suffix *-ernd*, where a perfect participle would be expected. The syntactic violation here indicates that unconscious and preconscious language processing—dreamwork language processing—has not yet graduated to the accepted syntactic habits of the German language, indicating that syntactic categories do not exist a priori in the unfolding of language. This can be compared with the study of the idiom "*das zu lesende Buch*", which displays a similar syntactic violation, but here, it is a conventional idiomatic utterance (see Chapter 11).

Kraeplin also supplies examples of compression and condensation, e.g., *Ich habe einen Grund, einen Würzgrund*. The string carries an allusion to the city of Würzburg and contains numerous puns on *Gründe* ("grounds") *Gründe* ("reasons"), *Würze* ("seasoning"), and *würzen* ("to spice"). Thus there is a play on grounds, reasons, spices, and the city of Würzburg. The parapraxis accesses the semantic fields of *Grund* and the stem *Würz-* and condenses them into one overdetermined pun, comfortably ignoring the lexical categories of verb and noun (14).

He notes the substitution in a dream of *Vendiasmen* for *Bestechlichkeit* (17). This is a multilingual pun. *Bestechlichkeit* is the word for "corruptibility" and derives from the verb *bestechen*, which means "to bribe". The condensation *Vendiasmen* contains the suffix *iasmen*, which is the plural suffix of *-i/asmus*, a bound morpheme corresponding to the English "ism", e.g., "enthusiasm" is *Enthusiasmus* in German. The morpheme is used in many medical terms, e.g., *Metabolismus*; *Dichromatismus* (a type of color blindness); *Miasmen* ("miasmas"). The *-us* morpheme derives from the Latin nominative singular *-us* (e.g., *maximus*, etc.). The first syllable *vend* is segmented off from the Italian *vendere*, "to sell". So the substitution would be "selling diseases" for "corruptibility". This is a wonderful multilingual condensation that scans syllables and morphemes and condenses them into a trilingual blend of German, Latin, and Italian.

Kraeplin also reports the combination *Wegegewaltige*, which consists of *Wege* ("ways, roads") and *gewaltige* (powerful ones), indicating people who presume the vehicular right of way. This neologism would be comprehensible in conscious discourse and is not redlined by a German spellcheck. One clearly sees here a condensation aided by repetitions of the velar stop [g]. This is a unification of themes via phoneme repetition, a subordination of semantics to phonology.

Kraeplin discusses some of the speech errors made by Prof. Johann Georg August Galletti, a *Gymnasialprofessor* in Gotha, whose "howlers" are well-known in German folklore. They indicate the dominance of metonymy/displacement in the production of language, e.g., "The difference between ancient and modern Persia lies mainly in the ignorance of language", and "The Aleutian Islands live in mud huts" (63–64). These are displacement errors caused by a confusion of identity and metonymy, where metonyms on the margins of the semantic field can substitute for the central referent.

A major contribution to the psychoanalytic understanding of language has been offered by Frank Heynick in *Language and Its Disturbances in Dreams*. Heynick ran an experiment trying to replicate Kraeplin's study. He collected 561 utterances from dream speech among Dutch subjects, and his findings parallel those of Kraeplin.

Heynick reads Freud as placing speech in the realm of secondary processes. He sees dreaming as a regression to a preverbal stage, which becomes verbal in its progression into waking recollection. This fits well into the psychoanalytic model, in which the root meaning of the dream is unknowable, due to repression. The recollected dream consists in symptoms (displacements and condensations) that receive their structure in the mechanics of secondary revision (Heynick, 1993, p. 13). And here, he holds that the secondary processes are "governed by the laws of grammar and formal logic" (13). This is akin to the imposition of structures of formal logic upon the generation of language. Heynick studies hypnagogic manifestations of language, those that occur just before falling asleep, and that are thus located in a liminal preconscious area. The notion of a preformal and preconscious generation of language is strengthened by Heynick's interesting observations on the dreams studied by Freud and Kraeplin: They contain very few examples of reading and writing. He holds that "all this accords with the psychoanalytic concept of dreaming as a partial regression to an earlier state of ontological development. Reading and writing are acquired later than listening comprehension and speaking" (56–57).

In this context, Heynick discusses the structural differences between transformational grammar and dreamwork. While transformations from infrastructure to superstructure are common to both, there are nonetheless major differences. There is no negation in dreamwork. Also, the UG model sees ambiguity arising from two distinct deep structures. Heynick supplies a good example in the phrase "questioning psychiatrists can be boring" (211), where the ambiguity is accounted for by deriving the phrase from a verb or a noun. But the manifest content of the dream can be a result of "a multitude of possible underlying meanings" (211), in which the phenomenon of overdetermination pays little attention to grammatical and syntactic difference, as has been seen. The constraints imposed upon speech "are far looser in the generation of dreams" (211). Again, syntactic laws are imposed upon the infrastructure of language and restrict and transform dream thoughts (latent) into dream content (manifest). And in the return of the repressed, the primary processes can transgress surface boundaries and generate parapraxes. This problematizes the traditional distinction between competence and performance. UG tends to posit an intact and "perfect" linguistic competence, and mistakes are relegated to the level of performance. However, "such loosening of constraints in actual performance makes speech more like dream images and events, by yielding displacements (word substitutions), condensations (word-blends), disjunctions of elements (syntactic ungrammaticality), and the like" (213).

Heynick refers to Chomsky's notion of the natural faculty of linguistic judgment, which defers to "native speaker" authority as the litmus test of acceptability. Thus our linguistic competence supposedly means that we are "able to determine slight distortions or misprints" when reading new sentences (Chomsky, 1959, p. 42). Freud, however, discusses at length the glossing over of misprints in his discussion of secondary revision. This has been recently validated by Cohen (1973), whose data shows that subjects have a tendency to overlook misprints, unless the misprint is excessively deviant. Competence, in short, derives from the accumulation of repeated habitual utterances. Habituation causes an utterance to "sound right or wrong".

Heynick notes that the oddities in dream speech are seldom corrected within the dream itself, unless these are thematized, i.e., unless the dream itself is about speech errors. He refers the reader to Freud's report of a dream he had about making mistakes in English, where he confused the prepositions "by" and "from", as both can be rendered by the German *von* (Freud, 1900, p. 456). The dream was clearly generated by an anxiety of insufficient knowledge of English. Freud notes a similar phenomenon in a dream about making mistakes in Latin (Heynick, 1993, p. 442).

Again, the process of secondary revision is important here. The recalled dream is a revision, and the syntacticality of the utterance in dream was most likely not there in the dream itself. Heynick and Kraeplin both note that the more nonsensical the dream neologism is, the harder it is to recall. Secondary revision can deem the memory unsalvageable. This is the entry port of grammar, as the utterance moves through the preconscious into consciousness.

Heynick poses the interesting question, "Can the label *homo somniens* serve as well as *homo sapiens* and *homo loquens* to distinguish species"? (281). All three are unique to the cognitive abilities of humans. "The dreaming animal" is an interesting hypothesis. We know, however, that some animals do dream, but we have no way of knowing if they dream in the same way that humans do. Nonetheless, the psychoanalytic model shows that the major cognitive mechanisms of dreamwork are continually present, even in conscious (linguistic) behavior.

In 1963, Werner & Kaplan published *Symbol Formation: An Organismic-developmental Approach to Language and the Expression of Thought*, in which they make important contributions to the understanding of dreamwork and its relation to language processing. They invoke a holistic approach to language, in which the elements of language are interrelated in a framework of overdetermination. This is not a perspective in which categories are fixed and immutable: "In general, the holistic assumption is opposed to any view that would treat an element...as if it possessed a fixed structure or meaning" (Werner & Kaplan,

1963, p. 4). Linguistic elements interrelate as do tonalities in music: "Tones identical in isolation may be functionally different in markedly distinct melodic wholes" (4). This contravenes the modular approach to language that sees it as consisting of units in isolation. In the organismic-holistic view, "every behavioral act, whether outward bodily movement or internalized cognitive operation, gains its significance and status in terms of its role in the overall functioning of the organism" (4–5). For the authors, the human is the symbolic animal, distinguished from other animals by the faculty of language, which they configure as fundamentally symbolic. Ergo, animal communication consists of "nonlinguistic asymbolic signals" (17).

Published in 1963, the authors' study is quite forward-looking and broaches the topic of inner speech, which has been controversial recently in theories of language processing. In their study of the handling of linguistic forms in dreams, they observe that "dream speech seems to be quite close to an extreme condition of inner speech" (241). Here, free association dominates: "The extreme fusion of addressor and addressee results in the symbolizer not being confronted with those demands for highly articulate representation" (241). This involves an early configuration of embodied cognition: "There is a very close tie between bodily states and representation in any form…bodily states and post-gestural representation very easily glide over into verbal expressions, which 'stick close' to the bodily patterning" (243). These amount to visual puns. For instance, with the urge to urinate, the dreamer would dream of a waterfall, or pressure hose, or river. With Piaget, they observe that dreams tend to concretize or literalize abstract expressions, as does the cognition of preoperational children.

The authors hold that verbal utterances in dream are arranged without regard to syntax—they are dystaxic. Condensation and dystaxia

> may actually be virtues rather than defects. Such characteristics eliminate unnecessary redundancy, and facilitate rapidity of thinking; they also serve to bring together diverse trains of thought, promoting that connection of disparate ideas which is at the basis of productive thinking.
>
> *(323)*

They say of condensation, that it occurs when the relationship between two things is other than similarity—a nice concise description. They add that this may "reflect primitive attempts to express a causal relation" (471).

There are also examples of para-semantic words—unexpected words that substitute for the normal ones—in which "the literal meanings of the words uttered in the dream are only remotely related to the intended meanings" (245). This preconscious ideation of language (e.g., "He bit off more than he could chew") may perhaps be the source of idiomatic (metaphorical) expressions. This theme will be revisited in Chapter 12 on metaphor.

They discuss logical relations in dreams, saying that for Freud, "Dreams have no inherent means of representing logical relations between thoughts" (467–468); inversion and denial are not the stuff of logic: "Dreams do not transform a counterfactual into a contrary but treat the counterfactual state of affairs as if it were actual (Not $A = A$)" (471). (So much for logical propositions!) Dreams also treat similarity differently than in logical relations. The dream does not say, for instance, that Fred is like Alice. It just supplies the image of Alice, and one is supposed to figure out that the subject is Fred. The same is true in compositions, where two people are fused into one.

They also deal with the phenomenon of switching out opposites in the same semantic field:

> Because contraries emerge from a common matrix, a contrary may be implied in any aspect of a dream image that potentially admits of a contrary: For example, something 'going up'…may also signify 'going down'; something 'hot'…may also signify 'cold'; and so on.
>
> *(472)*

They propose that such phenomena "are also employed in the imagery of the waking state" (472). And this is certainly true in the case of verbal slips.

They raise the possibility that polysynthesis could express an earlier state of language when languages possessed noun-verbs, and not separate nouns and verbs, which distinctions would have arisen gradually. Whorf notes this in his discussion of the Hopi phrase "it is summering", where one sees a noun-verb unity, and also in his discussions of Nootka, a Wakashan language in the Pacific Northwest, spoken on the west coast of Vancouver Island. Nootka inflects nouns, e.g., "it houses". Inflected for duration and temporality, they appear to us as verbs. They express "eventing" (Whorf, 1964). Here, "the properties of objects are perceived as dynamic, kinetic, or physiognomized qualities" (Werner & Kaplan, 1963, p. 484). The absence of noun-verb distinction is common in Amerindian languages. If this does correspond to an earlier state in the development of language, it can aid in the understanding of the ease of function shift in English, e.g., "to wash" becoming "a wash".

Werner and Kaplan cite research holding that Amerindian languages tend to be literal and nonabstract. They state that Navaho generates expressions "with great exactness by manipulating the wide choice of stems…by fusing prefixes and other separable elements in an almost unlimited number of ways". In contrast with abstracting languages like English, "Navaho thought is prevailingly much more specific, so much more concrete". Such languages use "holophrastic symbols…unitary forms that refer to a complex state of affairs" (486). They use linguistic codes that are less distant from their referents than those in English. In Klamath, a polysynthetic language of the Pacific NW, now extinct, one finds *shlelxtchanólatkó*, meaning "dropped and left behind altogether something garment-like while walking" (486–487). The authors explain the common absence of tense in polysynthetic languages as due to the minute specificity of description, and propose that tense evolves with abstraction (cf. Evans and Levinson, 2009).

One footnote to the discussion of dreams: It raises the question of where dreaming comes from in the first place, i.e., why would it have been selected for in evolution? We know that we dream in REM sleep, a stage of heightened brain activity, from which one can be easily awakened. Valli and Revonsuo, in "Evolutionary Psychological Approaches to Dream Content" (2007), propose that REM is a sentinel device to keep us alert when sleeping, in order to alert us to dangers. Clearly, the psychoanalytic mechanisms of displacement, condensation, overdetermination, repetition, etc., which are fundamental to language and cognition, continue to operate in sleep, but these are found in a playing field that is much less limited than that of conscious behavior, a zone of free play. In "The Nature and Functions of Dreaming" (2007), Hartmann maintains that the far-flung connections in dreams help us imagine new relations in waking life. Interconnectivity would maintain problem-solving strategies, thus a kind of rehearsal.

Wilson and Weinstein (1990) think that it is only through psychoanalysis that one can "resurrect the original meaning-situation which has become 'fossilized', that is preserved in some way in its original form" (Wilson & Weinstein, 1990, p. 37). This is a much more ambitious assertion than would have been made by Freud himself, who insisted that the unconscious is fundamentally unknowable, a kind of black hole that swallows the light of analysis. And post-Freudians such as Lacan and Žižek agree that we know the unconscious only through secondary symptoms, i.e., displacements, condensations, and other defense mechanisms.

In 1992, the authors published "Language and the Psychoanalytic Process: Psychoanalysis and Vygotskian Psychology. II", where they state that repression is connected to "the formation of the superego. Repression proper becomes necessary because during the oedipal period, for the first time the dangerous impulses of the id must be permanently excluded from awareness at the behest of the superego" (Wilson & Weinstein, 1992, p. 729). And they make the following observation: "Dynamically repressed mental content is made conscious through fantasies, memories, parapraxes, dreams, jokes, and puns" (732). And this is what happens in verbal parapraxes, when the separation of word and thought does not hold, and the thought forces the word to emerge in warped form—in the slip of the tongue.

They characterize the basis of repression as "the unavoidable futility of the child's attempt to translate between language and thought. Until language can meet thought on near equal footing, some precision must be lost in translation" (734). This can be related to Piaget's studies, which offer a similar non-pathological explanation of the issue. It concerns the underdevelopment of language and its inability to express thought. Repression occurs in the theater of language, and it is incomplete, as language is an unstable medium.

The authors make an excellent observation, one that helps the psychological enter in to the theater of metaphorical extension: "Vygotsky's explication of word sense as opposed to the decontextualized meaning of a word highlights the affective elements inherent in its metaphoric extension" (740). And the idea that one can arrive at a root meaning, a "prior affective meaning" (741), can be modified, as the entry into the theater of metaphor is like an entry into a circus hall of mirrors. However, one can intuit that there is "a prior affective meaning" that the individual is disinclined to change: "A patient's metaphoric use of language brings into the hour the rudiments of a self-interpretation" (741). They add that

> the metaphoric allows the introduction of warded-off experience into the psychoanalytic situation because both permit a wider accrual of linkages between the past and the present than those available to secondary-process thought. The metaphoric functions as action outside of awareness.
> *(743)*

They see a progression from egocentric speech, to inner speech, and then to conventional speech:

> Egocentric speech appears at about the age of three, disappears at about seven, and peaks in the middle. *Parallels to the oedipal stage are no coincidence.* The process of egocentric speech being transmuted into inner speech accompanies the internalization of the self-regulating functions characteristic of the development of the superego.
> *(749–750)*

One normally situates the oedipal stage at three to five years of age.

The authors discuss the phenomenon of inner speech as viewed by Vygotsky, and they emphasize the difference between egocentric (idiosyncratic) speech and allocentric (conventional) speech. There are three defining semantic features of inner speech: agglutination, the domination of sense over meaning, and the infusion of sense into a word. In agglutination, word parts synthesize into one word, a form of condensation. The authors hold that "agglutination is somewhat similar to condensation, except in agglutination the result of the combination is always a unified word that is recognizable" (744). This corresponds to the preconscious–conscious distinction, with the former being the locus of dreamwork condensations, which are less clear. Nonetheless, this shows the fluidity of word boundaries. Inner speech is not fully conscious;

thus it still displays primary processes and preoperational features: "The predominance of sense over meaning suggests that the concurrent intralinguistic context predominates over the stable denotation of the word" (745). Inner speech, directed to the self, "has different syntactic and semantic properties than speech directed to the other". It is "abbreviated, telegraphic, predicative (subjectless)", but "these aspects of speech also merge in conversational language usage" (746).

They also discuss predicativity, the dropping of the subject, as in, e.g., "Went to the store. Got an eggplant". This happens in analysis, where inner speech emerges and the analysand assumes contextual understanding on the part of the analyst (745). They see a continuum with inner speech at one end and, on the other, written language "being the most decontexted, fully explicated form" (746). They also emphasize that written language is an imposition upon language.

Similarly, Pinker and Jackendoff hold that language, like human behavior, is dynamic. One of the major factors involved in language change is the process of in-group identity formation: "Whatever mechanism underlies inner speech—presumably the phonological loop that makes up a major component of working memory—it is not subject matter of any familiar theory of grammatical competence" (Pinker & Jackendoff, 2005, p. 224). They note that the purpose of the language faculty "is for learning language from the community, not for inventing language. One cannot have inner speech without having words, and words above all are learned" (225). One would better substitute "words" with "linguistic representations", due to the transgressive fluidity of inner speech, which Freud has termed "thinking in pictures", as language and ideation form a unity in inner speech.

Wilson and Weinstein review their earlier assertion that one can "resurrect the original meaning-situation which has become 'fossilized', that is preserved in some way in its original form" (Wilson & Weinstein, 1990, p. 37), but here, one must admit that this takes place in displaced form:

> The Vygotskian view suggests that the earliest communicational climates between infant and caregiver become ground into the composition of the word itself…the succession of senses through which a word acquires connotations over time carries the imprint of one's affective history.
>
> *(736)*

But one must recognize that sense is lost in the succession of senses. One must extrapolate, as the analyst does from the intonations of the analysand: "How the word is uttered, i.e., the *prosodic* aspects of language which include pitch, rhythm, and tonality, can be a manifest form through which crucial material excluded from consciousness by primal repression can be glimpsed" (736). "Refracted" would be a better term than "glimpsed".

The *prosodic* aspects of language—pitch, rhythm, and tonality—can be seen as modes of language that act as windows to the preconscious.

Jackendoff and Lehrdahl, in "The Capacity for Music: What Is It, and What's Special about It"?, posit the existence of a "musical grammar" and pose questions concerning the capacity for music that "are entirely parallel to the familiar questions that underpin the modern inquiry into the language faculty". Comparing music with language, they posit the existence of a "broad musical capacity, which includes any aspect of the mind/brain involved in the acquisition and processing of music, and the narrow musical capacity" (Jackendoff & Lehrdahl, 2006, pp. 34–35).

After an enjoyable study of the musicality of several Beatles tunes, they conclude that

> it has proven virtually impossible to disentangle the parts that belong to the narrow musical capacity, those that are shared with other art forms, those that are shared with general auditory perception, those that are shared with vocal communication, and those that partake of more general cognition…These specifically musical features are richly interwoven with many other cognitive and affective mechanisms in such a way that it is impossible to think of music as a module…we would expect the existence of overlaps with language as well as dissociations from language, as have been observed. We have proposed that the aspects of musical affect that distinguish it from other sources of affect should be pursued not directly, but rather in terms of the interaction of musical structure with motor patterns that evoke affect. In these terms, a leading question ought to be how temporal patterns in audition can be linked with temporal patterns in posture and gesture, and how these are in turn linked with affect. These are issues for venues larger than music cognition alone, but music can provide a superb source of evidence.
> 
> *(68)*

Of this article, Kenneally says that

> large structures in music can be like dramatic arcs in narratives. The slow buildup of tension, a climax, and then denouement can be found in both musical pieces and stories. It may be that both music and language exploit a human predisposition to understand events in terms of tension and resolution.
> 
> *(Kenneally, 2007, p. 170)*

The sinusoidal alternation of tension and resolution has clear sexual connotations. Indeed, some psychoanalytic theory sees the alternation as a sublimation of sexual tension and release.

But it is not only the dynamic of tension and resolution that determine the "musical grammar", but also the human love affair with echolalia, with rhyme and phonetic allusion. If the two grammars—music and language— are inseparable, then musicality is, indeed, present in language production and processing, and it can widen the overdetermined network of language and cognition.

The study of dreamwork illuminates the unconscious and preconscious processing of language and shows that these processes are continual in adult speech, although controlled by the mechanisms of secondary revision and the related function of conscious reflection. It was George Steiner who said, "Language is, in a sense, an attempt to interpret, to narrate dreams older than itself" (Steiner, 1983, p. 7).

The next chapter will illuminate the presence of psychoanalytic processes in speech errors and humor.

## References

Chomsky, N. (1959). Review of B.F. Skinner's *Verbal Behavior*. *Language* 35, 26–28.

Cohen, A. (1973). Errors of speech and their implication for understanding the strategy of language users. In V. Fromkin (Ed.), *Speech errors as linguistic evidence* (pp. 88–92). De Gruyter.

Evans, N., & Levinson, C. (2009). The myth of language universals: Language diversity and its importance for cognitive science. *Behavioral and Brain Sciences* 32, 429–492.

Freud, S. (1900). *Die Traumdeutung*. Gesammelte Werke (Vols. 1–2, pp. 1–724). Imago. [English edition: Freud, S. (1953–1974). *The interpretation of dreams. The standard edition of the complete psychological works of Sigmund Freud* (Vols. 4–5, pp. 9–686). Hogarth].

Freud, S. (1913). *Das sprachwissenschaftliche Interesse*. Gesammelte Werke (Vol. 8, pp. 403–407). Imago. [English edition: (1953–1974). *The philological interest of psycho-analysis. The standard edition of the complete psychological works of Sigmund Freud* (Vol. 13, pp. 176–178). Hogarth].

Freud, S. (1923). *Das Ich und das Es*. Gesammelte Werke (Vol. 13, pp. 235–289). Imago. [English edition: Freud, S. (1953–1974). *The ego and the id. The standard edition of the complete psychological works of Sigmund Freud* (Vol. 19, pp. 1–66). Hogarth].

Heynick, F. (1993). *Language and its disturbances in dreams*. Wiley.

Jackendoff, R., & Lehrdahl, F. (2006). The capacity for music: What is it, and what's special about it? *Cognition* 100, 33–72.

Kenneally, C. (2007). *The first word*. Viking.

Kraeplin, E. (1906). *Über Sprachstörungen im Traume*. Engelmann.

Pinker, S. & Jackendoff, R. (2005). The faculty of language: What's special about it? *Cognition* 95, 201–236.

Steiner, G. (1983). The historicity of dreams (two questions to Freud). *Salmagundi* 61, 6–21.

Valli, K., & Revonsuo, A. (2007). Evolutionary psychological approaches to dream content. In D. Barrett & P. McNamara (Eds.), *The new science of dreaming (Vol. 3). Cultural and theoretical perspectives* (pp. 95–116). Praeger.

Werner, H., & Kaplan, B. (1963). *Symbol formation: An organismic-developmental approach to language and the expression of thought.* Wiley.

Whorf, B. (1964). *Selected writings of Benjamin Lee Whorf.* MIT Press.

Wilson, A., & Weinstein, L. (1990). Language, thought, and interiorization. A Vygotskian and psychoanalytic perspective. *Contemporary Psychoanalysis 26*(1), 24–39.

Wilson, A., & Weinstein, L. (1992). Language and the psychoanalytic process: Psychoanalysis and Vygotskian psychology. II. *Journal of the American Psychoanalytic Association 40*(3), 725–59.

# 5
# SPEECH ERRORS AND HUMOR

*In principio non erat verbum*

Freud's main work on the psychopathology of speech errors, commonly known as "Freudian slips", is found in *Zur Psychopathologie des Alltagslebens* (*The Psychopathology of Everyday Life*). Here, Freud uses the categorizations made by Meringer and Meyer (1895), which are still current in linguistics: transpositions, anticipations, perseverations, contaminations, and substitutions. He notes that in this particular taxonomy, "It makes no difference whether the transposition, distortion, amalgamation, etc., is concerned with single sounds in a word, with syllables, or with complete words forming part of the intended sentence" (Freud, 1901, p. 62).

It is important to note that slips studied are not limited to language. Indeed, Freud the neurologist places the linguistic slip in the larger complex of parapraxes (i.e., errors) in general, and here, he is perhaps the good part of a century ahead of his time in relating language to other neurological functions, as opposed to postulating a discrete language organ with isolated modules. He studies linguistic parapraxes—oral, written, and auditory—as well as embodied parapraxes (bungled actions).

Recent linguistic research on slips of the tongue does indeed discuss Freud's work, but almost invariably focuses only on the chapter on slips and thus does not contextualize it within the development of the arguments laid out in the entire work. Most importantly, it leaves out the related phenomena of embodied cognition and the structure of physical parapraxes, which demonstrate the basic psychoanalytic mechanisms of displacement and condensation, in other words, a kinesis of language.

It is important to begin with the discussion of the forgetting of names. It is also advisable to keep in mind how the mechanisms outlined in the *Interpretation of Dreams* and in *Jokes and Their Relation to the Unconscious* also

DOI: 10.4324/9781003180197-6

inform the analyses of slips, errors, and forgetting laid out in the *Psychopathology*. The observation that aligns the chapter on the forgetting of names with the mechanisms of slips is that the forgetting of names is not just that—the names are often wrongly remembered. In other words, one substitutes another name for the original one. This is similar to the slip of the tongue, where one utterance takes the place of another. The dreamwork process of displacement is used here to describe the detour away from the right name (6), which is an avoidance tactic. The example used is taken from one of Freud's own experiences of forgetting the name of the painter Signorelli and instead substituting the names of the painters Botticelli and Boltraffio, and also recalling Bosnia and Herzegovina, two areas in the country of Bosnia, which was part of the Austro-Hungarian Empire at the time Freud was writing the *Psychopathology*. But he recalls it in a reversal of the normal alphabetical order as "Herzegovina and Bosnia". This happened to Freud in a conversation about the Turks living in that country and the great faith they have in doctors (6–9).

The name "Signorelli" was not completely forgotten; the bound morpheme *-elli* was retained, and the free morpheme *Signor* was omitted. The mechanism producing the displacement sought to proceed along the semantic syntagm "painter", arriving at Botticelli, which preserves the syllabicity and stress of the name Signorelli (_ _ /_), but which submerges the meaning of *Signor*. The question remains as to the motivation of that submergence or repression.

*Signor* means, of course, "sir", and also "mister/master". The German equivalent is *Herr*, which carries the same meanings. It can also refer to God, as does the English "Lord". The phonetic presence of *Herr* is found in the place name *Herzegovina*, which he puts ahead of Bosnia. What is repressed is the figure of the master here, displaced onto the string "Herzegovina and Bosnia". The second string of displacements proceeds by alliteration with *bo-* and terminates with Boltraffio.

The etiology of the disturbance that precipitated the chain of substitutions is to be found in Boltraffio. Freud had recently learned that one of his patients who resided in the Austrian town of Trafoi had committed suicide. Now this would be, obviously, a difficult experience for a psychiatrist, whose job it is to maintain the stability of his patients. Here, Freud was not master (*Signor/Herr*) of his trade. Moreover, he was reduced by it: The Italian diminutive suffix *-ello*, here found in the plural, makes him "a little master", less than master.

This example of a mnemonic lapsus, a slipping from one word to others associated with it, reveals that the processes are phonetic, semantic, and motivated by affective experience. It is important to note that the syntagmatic progression chose the psychically less intense morpheme *elli* and avoided the hypersensitized word *Signor*, which it in turn displaced onto [hɛr] *Herr*, embedded, however, in *Herzegovina*.

It is important to note the processing of language via the associative properties of syllables and morphemes, both free and bound. This is clear in the usages of the productive diminutive morpheme -*elli*, along with *Signor* which, however, reflect Freud's fear of being "a little master" or no master at all of his profession. It is important to note that the anxieties of the subject (Freud) determine word segmentation. Herzegovina alliterates with the German *Herr*, as has been noted, but also with *Herz* (heart) [hɛrts]. The subject's anxieties, however, cause the separation of [r] and the affricate [ts], so as to yield *Herr*.

The same is true of the segmentation of Boltraffio, which would normally be syllabified into Bol + traffio, as Italian does not license /l/ + /t/ in word onset. Here, normal syllabification is rerouted so as to align with "Bosnia".

Freud informs the reader that the wrongly remembered names function here as rebuses, thus the process is similar to the processes found in dreamwork. Freud concludes the chapter on the forgetting of proper names with a caveat: This is not a blanket model for all such cases. He inserts in spaced letters (a German equivalent for italics): "In addition to the simple forgetting of proper names, one finds a forgetting that is motivated by repression" (12). Again, one may conclude that this is a recommendation for a suspicious hearing: Look for the psychological cause. It is a buried treasure hunt laid out on an indirect map.

I may here offer an instance of forgetting that occurred in my seminar on psychoanalysis in spring 2014. Having discussed the psychoanalytic account of forgetting, one of my students said that recently she could not recall the name of the cereal Rice Krispies. Skeptical, she wondered how on earth something like that could be motivated by repression. Repressing Rice Krispies? What could that have to do with anything?

I reflected on the possibilities, and at the beginning of the next class, I asked her if she was sensitive to issues of violence against women. She responded that she most certainly was. I then asked if she knew who the football player Ray Rice was. She immediately responded with a kind of Eureka! reaction, saying that she remembered getting breakfast cereal (Rice Krispies) in the dining hall when the news came on one of the TV monitors that Ray Rice had been arrested for punching his fiancé in an elevator. The assault was captured on tape, and Rice was arrested in March 2014. Here, an apparently far-fetched possibility turns out to be accurate. For this student, the traumatic experience of hearing this news blocked out the word rice and, consequently, the string Rice Krispies.

The *Psychopathology* then discusses the forgetting of foreign words (13–20). The first example involves an acquaintance of Freud who could not recall the entire Latin phrase: *exoriare aliquis nostris ex ossibus ultor* ("Let someone arise from my bones as an avenger"). He had omitted the word *aliquis* ("other", here: "someone else"). Freud asked what associations were evoked by the repressed word, and the acquaintance offered the associations of relics, liquid, and the Catholic rites involving the symbolism of blood. The common syllable [lik] served as the link for the sequence of associations. Freud neglects to mention that the full declension of the word is m. *aliquis*, f. *aliquis*, n. *aliquid*, thus, along the chain of associations, one approaches near homophony. The repression was motivated by the recent shocking news from the girlfriend of the acquaintance, that her periods had stopped. The bleeding had stopped: She was pregnant. The highly emotionally charged memory was repressed and displaced into phonetic associations, namely the alliteration of [lik], along the syntagmatic associations of liquidity. Thus one sees that the rhyming mechanisms can be determined by a psychologically charged meaning.

Here, looking for the psychological motivation for the apparently random forgetting yields a probable cause. The repressed word yields partially homophonous strings, e.g. liquid, relic, and also the thematically related phenomena of Catho*lic* ritual in a phonetic and semantic associativity that supersedes the logical meaning of the phrase, here evident, as the phrase is in another language.

The subsequent chapter on the forgetting of names discusses the phenomenon of forgetting names that are like one's own. Freud supplies several examples of this and remarks, "One cannot but feel slightly uncomfortable when one meets someone with the same name" (*Man kann sich einer leicht unangenehmen Empfindung nicht erwehren, wenn man seinen eigenen Namen bei einem Fremden wiederfindet*) (31). And here, one sees an incursion into ego boundaries, the persistence of a primitive notion of self that stands up to no logic at all. I clearly know that I am not the other person, but the unconscious effect is another matter.

Similarly, we often find that when a name is forgotten, it is because the name reminds us of a person with whom one has negative associations. The blockage here is affective and linguistic at the same time. Freud notes that when war broke out between Austria and Italy in 1915, he suddenly had trouble remembering Italian place names (40).

We are continually phonetically processing, but we should not leave out the psychological motivation.

The chapter on slips of the tongue, *Das Versprechen*, literally the "misspeaking", discusses the work done by Meringer and Mayer in *Versprechen und Verlesen*, which, as said above, uses the still current distinctions of transposition, anticipation, perseveration, contamination, and substitution.

In the first example of a perseveration, an employee was toasting to his boss and said, *Ich fordere Sie auf; auf das Wohl unseres Chefs aufzustossen* (62), which is an invitation "to burp to our boss" instead of "to toast to our boss". The proper infinitive verb form would have been *anzustossen*. Now this is a morphological substitution; the separable prefix *auf*, which is a free morpheme used in agglutination in German, substitutes for the partially similar prefix *an*. The perseveration is aided by the repetition of *auf*, said twice, and the momentum codetermines the perseveration error.

There is an odd translation problem common to the English translations of the works of Freud, which render it as "to hiccup" to our boss, which is a bit less amusing. (This would normally be *schluckaufen* in German). Also, burping would be more readily associable with drinking beverages. The question, however, is whether or not this slip is motivated by a sort of resentment toward the boss. In other words, is it phonetically and psychologically conditioned, or just phonetically? There is a structural and formal processing of morphemes here; is it independent of meaning, or is it semantically codetermined? The possibility of a psychological motivation to ironize the occurrence should not be excluded. This is the door of suspicion that psychoanalysis likes to keep open.

One of the points of contention raised by Freud concerns Meringer and Mayer's view that the substitutions made in the lapsus focus first on the initial phoneme in the root syllable. As German has initial stress in the root syllables, those are considered by Meringer and Mayer to have the greatest psychic intensity (*Intensität*), and thus are the first to be recalled after the forgetting. Freud shows time after time that the string with the highest psychic intensity is the one to go under, and this does not always follow rules of intonation. This is the case in the *Signorelli* example, which must follow Italian intonational patterns, as indicated above: (_ _ /_), with the stress falling on the penultimate syllable. The same phenomenon is found in the *aliquis* example, which would have been pronounced with word-onset stress. Instead of the first syllable, what surfaced was the unstressed string [lik].

Early on the discussion of slips, Freud invokes the mechanism of condensation found in dreamwork. He holds that any kind of similarity between two unconscious elements will cause a third element to be created, a highly contradictory mixture of both. He says, "The formation of substitutions and contaminations in lapsus (*beim Versprechen*) is the onset of a process of condensation that we find most actively involved in the construction of dreams" (67). One can add displacement to this, as is seen in the *Signorelli* example. Condensations are found in the diminutive *-elli* and in the morpheme *-her*, and the theme of fear of inadequacy is displaced onto the forgetting of the name of an artist.

Freud analyzes the following slip reported to Meringer and Mayer. A person was discussing occurrences that he found revolting, but he tried to find a neutral expression for them. He said, *Dann aber sind die Tatsachen zum Vorschwein gekommen* (Freud, 1901, p. 57), substituting *Vorschwein* for *Vorschein*. A possible rendering in English would be, instead of saying, "Light began to shine on the facts", saying in its place, "Light began to swine on the facts". Thus the slip found a condensation between illumination and disgust. An accurate light shining on the issue would reveal its disgusting nature. Here, as well, the trochaic intonation is preserved: (/_). And Meringer and Meyer bracket the element of disgust from their analysis of the slip, whereas for Freud, the affective element is the determiner of the lapsus.

A female patient (72) discussed an adolescent memory of an uncomfortable contact with a boy, but had difficulty recalling the details. When she was subsequently asked about her summer home, she said that it was located on the

*Berglende* instead of the *Berglehne*. Strachey offers an excellent translation of "hillthigh" instead of "hillside", which captures the issue well and maintains the voiceless fricative. *Lende* actually means "loin". Another good rendering might be "on the slip", instead of "on the slope".

It is important to emphasize that the reduction of inhibition facilitates the lapsus. Freud discusses two conflicting tendencies. On the one hand, there is the normal human condition of an uninhibited stream of associations, and on the other, a repressive attentivity (*hemmende Aufmerksamkeit*) that keeps these associations in check. (This is the work of the secondary process and of secondary revision.) When attention is diverted, the repressive tendency lessens, and the associations surface. In the slip, they emerge indirectly in an unstressed syllable, i.e., the reduction of stress, in both senses, causes the thought to express itself in a displaced and detensified manner. And here, the condensation is quite good: [bɛrklenə] becomes [bɛrklɛndə]. Only one phoneme is slightly modified, becoming tense and lengthened: [ɛ] → [e], and one other is introduced: [d].

One woman who ran a boarding house wanted to say that she had such a cold that she could not breathe through her nose (71). She transposed syllables and demonstrated an unconscious prioritizing of syllable over word boundary and meaning. She wanted to say, *Ich kann nicht durch die Nase atmen*, but wound up saying, *Ich kann nicht durch die Ase natmen*. This is similar to the French *naperon* entering English as "an apron". Or "a whole nother" instead of "another whole". This shows the perception of syllabic stress over lexical boundary. She offered an explanation: She had a French guest who had the habit of dropping initial /h/ in words.

A man who was distracted by a woman's décolletage (a plunging neckline) (79) at a party asked her if she had seen the new display at a certain department store and remarked that it was very *decolletiert*, "decollated". Now this is a condensation of the German *dekoriert* "decorated" and the French *décolleté*. The slip is motivated by an affective reaction to the woman's appearance and is facilitated by the similarity of the liquids /l/ and /r/.

A woman was asked what division her son was serving in during WWI (81). She responded, "the 42nd murderers", instead of "the 42nd mortars". The substitutions in the original German are similar: *Mörder / Mörser*. The German slip replaces a voiced alveolar stop with a fricative. The slip here reveals the subconscious perception of the true nature of war—legalized murder, which was normally suppressed from "polite" Austrian discourse during WWI. One would not have asked, "How many Italians did your soldiers murder today"? Again, the psycholinguistic application of condensation finds the homologous sequences of phonemes around which to construct the pun, here [møʁ] + [ə], and through which to permit the suppressed perception.

The subsequent chapter concerns misreading and miswriting (*Verlesen und Verschreiben*).

The instances of misreading are the ones where the psychological motivation is most evident. Freud offers the example of a young man whose friends are much stronger and more physically fit than he is. Reflecting on this, he reads a sign as *Eisenkonstitution* ("iron constitution"). Looking more closely, he sees that it reads *Eisenkonstruktion* ("iron construction"). The string [rʊk] is replaced by [itʊt], with the rest of the phonemes remaining identical.

Another anecdote concerns a man looking for a WC and misreads *Korsetthaus* as *Klosetthaus*, which would be an unusual rendering of *Klosett*, a shortening of *Wasserklosett*, a loan from the English "water closet". The slip is a metathesis and a substitution of semi-vowels: [o] + semivowel → semivowel + [o]. The shop actually sold corsets.

The slips of the pen (*Das Verschreiben*) that Freud discusses illuminate well the psychological motivations behind the slip. One amusing example concerns a physician who on several occasions prescribed overdoses of the drug belladonna, a suppository used for constipation, to elderly woman patients. The physician was living with his elderly mother and felt that the situation was interfering with his love life. The unconscious hostility that he felt toward his mother and the desire to "rid" himself of the burden were displaced onto other elderly women. Belladonna serves as an excellent condensation here. It means "pretty woman" in Italian and captures his desires as a bachelor. But *donna* in Italian is also used as a title, e.g., *Donna Gina*, to refer to a woman of stature, usually older. Thus the word combines the semantic antitheses of satisfaction and dissatisfaction, along with the issue of respect seen in the word *donna*, into one condensation. And the parapraxis seems to delight in doing so. The parapraxis reveals the conflict between freedom and responsibility. It was the psychologically charged meaning of the word that codetermined the slip of the pen.

Chapter 8 of the *Psychopathology* is entitled "Bungled Actions" (*Das Vergreifen*), an odd term in English. "Blunders" might be better. The French translation fares well in offering *Le geste manqué*. The chapter studies motor parapraxes, i.e., slips of the body. It begins with a recognition by Meringer and Mayer of their structural similarity with slips of the tongue. They assert that slips of the tongue are not isolated phenomena, but correspond to blunders committed in other activities, for which we commonly use the term "forgetfulness" (179).

Freud discusses the well-known phenomenon of pulling out one's house key when entering another residence and cites examples of this by several psychiatrists. In one of his own blunders while making a house call to one of his favorite patients, instead of knocking, he pulled out his own housekey, only to put it back. He reflects upon "feeling at home" when visiting the patient.

Other examples reverse the mistake, e.g. when, at work, the housekey is inserted instead of the office key. Here, one would rather be at home than at work. But in both cases, the condensation is the desire to be "at home", either in the other place or away from it (179–182). He cites another example from his own experience. In the days preceding his daughter's wedding, family members "accidentally" broke a lot of glass and china. It is a custom at Jewish weddings to break glass.

Some of the observations in the discussion of blunders do not translate well and thus escape full analysis. A particularly notable example is found in the anecdote about the woman who cut herself in the ring finger while trimming her nails. Freud writes:

> Dass sie sich beim Nägelschneiden „ins Fleisch geschnitten, während sie das feine Häutchen im Nagelbett abzutragen bemüht war"…es war wirklich der Ringfinger…der Finger, an dem man den Ehering trägt. Es war überdies ihr Hochzeitstag, was der Verletzung des feinen Häutchens einen ganz bestimmten, leicht zu erratenden Sinn verleiht.
>
> *(213)*

> That she had been cutting her nails the day before and had "cut into her flesh while she was trying to remove the fine cuticle/hymen at the bed of the nail"…it was "the ring-finger, the one on which a wedding ring is worn. It was also her wedding anniversary, which gives the injury to the fine cuticle/hymen a very definite and easily interpreted meaning".

The German *Häutchen* means "cuticle" (literally "little skin"), but it is also the word for "hymen". It is revealing that the woman herself produces the pun. Moreover, she chooses the term *Nagelbett* "nail bed". The fact that she cut her ring finger on her wedding anniversary is a crasser example of the "accidental" forgetting of the wedding ring when one goes out. It is important to note here that the blunder was *linguistically codetermined* via the homophony of *Bett* (the bed of the nail and the marriage bed), and by the homophony of *Häutchen* (cuticle and hymen). This indicates the unity of word/image/referent in the blunder. This can be seen as a mild conversion disorder.

Freud refers the reader to the work done by other psychoanalysts on the unconscious processing of songs. He says that if you pay attention to the melodies "that you find yourself humming, without intending to do so, and often without noticing it at all, the connection between the lyrics and the subject that is preoccupying you will regularly be revealed" (240). I have a host of my own examples that I use in my psychoanalysis seminar. They are invariably parodies of what I am preoccupied with. While working on the current project at the tail end of my sabbatical leave, far away from colleagues and teaching, I found that I was missing the university environment a bit. I often "heard" the refrain from a popular song playing in my head: "Man you wish you got a job". And often, the melody of a song, but not the lyrics, can enter into the preconscious, the melody serving as a metonymy (displacement) for

**76** Speech errors and humor: *In pricipio non erat verbum*

the sensitive issue. This recalls the parallels made by Jackendoff and Lehrdahl (2006) on the musicality of language and the language of musicality.

Freud also observes that patients who do not want to end the therapy session will often leave objects behind in the doctor's office, such as umbrellas, gloves, purses, etc. (Freud, 1901, p. 231).

Salvatore Attardo, in *Linguistic Theories of Humor*, claims that Freud has 20 different mechanisms for humor (Attardo, 1994, p. 55), and that they are all subsets of displacement and condensation. He notes that condensation and displacement correspond to paradigmatic and syntagmatic relationships, as covered by Jakobson and Todorov (55). He notes, "Freud's analysis is not so much specific to humor, but rather serves as an analysis of the linguistic tools that express it which are not peculiar to humor" (55). Freud says as much himself.

Attardo holds that slips operate in the same manner as puns, with the difference being that the intention of the pun is visible in its superstructure, while that of the slip is visible in its infrastructure. In other words, the former is conscious, and the latter unconscious or preconscious. He offers some amusing examples of puns, where it is easy to see the agenda behind the pun: "Clubs are good for children only if nothing else works"; "You can't have your cake and Edith too"; "Departmental newslitter" (149).

Victoria Fromkin contributed the study "Grammatical Aspects of Speech Errors" to the Cambridge survey on linguistics, in which she offers a taxonomy of errors:

> There are two major kinds of errors: Those involving linguistic units, e.g., disordering, deletion, or addition of intended segments, morphemes, words; and those involving grammatical rules, e.g., application of a rule which should not apply, or failure to apply a rule which should.
>
> *(Fromkin, 1988, p.121)*

Fromkin demonstrates some phonological switches showing that the speaker is processing phonetics over semantics: feed the pooch → food the peach; keep a tape → teep a cape; baked macaroons → maked bacaroons. And she includes, as well, the well-known "clear blue sky → glear plue sky; big and fat → pig and vat" (124–125). She poses the basic problem: "One would then need some plausible explanation for how such errors arise in spontaneous speech" (125). This study holds that the errors are determined by musicality. Semantic motivations are evidenced, but these are of secondary importance. Fromkin supplies numerous examples of phonetic and morphological confusion, as well as confusion within the same sematic field.

She also discusses some lexical errors, but leaves unexamined the affective motivation, e.g., in the following examples, in which the affective motivation is fairly clear:

- Del Amo fashion square → Del Amo passion square
- the Mafia moved into Boston → the Mafia moved into Italy
- hot under the collar – hot under the belt
- making headlines → making hairlines.

(132–133)

Concerning blends, she makes the following generalization: "Blends reflect lexical indecision—the selection of two semantically related words". Examples are: "edited/annotated → editated"; "instantaneous/momentary → momentaneous" (132–133). Here, a decision-making process really does not seem to play the dominant role—it is instead the pleasure in rhyme. It is important to note the presence of dreamwork in blends found in normal speech, e.g., smoke and fog → smog; breakfast and lunch → brunch, etc. These operate as condensations. She also notes semantic combinations emerging from the same semantic field, but again, it is important to note that rules of logic play no role in the confusion, e.g., uncle for aunt, short for long, uptown for downtown.

Fromkin also published an excellent anthology, *Speech Errors as Linguistic Evidence* (1973a), which begins with her own introduction, followed by Freud's "Slips of the Tongue" (*Das Versprechen*), a chapter from the *Psychopathology*. Her study predates the progress made in neurolinguistics, nonetheless it is useful. The anthology reprints one of the most important contributions to the psychoanalytic study of speech errors. It is the study by Charles Hockett from 1967, "Where the Tongue Slips, There Slip I". Hockett here alludes to Freud's famous statement, *Wo Es war, soll Ich werden* (Freud, 1933, p. 86) ("Where the id was, the ego shall be"). The statement indicates that the notion of self and identity replaces the libidinal drives and most succinctly captures how the ego is based on repression. Hockett notes that in the *Psychopathology*, Freud suggested that studying slips of the tongue may shed light on the generation of speech. He emphasizes: "I propose here to take Freud's suggestion seriously" (Hockett, 1973, p. 93).

Freud's assertion reads in the original as such:

> Im Falle der Störung durch Einflüsse außerhalb des nämlichen Satzes oder Redezusammenhanges würde es sich vor allem darum handeln, die störenden Elemente kennen zu lernen, und dann entstände die Frage, ob auch der Mechanismus dieser Störung die zu vermutenden Gesetze der Sprachbildung verraten kann.
>
> *(Freud, 1901, p. 64)*

> In the case of disturbances caused by elements external to the particular sentence or speech context, one would first of all have to identify the disturbing elements, which then would yield the question as to whether

**78** Speech errors and humor: *In pricipio non erat verbum*

> the mechanism of this disturbance could demonstrate the presumed rules of the configuration of language.

Hockett thinks that we focus too much on the structure of sentences instead of the processes that produce them. He also thinks that the dominant view of speech defects and lapses has been

> that paralallies are pathologies external to the language, intrusions from some other realm or system…and a bother to linguists because one must somehow work around and past them to get at what really counts… criticized by Freud, it is, with considerable elaboration, Chomsky's view today.
> 
> *(Hockett, 1973, pp. 94–95)*

It is important that Freud discussed speech errors under the rubric of the "psychopathology of everyday life", which indicates a normalization of the pathological. Humans are not enlightened beings motivated by logic—their behavior is determined by unconscious internal psychological conflicts. The model that I am suggesting here is that the alliterative dynamics of language, i.e., the things that cause the slips

- are always present below the surface
- are overdetermined
- are normally repressed from expression
- can occasionally surface
- their surfacing can be codetermined by psychological factors

Hockett offers a good example of overdetermination in his examination of the blending of "shout" and "yell" to yield "shell" in the utterance: "Don't shell so loud", uttered by a father "exasperated by his noisy children" (95). He suggests that the blending could have yielded "yaut" /jaʊt/, but instead yielded "shell", because "shell" is an existent word and "yaut" is not. Thus the error is determined by the semantic and phonological habits of the particular language. But he adds that the motivation could be awareness at some level that ears are shaped like shells (99). He then suggests a passage to the shrill sound of guns and shells, i.e., shelling. This seems more likely, as it engages the affective problem: The father felt that his children were shelling him with a barrage of sounds, and perhaps he would like to shell them back. Hockett makes here an important observation concerning the motivations for the slip: We can discuss plausibility, but not truth in our interpretations (99).

He offers another example of blending in the string: "We weren't sure we could avord—affoid it", which combines "afford" and "avoid". This was uttered in discussing the acquisition of a luxury item. He says of this, that "the speaker was clearly both boasting and apologizing" (101). This could serve as a good example of dreamwork saying two things at once with no difficulty. These examples show that the mental blending and the phonetic blending go hand in hand. The unconscious does not see contradictions. Just as the dream will seek out the points of condensation, so does the phonology. Neither is concerned about nonsense.

He discusses Jespersen's report of a child who said, "It's three hot in here" (Jespersen, 1922, p. 122). The child was performing an analogy with the sequence two, three, as in:

I'd like two pieces: I'd like three pieces
We waited two minutes: We waited three minutes
It's too hot in here: It's three hot in here

It is important to note that the child is not distinguishing between adverb and noun, and that the analogic process is jumping categories, just as is the case with phonetic and morphemic associations. Children will pattern upon auditory input. Another parent told their child, "Don't interrupt"; the child heard, "Don't interrup", and parsed it into "inter" and "up", and told the parent, "You're interring up"! (115).

Hockett places parapraxes and conventional fluid speech on the same continuum and says that "the difference between smooth and blunderful speech… is one of degree, not of kind" (117). This fits well into Freud's analysis of parapraxes in *the Psychopathology*, where the abnormal and the normal are also found on a continuum. The neologism "blunderful" is itself a nice pun, as speech errors can manifest quite interesting expressions.

He also takes issue with the competence and performance distinction here, which he summarizes as such: A sentence "must first be constructed by the internal competence of the speaker" and licensed by their grammar. It must then be performed "either overtly so that others may hear it, or covertly, so that it is perceived only by the speaker himself. It is in this second step that blunders may appear" (117). And UG sees internal competence as the seat of the linguistic intention of the speaker, of what they want to say. It is "the only real concern of linguistics; blunders in actually performed speech are intrusions from elsewhere" (117). In a footnote he says, "This, or something very much like it, is the only interpretation I can make of what Chomsky says" (117). He adds: "I believe this view is unmitigated nonsense, unsupported by any empirical evidence of any sort" (117).

Instead, he thinks that all speech is produced by three mechanisms: analogy, blending, and editing. Editing would be the last stage, the overt correction. This can be compared with the psychoanalytic concepts of the secondary process and secondary revision. He thinks that individual language is a set of habits, i.e., patterned analogies. He specifies: "Speech actualizes habits—and

**80** Speech errors and humor: *In pricipio non erat verbum*

changes the habits as it does so" (117). If language is based on analogies, then it is based on metaphor (and metonymy, the syntagmatic slide), which correspond to displacement and condensation, in the psychoanalytic perspective. He makes distinctions in the generation of speech that recall psychoanalytic concepts. The inner stage he calls "primary generation. This goes on partly in and partly out of awareness. It is 'thinking in words'" (118). This clearly resonates with the concepts of the primary process and of the preconscious.

It is at the level of the preconscious that speech is formed, based on the linguistic repertory we have, not on competence. The repertory is the toolshed that we raid to perform our utterances. Hockett notes that he has heard slips and blunders in his own inner flow. Poets do this all the time—they raid the multivalent allusions that are continually active below the surface and work these into creative combinations, even neologisms. One would have to subdivide Hockett's notion of editing into covert editing, where we survey our words before announcing them, and overt editing, which is what we wind up saying aloud. Hockett claims that beyond these three factors, a language has no design: "The search for an exact determinate formal system with which a language can be precisely characterized is a wild goose chase, because a language neither is nor reflects any such system" (Hockett, 1973, p. 119).

The similarities between Hockett's model and the psychoanalytic one become more evident in Boomer and Laver (1973), "Slips of the Tongue", also in Fromkin's anthology. The authors introduce their essay with the phrase: "The speech pathology of everyday life" (Boomer & Laver 1973, p. 120) and make a productive distinction between conversation and spoken prose, in which they see spoken prose as declamatory and conversation as zigzag and often ungrammatical, consisting in hesitations, lapses, etc. Here, one may invoke the distinction between formal written language (e.g., Ciceronian Latin)—which is, in effect, an imposition on language itself—and the normal phases of interactive conversation (e.g., Vulgar Latin). They note:

> Capsule demonstrations of the operation of a given linguistic model on carefully selected citation utterances are not compelling since any instance of spoken prose may be equally consonant with a number of internally consistent systems which have been expressly constructed to generate spoken prose.
>
> *(121)*

They lament that slips of the tongue are considered to be "deviant", and thus by association "abnormal" and excluded from study. They offer a simple taxonomy showing that the slips involve the switching of segments.

Meringer and Meyer showed systematicity in slips in their study from 1895. Subsequently, Meringer (1908) said that coincidence is fully excluded in slips, and that all slips are rule-governed. As stated, Freud disagreed with the mechanistic model of Meringer and Meyer, which excluded psychological motivations. And it is important to emphasize that Freud never insisted on the presence of psychological motivations in slips, he simply recommended that one consider it as an option. One may apply here the psychoanalytic distinction between innocent jokes and tendentious ones—those with an agenda—as outlined in *Jokes and Their Relation to the Unconscious*. Innocent jokes are those found, for example, in nursery rhymes, which communicate purely and simply the pleasure of play, such as "eeny meeny miny moe", as already mentioned. The tendentious joke, on the other hand, uses puns and blends as disguised criticisms.

Freud offers an anecdote by the poet Heinrich Heine, who had been introduced to the Baron Rothschild, and who commented on the meeting by saying, "He treated me quite as his equal—quite famillionairely" (Freud, 1905, p. 17), indicating, through displacement and condensation, that the Baron's attitude, while apparently communicating equality, was clearly aimed to remind Heine of the difference of status between the two of them. In both cases, however, those of the innocent and of the tendentious joke, the principles of morphophonemic combination are the same. The interesting aspect is that the addition of the psychological does not change the rule-governed nature of slips. The psychological motivation follows the established channels.

The primacy of humor in human behavior and cognition has been noted by Johann Huizinga in *Homo Ludens. A Study of the Play Element in Culture*. First published in 1938, the book opens at such:

> A happier age than ours once made bold to call our species by the name of Homo Sapiens. In the course of time we have come to realize that we are not so reasonable after all as the Eighteenth Century, with its worship of reason and its naive optimism, thought us.
> 
> *(Huizinga, 1944, p. ix)*

He said this in the year before Germany invaded Poland.

Huizinga observes that animals play just as do humans and supplies the charming phrase: "We have only to watch young dogs to see that all the essentials of human play are present in their merry gambols" (1). He also firmly holds that that ritual is play:

> Formally speaking, there is no distinction whatever between marking out a space for a sacred purpose and marking it out for purposes of sheer play. The turf, the tennis-court, the chessboard and pavement-hopscotch cannot formally be distinguished from the temple or the magic circle.
> 
> *(20)*

He specifies that play is

**82** Speech errors and humor: *In pricipio non erat verbum*

> older than culture itself and pervades all life like a veritable ferment. Ritual grew up in sacred play; poetry was born in play and nourished on play; music and dancing were pure play. Wisdom and philosophy found expression in words and forms derived from religious contests. The rules of warfare, the conventions of noble living were built up on play-patterns. We have to conclude, therefore, that civilization is, in its earliest phases, played. It does not come from play like a babe detaching itself from the womb: It arises in and as play, and never leaves it.
>
> *(173)*

This is quite a sweeping statement, but it sets up a large context for viewing language as originating in play, clearly evident in the linguistic play of children, thus both phylogenetically and ontogenetically. The play element in language is clearly connected to the production of speech errors; a continual morphophonemic processes of association is common to both.

Archibald A. Hill, in "A Theory of Speech Errors", cites some amusing slips that clearly betray a psychosexual subtext, for instance, the substitution of "University of Virginity" for "University of Virginia", which he terms "a fairly highly charged word...heard in a public address" (Hill, 1973, p. 210). He also cites a transposition of noun and particle in "his bubble would be pricked", an error that produced "a new and grammatical, if unfortunate, sentence... which occurred in a serious and polite discussion of church affairs" (209–210). Apparently, concerns of prudence in the early 1970s prevented him from spelling out the error "his prick would be bubbled". He notes, in consonance with the observation of Hockett and Freud, that "we all carry on a continuous flow of internal images"; this "makes it possible to understand thinking and daydreaming in language. That is, a flow from image to word is not ruled out, but the reverse flow, from word to image, is strongly suggested" (210). This is a very good point, as there is no firm frontier between full wakefulness and daydreaming.

He also makes a wonderful point concerning the transcendental properties of speech sounds:

> Sounds are manipulable units, and when a blend forces them out of one position, they are bodily transported to another...sounds exist as internal realities, abstractable from words, much as the conscious mind makes realities of words by abstracting them from sentences. In fact, speech errors are one of the two most important evidences for internal reality of sounds, rather than of morphophonemes.
>
> *(212)*

Here, sounds take precedence over morphophonemes.

Rulon Wells, in "Predicting Slips of the Tongue", observes that "linguistics doesn't enable us to predict" (Wells, 1973, p. 85). (I once heard a student ask a professor if linguistic science can predict language changes, and the professor answered, "No, but we can postdict them".)

Wells offers three laws:

- slips are almost always phonetically possible sounds in the phonology of the particular language
- a blend of two rhythmically similar words will rhythmically resemble both of them, e.g., behavior + deportment = behortment
- words containing the same sound in the same position will blend with that sound in that position, e.g. essay + dissertation = essertation (V + s). (86–87).

A. Cohen's data in "Errors of Speech and Their Implication for Understanding the Strategy of Language Users" shows that of the three categories examined—anticipation, perseveration, and transposition—anticipations comprised 78% of the lapses. The average syllable span was 2.1 syllables for anticipations and perseverations (Cohen, 1973, pp. 88–92).

One of the most important findings relevant for a psychoanalytic approach to morphology can be found in the research done by Carstairs-McCarthy in the article "The Evolutionary Origin of Morphology". He sees the syllable as forming the evolutionary basis of syntax. In an exaptation of syllables for syntax, the syllabic nucleus would become the verb, and the coda its object. The syllable rhyme would then become the verb phrase, and syntactic movement would have simply arisen from emphasis, as is the case in the current English alternate interrogative, "You did *what*"? He sees allomorphy as "the blurring of the boundaries between neighboring items in speech production" (Carstairs-McCarthy, 2005, p. 168). The most important observation here is that allomorphy occurs prior to morphology and is an "assimilatory blurring…characteristic of speech well before fully modern grammar had come into existence" (168), such as is common in infant speech. The transition to morphology would have evolved when adjacent elements in the protolanguage influenced each other phonologically.

He introduces the clever distinction that speech is analog rather than digital, analog in that elements can influence other elements. He notes that "in speech production, individually meaningful units, or morphemes, are not diamond-hard and immutable, but are subject to influences (usually assimilatory) from their neighbors in the speech chain…speech is 'analog' rather than 'digital' in character" (172–173). In digital technology, each element is discrete. In analog technology, signals are prone to corruption by ambient noise during transmission; digital signals are discretely encoded and thus immune to interference. A useful comparison would be the analog TV signal broadcast with an antenna, susceptible to ambient interference, versus the digital one. He posits that, in the evolution of language, the blending of sounds would have been the rule rather than the exception. This is evident in the understanding of language in the mind of the preliterate child, as well as the mind of the illiterate adult. Now this corresponds very well to the psychoanalytic configuration of speech errors as determined by condensation, displacement, and overdetermination. The interconnectivity is enabled by the process of overdetermination. Morphology would have arisen post-facto in the process of linguistic habituation.

Calvin & Bickerton, in *Lingua Ex Machina. Reconciling Darwin and Chomsky with the Human Brain*, specify that

> a word is a combination of a mental representation of something, which may or may not exist in the real world, with a mental representation of a set of symbols (phonetic, orthographic, manual). What you write are not words, but only the phonological representations of words...If all you did was to link these representations, all you would have would be a language of isolated words: Bread. Life. Oak tree. Silence. These would have meaning, but not a lot of it. To get anywhere serious, words have to be put together.
>
> *(Calvin & Bickerton, 2000, p. 24)*

There is a notion here of the composite nature of words, but not one of the segments of a perception of an utterance. Do we really perceive separate words unconsciously and preconsciously? Clearly, preliterate and illiterates do not. Words were originally not snapped together like Lego toys.

In their discussion of "protolanguage", which varies between toddler talk and speculations about the speech of early humans, they note that "all protolanguage varieties can only string together a small handful of words at a time" (30). And a protolanguage is a priori a proto-grammar. They note that

> a grammar with a fixed order in which subject precedes predicate and the verb of the predicate, if transitive, precedes its object, works just fine, so long as all you have are nouns and verbs and no more than one verb per utterance.
>
> *(31)*

They note that "in protolanguage, all words are equal" (41). And such a protolanguage would consist "of nouns and verbs without modifiers of any kind" (32).

Fromkin's contribution to her anthology on speech errors as linguistic evidence: "The Non-Anomalous Nature of Anomalous Utterances" starts with the same question from Freud that Hockett poses, and which she, as well, takes seriously. She studies the experience of having a word on the tip of one's tongue, but not being able to recall the word itself. While the word slips away, the number of syllables in the word remains (the metrical beat of a word). She concludes that we may store a category of monosyllables and then disyllables, and so on (Fromkin, 1973b, pp. 215–242).

Cutler, in the article "The Reliability of Speech Error Data", holds that

> there is no logical reason why the occurrence of an error via one or another mechanism (anticipation, perseveration, etc.), or alternatively the failure of an error to be detected and corrected by internal monitoring systems prior to output, should not be rendered more likely by the fact that the error form is associated with secret desires or thoughts.
> *(Cutler, 1982, p. 21)*

Andrew Ellis, in "On the Freudian Theory of Speech Errors", observes that the research on slips of the tongue "has been motivated by predominantly psycholinguistic, rather than psychoanalytic interests". He believes that, with the exception of Hockett's work, most investigators assume that "the mechanics of slips can be studied linguistically without reference to their motivation" and "independent from psychopathology" (Ellis, 1980, p. 123). He seeks to ascertain to what extent psychoanalytic explanations are needed in addition to the "the mechanical-psycholinguistic" ones (123). He reiterates the psychoanalytic distinction between the conscious intention and the unconscious disturbing intention that produces the slip. He notes that 60% of Freud's examples are lexical substitution errors, of which there are two types: phonetic and semantic, and these do not differ from the data supplied by psycholinguists. In other words, they can be explained without reference to unconscious motivation.

Ellis notes:

> Freud did, on occasion, perceive errors for which he could not provide a satisfactory explanation in terms of conflicting intentions. Thus, his assertion that all slips of the tongue require a depth analysis amounts more to a statement of a priori belief than to an empirical generalization. It is certainly not falsifiable.
> *(127)*

He does well to note that most recent investigators categorically assert that Freudian explanations cannot be verified or reproduced, and that they must be discarded "in a systematic analysis" (127). These investigators work on an information-processing model of speech production. If the model "can be shown to be capable of simulating naturally occurring speech errors, then it will do so without recourse to a hypothesized secondary intention interfering with the conscious intention". He concludes that "in the current state of the art the problem is, however, insoluble" (128).

It should be noted that Freud never said that all speech errors are motivated. He merely said that one should not forget to look for the motivation; this is basically the essence of Freudian theory: One should engage in a suspicious observation of behavior that looks for *the possibility of a psychological motivation*. In this sense, Freudian theory does not violate the principles of falsifiability, as described by Popper (1934), which state that, in order for a theory to have scientific validity, it must be testable in an experiment that would find an exception to the generalization. Clearly, UG theory, in its vision of parameters, violates the principles of falsifiability much more than do the conceptions seen in Freudian theory. UG theory holds that, if language X does not display a certain grammatical feature Y, the parameter for Y—the switch—is there anyway, but it is not turned on. But concerning the principles of falsifiability in general, one should be reminded that a vast majority of our daily decisions do not await scientific validation. How many of our daily disagreements are fought over falsifiability criteria?

He observes that the recent studies of blends hold that the two words are often equally appropriate synonyms. He cites the *Vorschwein* example as a counter example, but then goes on to hold that most of the blends can be explained on purely phonemic grounds, i.e. perseveration, anticipations, etc. (129). He thinks that in many instances,

> The speaker's introspections reveal that the disturbing word that blends with the intended word had been in the speaker's thoughts before the utterance was produced. Arguably the disturbing word had been 'spoken' subvocally, so that the intended word could have blended with a lingering phonemic trace of the disturbing word. Such errors would, indeed, be revealing as to the thoughts that the speaker wished to conceal, but those thoughts could not have been truly unconscious prior to manifesting themselves in the slip.
>
> *(129)*

Here, he demonstrates an insufficient knowledge of the progress from the unconscious, to the preconscious, and then to consciousness.

Nonetheless, Ellis does astutely observe that

> Freud's formulations may be rejected on the grounds of current untestability, but they should not be rejected as vague, or as incompatible with an information processing approach...Freud's theory can be translated into the language of modern speech production models without excessive difficulty. The theory requires that the cognitive system which molds semantic messages into phonemic form should be capable of processing

two rival messages simultaneously...speakers should (sometimes) be unaware of cognitive-linguistic activity until its products are crystallized into phonemic form.

(130)

The processing of two simultaneous rival messages corresponds well to the general phenomenon of cognitive dissonance. Freud examined many such examples in his works, and the "kettle joke" (*der Kesselwitz*) stands out as the most well-known. In his work on dreams and jokes/wit, Freud tells the story of a man who borrowed a kettle from his neighbor and returned it damaged. The owner of the kettle sued him, and the borrower offered three mutually exclusive defense arguments in court:

—  I never borrowed a kettle from him in the first place;
—  It was already damaged when he lent it to me;
—  I returned it intact.

(Freud, 1905, pp. 65–66)

It was Jacques Derrida who popularized the kettle joke, calling it *la logique du chaudron*. This is a form of shell game, which reveals the persistence of unconscious primary processes, e.g. dreamwork, in everyday life: hence the rubric of *The Psychopathology of Everyday Life*. As Freud noted, dreamwork is blind to contradiction. It is important to note that the borrower here, in jumping freely among mutually exclusive justifications, is motivated by a sense of guilt.

Fromkin's anthology includes Michael T. Motley's article "'Freudian Slips' and Semantic Prearticulatory Editing". Motley agrees with Ellis and says that

> Freud's more general insight is one for which this study lends strong support: Semantic influences that are independent of a speaker's intended utterance can influence verbal slips to be closer in meaning to those semantic influences than to the originally intended utterance.
>
> (Motley, 1980, p. 145)

He uses the data from the Mosher Sex-Guilt Inventory Test (Mosher, 1965), which assessed the sexual anxiety level of college male subjects, dividing them into three categories: high, medium, and low sex anxiety. The questionnaires surveyed students on controversial topics, such as masturbation, premarital sex, etc. Motley conducted his experiment at Ohio State University and found that the most sexually repressed subjects tended to make the greatest number of "Sex-Error spoonerisms" (142). He gives no examples, unfortunately, and the errors are left up to the reader's imagination. This is basically a pressure cooker model, where repression causes the impulse to be displaced into the medium of language. This fits nicely into the psychoanalytic model, which does not see an independent domain for language; impulses under the surface can interrupt verbal articulation.

Similarly, MacKay, in the study "Mental Diplopia: Towards a Model of Speech Perception at the Semantic Level", shows that an anterior meaning that disturbs semantic clarity is subject to partial awareness, locatable in the preconscious, and then undergoes repression. Diplopia is commonly called double vision, and the term is used as a metaphor for rival messages (MacKay, 1970).

Fromkin's anthology also includes Aitchison and Straf, "Lexical Storage and Retrieval: A Developing Skill"? The authors study 680 malapropisms made by adults and children, with age 12 being the cutoff point. They found that both groups retrieve words by looking for the same salient phonological features. Adults give a higher priority to initial consonants, but children look at other facets, such as the number of syllables and the stressed vowel. Children pay more attention to rhythm and word endings (Aitchison and Straf, 1980). As stated earlier, children process language by rhythm, rhyme, and musicality in general. The less frequent presence of prosodic aspects in adult language processing and the concentration instead on initial consonants may be a result of literacy. Adults would, however, still be processing the musical aspects of language, but at a preconscious level.

None of the studies in Fromkin's anthology looks at the structural similarities among parapraxes in general, e.g., slips of the pen and bungled actions. As stated earlier, the similarities between verbal and nonverbal parapraxes helps situate language within cerebral interconnectivity, especially as concerns the embodiment of language. These similarities are structured by the master cognitive mechanisms of displacement, condensation, overdetermination, and repetition.

Don Norman has offered an excellent study of bungled actions in the article "Categorization of Action Slips". He summarizes:

> Freud believed that slips resulted from competition among underlying mechanisms, often working in parallel with one another and almost always beneath the consciousness of the owner. The resulting notions were of mental operations controlled by a quasi-hierarchical control structure, with parallel activation of thoughts and memories and with conscious access to only a limited amount of this activity. The ideas are sophisticated even for today's theorists, who only recently have introduced the differences between conscious and subconscious processing into their models of cognitive functioning and who are just beginning to develop notions of independently operating computational units…it is indeed true that slips appear manageable and that they cry out for interpretation. The examination of any large collection of slips reveals that they can be categorized and that they fall into patterns. However, the meaning in them is not at all clear; their categorization and interpretation

are theory dependent, yet contemporary theories of cognitive behavior are not really up to the task.

*(Norman, 1981, p. 2)*

This gap in the theory of parapraxes is one of the major points of entry for a psychoanalytic science of language. Norman also studies the structural similarity between misspeaking and bungled actions and shows that they are controlled by sensorimotor cognitive structures or schemas (3).

Jeri Jaeger's *Kid's Slips: What Children's Slips of the Tongue Reveal About Language Development* offers the largest collection of slips of the tongue made in English by children from about one-and-a-half to six years of age. In this exhaustive collection of over 700 pages, the corpus is taken mostly from the slips made by her own three children, all monolingual anglophones. She finds that when children start committing slips of the tongue at the age of one year and seven months, "the representation of words…is largely based on individual segments, consonants, and vowels" (Jaeger, 2005, p. 214), i.e., the word is not yet a concept; the syllable becomes the basic unit of processing (215). In addition, in lexical errors, semantics plays the major role, as do the context and environment of the word. She sees the semantic stage as preceding a syntactic one, as syntactic errors emerge later in childhood.

Jaeger observes that children produce nearly all the same types of errors as adults (51). These are collected in a corpus of unmotivated slips, i.e., ones not yet subject to mechanisms of repression. In her analysis, Jaeger does not supply the necessary psychoanalytic framework for observing these speech errors. She holds that

> the psychoanalytic framework assumed that when a person spoke a word different from the intended word, or made a phonological error which resulted in an unintended real word, this was caused by some repressed thought or phantasy which had surfaced unintentionally. It should be abundantly clear from the data in this book that very few errors can be interpreted in this way, since very few of them result in the speaker producing an embarrassing or offensive word.

*(279)*

Since the motivated slip is a product of repression, and since repression is an ontogenetic latecomer in human development, it should come as no surprise that children produce few of them before the age of six. What they produce would be innocent mechanical errors. Moreover, any parent knows that children are much less repressed than adults, and that learning self-control, especially over bodily functions, is one of the major projects facing parents in the acculturation of children. The transition from childhood to adulthood is, however, a task that many adults, unfortunately, have not properly completed themselves. It is also important to reiterate that the mechanisms of slips proposed by psychoanalysis do not require the utterance of an obscenity. They merely show that there may be a competing thought normally excluded from expression. This may, however, need contextual biographical information on the speaker.

This chapter has demonstrated the presence of anterior affective motivation in the production of speech errors, and also how these errors are influenced by the persistence of precognitive and preconscious modes of thought in adult speech, especially by the chief mechanisms of dreamwork. Thus there is a codetermination here of language and thought, but it should be emphasized that the thought processes present here are not those of logical conscious reflection.

The following chapter will examine the presence of language in the construction of identity.

## References

Aitchison, J., & Straf, M. (1980). Lexical storage and retrieval: A developing skill? In V. Fromkin (Ed.), *Errors in linguistic performance: Slips of the tongue, ear, pen, and hand* (pp. 97–241). Academic Press.

Attardo, S. (1994). *Linguistic theories of humor*. De Gruyter.

Boomer, D., & Laver, J. (1973). Slips of the tongue. In V. Fromkin (Ed.), *Speech errors as linguistic evidence* (pp. 120–131). De Gruyter.

Calvin, W., & Bickerton, D. (2000). *Lingua ex machina. Reconciling Darwin and Chomsky with the human brain*. MIT Press.

Carstairs-McCarthy, A. (2005). The evolutionary origin of morphology. In M. Tallerman (Ed.), *Language origins: Perspectives on evolution* (pp. 166–184). Oxford University Press.

Cohen, A. (1973). Errors of speech and their implication for understanding the strategy of language users. In V. Fromkin (Ed.), *Speech errors as linguistic evidence* (pp. 88–92). De Gruyter.

Cutler, A. (1982). The reliability of speech error data. In A. Cutler (Ed.), *Slips of the tongue and language production* (pp. 7–29). De Gruyter.

Ellis, A. (1980). On the Freudian theory of speech errors. In V. Fromkin (Ed.), *Errors in linguistic performance: Slips of the tongue, ear, pen, and hand* (pp. 123–131). Academic Press.

Freud, S. (1901). *Zur Psychopathologie des Alltagslebens. Über Vergessen, Versprechen, Vergreifen, Aberglaube und Irrtum. Gesammelte Werke* (Vol. 4, pp. 5–321). Imago. [English edition: Freud, S. (1953–1974). *The psychopathology of everyday life. The standard edition of the complete psychological works of Sigmund Freud* (Vol. 6). Hogarth].

Freud, S. (1905). *Der Witz und seine Beziehung zum Unbewussten. Gesammelte Werke.* (Vol. 6, pp. 1–269). Imago. [English edition: Freud, S. (1953–1974). *Jokes and their relation to the unconscious. The standard edition of the complete psychological works of Sigmund Freud* (Vol. 8, pp. 1–236). Hogarth].

Freud, S. (1933). *Neue Folge der Vorlesungen zur Einführung in die Psychoanalyse. Gesammelte Werke* (Vol. 15, pp. 1–118). Imago. [English edition: Freud, S. (1953–1974). *New introductory lectures on psychoanalysis. The standard edition of the complete psychological works of Sigmund Freud* (Vol. 22, pp. 1–79). Hogarth].

Fromkin, V. (Ed.). (1973a). *Speech errors as linguistic evidence*. De Gruyter.
Fromkin, V. (1973b). The non-anomalous nature of anomalous utterances. In V. Fromkin (Ed.), *Speech errors as linguistic evidence* (pp. 215–242). De Gruyter.
Fromkin, V. (1988). Grammatical aspects of speech errors. In F. Newmeyer (Ed.), *Linguistics: Cambridge survey* (Vol. 2, pp. 117–138). Cambridge University Press.
Hill, A. (1973). A theory of speech errors. In V. Fromkin (Ed.), *Speech errors as linguistic evidence* (pp. 205–214). De Gruyter.
Hockett, C. (1973). Where the tongue slips, there slip I. In V. Fromkin (Ed.), *Speech errors as linguistic evidence* (pp. 93–119). De Gruyter.
Huizinga, J. (1944). *Homo ludens. A study of the play element in culture*. Routledge.
Jaeger, J. (2005). *Kid's slips: What children's slips of the tongue reveal about language development*. Erlbaum.
Jackendoff, R., & Lehrdahl, F. (2006). The capacity for music: What is it, and what's special about it? *Cognition* 100, 33–72.
Jespersen, O. (1922). *Language: Its nature, development and origin*. G. Allen & Unwin ltd.
MacKay, D. (1970). Mental diplopia: Towards a model of speech perception at the semantic level. In G. Flores d'Arcais, & W. Levelt (Eds.), *Advances in psycholinguistics* (pp. 76–100). North-Holland Publishing.
Meringer, R. (1908). *Aus dem Leben der Sprache*. Behr's Verlag.
Meringer, R., & Meyer, C. (1895). *Versprechen und Verlesen*. Göschen.
Mosher, D.L. (1965). Interaction of fear and guilt in inhibiting unacceptable behavior. *Journal of Consulting Psychology* 29, 161–167.
Motley, M. (1980). 'Freudian slips' and semantic prearticulatory editing. In V. Fromkin (Ed.), *Errors in linguistic performance: Slips of the tongue, ear, pen, and hand* (pp. 133–147). Academic Press.
Norman, D. (1981). Categorization of action slips. *Psychological Review* 88, 1–15.
Popper, K. (1934). *Logik der Forschung*. Springer. [English edition: Popper, K. (1959). *The logic of scientific discovery*. Routledge].
Wells, R. (1973). Predicting slips of the tongue. In V. Fromkin (Ed.), *Speech errors as linguistic evidence* (pp. 82–87). De Gruyter.

# 6
# LANGUAGE, CONSCIOUSNESS, AND IDENTITY

In 1923, Freud published *Das Ich und das Es* (*The Ego and the Id*), an important work for placing language acquisition in a psychoanalytic context. It articulates a connection among consciousness, language, and identity formation. It is important for two reasons: It locates both language and consciousness in the ego, and it presents *a linguistic configuration of consciousness and identity*. The title literally translates as: "The I and the It".

The first chapter is titled *Bewusstsein und Unbewusstes*, which is often well-translated as "consciousness and what is unconscious", but the latter often becomes reduced to "the unconscious" in English. *Unbewusstes* is an adjectival noun carrying the inflectional morpheme *es*, which fixes the meaning as a collection of things that are not conscious. Unfortunately, the locution "the unconscious" is dominant in English, which, due to the paucity of inflectional morphemes and the consequential function shift from adjectival noun to noun in English, gives the false impression that the unconscious is a place, a location. This is clearly not the case. The unconscious is simply a collection of things that are repressed from consciousness by various psychoanalytic defense mechanisms. They remain beneath the threshold of consciousness, in the preconscious, and continually threaten to transgress that threshold. These transgressions are responsible for the host of motivated parapraxes.

Freud notes that the conscious state is transitory; mental representations are not conscious for a long period of time. They slip in and out of consciousness, and most of them remain in a transitional phase—the preconscious (*Das Vorbewusste*). Consciousness itself is housed in the ego, as has been said, which constitutes the coherent organization of mental processes in the individual. Indeed, Freud holds that to see the psyche as existing in a conflict between consciousness and that which is unconscious leads into "an endless amount of

DOI: 10.4324/9781003180197-7

inaccuracies and difficulties"; he substitutes for this an opposition "between an integrated ego and the repressed that has been split off from it" (Freud, 1923, p. 244). Thus repression results from the activity of maintaining a coherent identity, which involves resisting information that threatens that identity. The repressed information remains in a liminal state and can attempt to gain reentry into consciousness. It is important to note that repressed information in this liminal state *can interfere with the articulation of language.*

In *Early Social Interaction*, Michael Forrester holds that "the mind is forever at odds with itself". For Forrester, the conscious–unconscious relationship is like "trying to keep a floating beach-ball under the water when swimming" (Forrester, 2015, p. 46). Thus the sense of self comprises contradictory forces, and concerning verbalization and pronunciation, there is always a subterranean force undermining the construction of the utterance. He observes an "ever-present and enduring sense of anxiety in the organism" (62) and holds that "when you learn how to talk, you learn how to repress" (65). For Forrester, speech and repression go hand in hand: "There is no repression before learning how to talk" (130). This configuration of language, which is the basis of errors and hesitations in speech, contrasts incompatibly with the model of natural language based on formal logic and information science.

The arrival at conscious expression evokes the following question posed in *The Ego and the Id*: "How does something become conscious"? Freud suggests that this question should be restated "more to the point…how does something become preconscious?" And the answer would be: "Through becoming connected with the corresponding word-presentations" (247). In the narration of the dream content, one sees that word formation is determined by a chain of associations operating among morphophonemic similarities. The word-representation (*Wortvorstellung*) emerges from a network of displacements and condensations. Again, one sees that the semantic and phonetic associations must have been operating continually in neural networks that connect associated sounds and meanings. Unconscious, preconscious, and precognitive in nature, they materialize in the process of the formation of thought and language.

One may say that there are here no discrete elements in the generation of language; each element is overdetermined in an associative nexus of neural interconnections, a nexus that is coarticulated by the formation of identity.

Wilson and Weinstein (1990), in their study on Vygotsky, observe that for Freud, when the word gets attached to a visual representation of an object, this constitutes the transition from unconscious to preconscious, and the separation of the representation of the word from its object is what constitutes repression. This corresponds to the observations made by Freud, in his study of the unconscious, *Das Unbewusste*, where he distinguishes between unconscious (Ucs.) and preconscious (Pcs.) systems ("Cathexis" refers to the choice of and desire for an object.):

> The system *Ucs.* contains the thing-cathexes of objects, the first and true object-cathexes; the system *Pcs.* arises when this thing-presentation becomes hyper-cathected [*überbesetzt*] via the connection with its corresponding word-presentations. It is probable that these hyper-cathexes bring about a higher psychical organization and make possible the dissolution of the primary process by the secondary process dominant in the *Pcs.* We can now specify what repression in the transference neuroses does not allow to the rejected presentation: The translation into words that ought to remain attached to the object. A presentation that is not put into words, or a psychical act that is not hyper-cathected, thus remains repressed in the *Ucs.*
>
> (Freud, 1915, p. 300)

Thus there is no full consciousness without words. He adds:

> In the last pages of the 1900 edition of *The Interpretation of Dreams*, it was demonstrated that thought-processes, i.e., the acts of cathexis separated from perception, are in themselves without qualities, and unconscious, and that they attain their capacity to become conscious only via connection to the residues of word-perceptions [*Wortwahrnehmungen*].
>
> *(301)*

Thus the preconscious becomes conscious through the word representations of the object. In repression, the word representations become detached from their objects or from the psychic act (*der psychische Akt*). The object or psychic act remains unconscious (but the affect remains) and then becomes subject to displacement. This can explain the forgetting of words. Words make possible the transition to consciousness, and when something is repressed, the linguistic channels are blocked.

Wilson and Weinstein observe that Vygotsky's views correspond to a gradualist process in language development and production. For Vygotsky, "thought is not expressed but completed in the word...before a thought can reach its fully formulated state, a person must go back and forth between thought and word searching for the proper articulation" (Wilson & Weinstein, 1990, p. 26). In this process, the utterance traverses networks of associations on its way to expression. The authors claim that this goes on "outside of awareness" (26). Consciousness is attained in and through "the proper articulation". Thus, with Freud, they hold that consciousness is a linguistic construct. And the old binary distinction of thought vs. language, which gets stuck in a chicken or egg debate, is surpassed by the proposition that "meaning is created by the unification of speech and thought" (28).

To be conscious is thus to be conscious of the self. Freud holds that a perception first enters into the preconscious by a connection to its word representations

(*Wortvorstellungen*), and he makes a very important observation in this regard: Thinking in images is a very incomplete form of consciousness and is most likely phylogenetically older than thinking in words. We consciously perceive something via the word representations associated with it—word representations in the wide semantic field of that which is perceived. This is the state of perception consciousness, where perceptions take on linguistic form; they begin with "verbal residues" (*Wortreste*—literally "word remains"). But what is the source of these verbal residues? They must be derived from auditory perceptions, from things that one remembers hearing, and as such, can be fragmentary; hence the term "remains". Word representations then turn thought processes into perceptions. Freud observes that the ego wears a "hearing cap" (*Hörkappe*), i.e., an auditory perception device (Freud, 1923, p. 252).

The ego is that part of the mental apparatus that has been influenced by the external world, which seems quite evident, as the concept of self is constructed in interaction with the environment, with the non-selves, and, most importantly for ego formation, by the voice of the parents, i.e., voices to which authority becomes attributed. And here, the familiar concept of the super-ego comes into play. This constitutes a moment of dialog that corrects and normalizes impulses, so as to socialize the individual. The ego-ideal

> fulfills all the claims made to the higher nature in humans. As a substitute formation for the longing for the father, it holds the germ from which all religions have been formed. The judgment of one's own insufficiency in comparing the ego with the ego-ideal gives rise to the religious sense of humility…in the subsequent process of development, teachers and authority figures continue the role of the father.
>
> *(265)*

One of the most important statements made by Freud about the constitution of the ego, is that "the ego is above all a bodily ego [*ein körperliches*]; it is not only a surface phenomenon, but the actual projection of a surface itself" (253), i.e., a representation to the individual of the individual's own body. This is a very early instance of the concept of the embodied ego, one that leads well into the field of embodied cognition. The ego is formed by a modeling in and through language, a modeling that is largely mediated via the auditory sphere. And this modeling proceeds through an embodied cognition of self, in dialog with non-selves, especially with others in possession of authority. Wilson and Weinstein also refer to "the exceptional position of the auditory sphere in the formation of the superego" (Wilson & Weinstein, 1990, pp. 749–750).

A major revision of the dynamics of the formation of the ego was offered by Jacques Lacan in his essay *Le stade du miroir* (first published in 1949), normally translated in English editions as *The Mirror Stage*. Lacan reflects upon the moment when an infant discovers its own image in a mirror, i.e., when the infant first knows that it is seeing itself in the mirror. Lacan contrasts that with the chimpanzee's experience of the same phenomenon. The chimpanzee thinks it is seeing another animal, while the infant becomes aware that it is seeing itself. For Lacan, this is a moment of reflective consciousness of the self, the initial state of metacognition. Most pet owners will validate what Lacan is saying. Our own dog thought that its image in the hallway mirror was another dog and, after a few moments of initial curiosity, concluded that the other animal did not enter into its own sphere of activity and quickly lost interest in the apparent other.

For Lacan, the initial moment of self-recognition, i.e., of metacognition, is both embodied and alienating at the same time. The infant experiences itself in an uncoordinated condition. It cannot yet walk, nor stand up, nor control its bodily functions, yet it sees an integrated image of itself in the mirror, which contrasts sharply with its own experience. The infant begins to identify with this image of itself, which Lacan calls the "ideal-I" (*le je-idéal*) (Lacan, 1966, p. 94). This sets up a model of self-identification that is, however, always incommensurate with its goal. In other words, it points the development of the self toward an integrated ideal that it will never fully attain.

Lacan works with the difference in French between the pronouns *je* and *moi*, or "I and me", the former being used only as the subject of the verb, and the latter as the object of the actions of the verb. Thus the *moi* is the real experience of self as the patient, as an object acted upon by its environment, while the *je* would be the one in control. The infant sees this image and thinks, "Is that me"?, and the answer is, no, it is I, an ideal image of myself, one that is never fully attainable. Lacan says that this instantiates the ego "in a line of fiction… in which becoming a subject is only attained asymptotically" (*dans une ligne de fiction…qui ne rejoindra qu'asymptotiquement le devenir du sujet*) (94). The use of line and asymptote is quite effective here, as the asymptote is a line that never touches a given curve; there is always a disjuncture. Lacan sees this as a given, a real consequence of the "specific prematurity of human birth" (*la donnée d'une véritable prématuration spécifique de la naissance chez l'homme* (96). And here, he is operating in the Freudian tradition, as Freud locates the source of human development, especially the neuroses, in the prolonged period of parental dependence. Since the human brain develops largely postnatally, in comparison with animals, human motor coordination takes much longer to develop and, in short, *necessitates the temporally extended family*.

Lacan offers a succinct summary: "The mirror stage is a drama whose internal thrust moves from insufficiency to anticipation, and which creates, for the subject, the phantasms that proceed from a fragmented body image to one that we can call orthopedic" (97). The use of the term "orthopedic" here is apt, as it is a Greek compound combining "straight" with "child", referring to the correction of deformities in children. He continues: "This fragmented body…appears regularly in dreams…in the form of disjointed members", as well as organs, and images of "intestinal persecutions" (*les persécutions intestines*) (97). He refers to Hieronymus Bosch and the grotesque images in the painting *The Garden of Earthly Delights*. These are "lines of fragilization that define the phantasmagoric anatomy, manifested in schizoid and spasmodic hysterical symptoms" (97). Thus the orthopedic embodied ego rests upon a fragmented foundation, one that is unconscious, and that appears in dreams as well as in neuroses, waking manifestations of dreamwork.

The mirror stage creates a construction of identity based on self-mirroring. Lacan notes that it is not just the image of itself that the infant is dialoging with, but also the environment surrounding that image. The infant responds with

> a series of gestures in which it playfully tests the relation between the movements assumed in this image and the reflected environment, and also between this virtual complex and the reality that it duplicates: its own body and the persons or objects around it.
>
> *(93)*

> une série de gestes où il éprouve ludiquement la relation des mouvements assumés de l'image à son environnement reflété, et de ce complexe virtuel à la réalité qu'il redouble, soit à son propre corps et aux personnes, voire aux objets, qui se tiennent à ses côtés.

In 1991, Alexander Guiora published "The Two Faces of Language Ego" in the Dutch journal *Toegepaste taalwetenschap in artikelen*. Guiora begins by posing the traditional question of why, in the course of language acquisition, children easily acquire local accents, but adults learning an L2 have greater difficulty doing so. He adds to this an odd claim that children can acquire L1 pronunciation in a "foreign" language *in situ* but not in their home country, in other words, a child raised in an English-speaking household in, say, Tokyo, would not acquire a "native" anglophone accent. No data is offered for this assertion.

Guiora bases his study on the idea of ego boundaries, which involve an interplay between fixed and fluid identities. He holds that most people have a fixed language identity and cannot tolerate two or more identities. In this context, he discusses research done on an Italian girl, bilingual in Italian and English, at the age of one year eight months, who would respond in each language if posed questions in that language, but not if the interlocutor had an accent from the other language, e.g., if engaged in Italian, she responded in Italian, but if engaged in Italian by someone who spoke Italian with an English accent, she responded largely in Italian but peppered her responses with English words. Guiora concludes that "the child gave the greatest weight to…the phonological channel" (Guiora, 1991, p. 6). Examples like this lead Guiora to "the formulation of a psychological theory, a theory of inhibition…based on the constructs of language ego and permeability of language ego boundaries" (6).

This has a psychological cause—inhibition—and is not due to "some genetically predetermined atrophy in the sound-producing apparatus" (7). Thus the child was engaging in a construction of identity on the axis of language, and via language ownership. She would respond fully in Italian only with L1 Italian speakers, selves who mirrored her own.

Guiora holds that the appearance of language "is developmentally relatively late, both phylogenetically and ontogenetically…yet, language is a central and critical element among, and for, what might be called identity formants and determinants" (7). And rightly so. He adds that language is the vehicle for "the integration of internal and external self-representation" (8). Guiora astutely calls pronunciation "the core of the language ego": "The way we sound marks us, defines us, in a singular fashion", he holds, and "no two people sound alike, no two people have the same fingerprints, and no two people, with the exception of identical twins, look alike" (8). Thus we "cleave to the linguistic marker of identity, i.e. the phonological pattern of their native tongue" (8).

As has been noted, Freud was perhaps the first to observe that the ego is above all a bodily ego, and that self-representation is extensively bound to our perception of our bodies in the eyes of others. This is evidenced by a host of idioms, such as "having a bad hair day", which broach the difficulties of aligning the way we see ourselves with the way others see us, and which can amount to two radically different versions of the same event. Language clearly arises and emotes from the body, and our discourse can be an object of the same anxieties and insecurities that we have relating to our bodies, hence Labov's notion of "linguistic insecurity" (Labov, 1972), which manifests itself in dialog, but not in monolog, not in "talking to oneself". We reflect on the way we speak, just as we reflect upon the way we look, and one aspect of naivete is the limited ability to know how one comes across, how one sounds in the perception of others. This is evidenced by idioms, as well, such as: "Are you hearing yourself"? The maintenance of a local accent is clearly related to identity formation, which, in turn, is related to a host of psychosocial factors involving ethnicity, regional or national pride, prestige, economic status, etc. This corresponds to Lacan's concept of the mirror stage, where the reactions of the interlocutor provide to us an image of ourselves in the eyes/ears of others. This involves reflection, consciousness, and recursion, i.e., the subject must be aware of the mirroring of self in the reactions of the other.

The fascinating case of "Monsieur 13 août" is important in this regard.

On August 13, 2017, a man was found in Marseille, France, who could not speak or write. He could, however, understand simplified communication. He had no identity papers on him, and his origin is a mystery, as is how he arrived in Marseille in the first place. The man has a pleasant appearance and smiles a lot. But he cannot tell you who he is. He was given the name "Monsieur 13 août", after the date when he was found (Franceinfo, 2019). The video of him fascinates the viewer, as he is an enigma who cannot articulate his own identity. Monsieur le 13 août suspends the dyad of mirroring in human interaction. He has the appearance and mannerisms of a stranger that you could meet, but there is no possible exchange of identities.

He mesmerizes us, because he cannot articulate his identity in any language, not even sign. He looks normal, even pleasant, can understand language, can work, and looks like he should be able to tell us who he is, but he cannot. There is no information on him. His figure foregrounds the fiction of identity, and hauntingly so. It asks us who we are and poses the question, "I cannot say who I am…and you"? He presents us with the possibility that our identity is a construction, a fiction. And this is due to the absence of language.

Many studies discuss the discrepancy between L1 and L2 performance, and the difficulties that second language learners have mastering the target language. Among the aspects of linguistic performance in the target language, L1 accent is the hardest aspect to attain, while grammar and vocabulary can well be mastered. There are plenty of L2 English speakers teaching at colleges and universities in the United States who regularly pass judgment on the performance of their L1 anglophone students, especially in written work. The L2 speaker's command of grammar and vocabulary can easily surpass that of the L1 speaker, but perfecting the L1 accent often eludes them. Why is it that an L2 pronunciation that "passes" is so difficult to attain?

For Guiora, the reasons are psychological. Pronunciation marks identity, and does not have, in his model, an adaptive function. He observes that mastering the grammar and vocabulary of a language will present no threat to the identity of the learner. On the contrary, high-register grammar and vocabulary can serve as indications of intelligence. And clearly, grammar and vocabulary utterances that deviate from the accepted norm can be easily, and unjustly, marked for lesser intelligence. But accent falls into a different category. Here, Guiora proposes a distinction between the "cognitive language ego and affective language ego", the first consisting in grammar and vocabulary and the second in pronunciation. In the case of "nonnatives" with a stellar command of grammar and vocabulary and an identifiable nonnative accent, the former can indicate impressive intelligence; the latter can indicate membership in another community, and can also indicate exotic status. Here, the maintenance of one's "home accent" can function as an act of preservation of the original identity. This raises the possibility that those who "pass" in the arena of the L2 are less concerned with maintaining their identity of national origin.

Guiora says that it is possible to acquire

> perfect affinity with the very soul of another language, have full command of its lexis and grammar, know every nook and cranny in the treasure-house of its idioms, and yet be not admitted to a privileged corner, closed beyond a certain age to most foreigners. And that privileged corner is native-like pronunciation.
>
> *(Guiora, 1991, p. 16)*

Guiora overstates the issue, oddly: "One cannot, simultaneously, maintain two schemata, two systems of external representation, i.e. two native phonological systems" (10). This is a curious statement coming from a psycholinguist. While they may be rare, there are clear cases of L2 learners passing for native.

But Guiora is not fully consistent on this. He also addresses this issue in the article "A Psychological Theory of Second Language Pronunciation", in which he holds that

> to sound like my fellow is to be at one with him, to be part of him and have him be part of me. Not to sound like me marks the other as one who is not at one with me, one who is not part of me, and of whom I am not a part.
>
> *(Guiora, 1990, p. 15)*

And here, one may refer back to the process of ego formation outlined in *The Ego and the Id*:

> When a sexual object has to be given up, there ensues a transformation of the ego, which one can term a reconstruction of the object in the ego itself...perhaps the ego permits or facilitates the abandonment of this object by means of introjection, which is a form of regression to the mechanisms of the oral phase...In any event, this is a frequent process, especially in the early stages of development, and can allow us to propose that the character of the ego is the precipitate of abandoned objects of desire—the history of these object choices.
>
> *(Freud, 1923, p. 257)*

The notion of introjection here as the core process of identity formation is quite valuable. The relinquishing of a sexual object would correspond to the core prohibition on incest—the relinquishing of family members as sexual objects. This results in an imitation of the relinquished others, a substitute incorporation of their behavior. One can expand the phrase "sexual object" to include desired objects in general, where erotic interests—both homo- and hetero-erotic—become sublimated into a theater of imitation and simulacra. This is evidently shown in the shared behavior of many social groups—behavior and modes of speaking, including pronunciation, intonation, vocabulary, etc. And Guiora's statement that "to sound like my fellow is to be at one with him, to be part of him and have him be part of me" would indicate this desire implemented in symbolic re-enaction, with an aspect of the other, a metonymy (displacement), standing in for the other.

I once asked a colleague at what point you begin to notice that someone has an accent. He responded, "When you don't like them". This is clearly an overstatement, but it sheds an exaggerated light on the issue of interpersonal dynamics in the audition of accent, especially the perhaps unconscious element of hostility present in those dynamics. A similar point can be made for the perception of race and ethnicity, which is often not the result of an objective observation, but is instead created by a motivated interest in race.

Returning to the theories of Guiora, one sees how he sets up a playing field with the possibilities of transgressing the ego boundaries that he seems to have rigidly set up: "Native pronunciation is the near-perfect litmus test of membership in this vital ring of identity. Native pronunciation becomes the hallmark, or the marker, of group language identity" (Guiora, 1990, p. 16), he notes, but at the same time, he seeks "to gain an understanding of what we took to be the psychological dilemma created by the need to sound, and thus to represent ourselves, as something we are not" (18). He says that "language and speech become the highest and the most vulnerable form of ego integration…grammar and syntax are the scaffolding of language ego, lexis the formal content that gives it body, and pronunciation its very core" (16).

He conducted experiments to test the fluidity of boundaries of identity articulated through accent. He cites the "alcohol study" that he and his colleagues performed at the University of Michigan in 1972, which administered alcohol mixed with sugar to students (the drinking age was 18 then) and then tested their performance in pronouncing Thai. The sugar–alcohol group performed sizably better than the control group. He concludes

> that pronunciation ability is apparently critically influenced by a psychological variable that can be successfully isolated from the larger web of ego functions. Our conclusion was that alcohol produced a temporary change in ego boundaries, in the form of greater permeability, and thus enhanced the ability to approximate native-like pronunciation in a foreign language.
>
> *(19)*

One would perhaps modify the statement that this imitative success is "successfully isolated from the larger web of ego functions", since self/non-self interactions cannot be seen as always prohibiting incorporation of the other into the self. He also cites other studies employing "other disinhibiting agents", one of which was hypnosis. The study showed that "deeply hypnotized subjects performed significantly better than less hypnotized subjects" on L2 pronunciation tests, and the experimenters concluded that "the results are consistent with…Guiora's line of reasoning about permeability of ego boundaries". Experiments with valium produced similar results, ostensibly because "the drug facilitated the empathic sensitivity of the subjects to the tester, significantly influencing their pronunciation performance" (19).

And his conclusion clearly qualifies his other statements on the impossibility of achieving an L1 accent: "The observed reduction in the flexibility of adult pronunciation behavior derives from the operation of psychologically significant inhibiting factors rather than from some genetically predetermined atrophy in the sound-producing deficiency in a foreign language". He adds that it "is not irreversible, and that it is manipulable, to a degree, under certain conditions. This theory can account for the both the relative flexibility and the extreme rigidity of the pronunciation barrier" (21).

Thus the inhibiting factors are psychological rather than physiological, and they tend to consolidate during and after the establishment of identity:

> Pronunciation delimits the boundaries of language ego and since most people cannot tolerate a split or a double identity, they cannot have a split or double language ego once their identities have matured and became firmly anchored, embodied in and expressed through native language.
> 
> *(21)*

The boundaries of the language ego—an excellent phrase—do clearly not consist only in accent, but also in tone, rhythm, volume, pitch, etc., which constitute the modalities of self-presentation through verbal language, i.e., in the composite way that one presents oneself verbally. However, experience has shown countless cases of individuals whose accent (and behavior) changes in self/non-self interaction.

For example, students often begin to change their accents when they are away from home their first year in college, and, in the same environment, often pick up the speech patterns and mannerisms of those in their social group. Now it should be emphasized that this is rarely a conscious decision, nor one that happens overnight—it occurs in a gradual, unconscious manner, one that the speaker is largely unaware of. The case of post-puberty L2 acquisition through dedicated study, however, offers a different scenario, in which the learner would be making a conscious effort to imitate the L1 accent. Thus it is the degree of consciousness of self that determines the inhibiting factors. Again, language is being processed here in an unconscious manner. As stated above, however, the inhibiting factors would not generally apply to the conscious acquisition of grammar and vocabulary.

Guiora also offers a study of "natural bilinguals", i.e., those who grow up with two L1s. In this case, it concerns 29 English and Hebrew speakers living in Israel. He finds that 27 of the 29 had a "non-native" accent in one of the languages, usually in Hebrew. This is the common condition of diglossia, where one language remains dominant. Guiora posits that

> natural bilinguals, as a group, are not different from others in that they will have only one authentic language identity, only one language ego. Natural bilinguals, like everybody else, will cleave to the linguistic marker of identity and protect their psychological and cultural integrity

by refusing to make phonological compromises affecting their language persona.

*(22)*

Nonetheless, 2 of the 29 participants demonstrated L1 accents in both languages. He notes that

> the early flexibility of ego boundaries is reflected in the ease of assimilating native-like pronunciation by young children; the later reduced flexibility is reflected in the reduction of this ability in adults. As conceived here, both required a temporary relaxation of ego boundaries and thus a temporary modification of self-representation.

*(20)*

The crux of the matter is that adults construct these inhibitions; they are *resistances to imitating*. And this reinvokes the earlier discussions of the role of verbal play and echolalia in the child's development of language, a phenomenon that becomes repressed in the transition to adulthood.

This could provide a moment of dovetailing of evolution and psychology. In the competition between cultural groups for niche dominance, the better organized group would have a persistence advantage. The better organized group is *the group that communicates better*. Accent can be placed in this context.

In 2014, Pietraszewski and Schwartz published "Evidence That Accent is a Dimension of Social Categorization, Not a Byproduct of Perceptual Salience, Familiarity, or Ease-of-processing", in which they investigate the atrophying of language acquisition faculties at puberty. The authors emphasize the difference between genotype and phenotype as an important distinction for studying language evolution. A genotype describes the genetic makeup of the individual, the heritable genetic identity, and phenotype describes the resultant expression of that identity in interaction with the environment. An easy way to characterize it would be to begin with the familiar binary distinction between nature and nurture, and to modify that with one that is not mutually exclusive, not "either-or", but both together, in an interactionist perspective. The distinction would be nature, on the one side, and, on the other, nature and nurture in symbiosis, i.e., the reality of the interaction between genes and culture.

The authors place the function of accent in such an interactionist perspective: "Natural selection has run through the culling process of trading off acquisition flexibility and costs, arriving at our modern phenotype in which language acquisition closes around adolescence" (Pietraszewski & Schwartz, 2013, p. 44). They are referring to the well-known critical period hypothesis, also referred to as the sensitive period. They observe that there are windows of opportunity for each component of what passes for L1 fluency, e.g. syntax, grammar, and pronunciation, but this has been problematized, as there are many L2 speakers, especially professionals, who have even surpassed average L1 facility in grammar, vocabulary, and syntax, but whose accents remain, as has been noted above. Again, it would seem that the "window" is much narrower for accent than for the other components.

Bates et al. (1995) show that the average child understands about 17 words at the age of eight months but does not produce any until about 12 months. They remark, "An adult who studied language without producing words for a year would most likely be considered an idiot, but we consider the same behavior by children quite normal" (Bates et al., 1995, p. 5). They add that "children do not acquire a language more quickly than adults". And they add that "with a lot of time devoted to language acquisition, adults can learn a second language to a high level of proficiency in the same amount of time it takes a baby to learn its first 20 words" (15–16). But eventually, there is a bifurcation between accent on the one hand and grammar, syntax, vocabulary, etc., on the other.

Pietraszewski and Schwartz explain the atrophying of language acquisition faculties after puberty in terms of a cost/benefit analysis. They conclude "that maintaining the acquisition machinery beyond puberty was not sufficiently beneficial" (Pietraszewski & Schwartz, 2013, p. 44); thus the brain turned its attention to learning other things besides a new language. This does indeed raise many questions, the major one being why the brain differentiates between "extra" languages and "original" ones. It clearly does not start to dim all the language faculties at the time of puberty. Why should it continue to develop the L1 but neglect the L2? The cost/benefit model does not really offer a sufficient explanation here, as intercultural contact is currently the rule and not the exception, and would have been so prehistorically, as well. There must have been a sort of reverse cost/benefit analysis.

Populations would have benefited from sealing off of their linguistic codes, developing a sort of aural/oral clan ID card. Thus the inverse may be the case; ossifying the acquisition machinery, especially accent, would have been beneficial for identifying outsiders and also for forming new subcultures that identify via shared sociolects. This may also tie into the exogamic function, as it would have facilitated the identification of possible mates outside of the clan, in addition to identifying exotic intruders. In the transition from child to adolescent, the other becomes a possible mate but also a possible threat with sufficient capabilities to penetrate the home culture. The authors also cite research indicating that young children prefer hearing L1 language production to L2. Thus a phenotype would have developed, enabling intracultural bonding, and also intercultural boundaries.

The authors perform a brilliant experiment using the well-known memory confusion paradigm, which is used to assess modes of social categorization:

> The logic of the paradigm is that if a particular feature—such as accent—is a basis of categorization, then people who are similar along that dimension

should be more readily confused with one another in memory. That is, when trying to recall information, memories about people who share the same accent will be more likely to be confused with one another, even in the absence of conscious awareness that this is happening. Thus, patterns of memory confusions reveal fundamental categorization processes.

(45)

Here, the "targets" in the experiment—the people who were to be categorized—were divided into two groups: those with British accents and those with American accents. The participants listened to recordings of the accent coupled with photos for each one. When asked to recall the correspondences and identify who said what, the participants erred and grouped according to accent. They would recall that one of the Brits had spoken the utterance but could not remember who. They would confuse among the Brits and among the Americans, but not between the two groups. Subjects were much more likely to misattribute the statement to someone who also had the same accent as the original speaker, as opposed to someone who had a different accent.

The authors conclude:

> These results demonstrate that accent—in this case, a native versus non-native accent distinction—was indeed the basis of strong social categorization. When participants incorrectly attributed statements to speakers, they were much more likely to choose a speaker who shared the same accent as the original speaker.

(46)

The authors also attempted to seek conformity and limit other distracting variables, and they settled on an amusing category; the targets "were all Caucasian men in grey t-shirts" (46). They add that, "for categorization to occur, participants must have encoded the speakers' native versus non-native accent information during the initial presentation phase and retained this category information during the recall task" (46). And they would have done so unconsciously.

The experiments clearly show a subliminal perception of accent that can influence social categorization and even override the visual. While the experiment is quite viable, there is a problem with the use of the terms "native speaker" and "native accent". One prefers nowadays the categories L1 and L2. In any event, aural perception here tags the speaker along the lines of self/other, i.e., "one of us or one of them".

Thus one sees that the production of accent operates under criteria different from those of the other "language skills". While the production of language in general involves the expression of identity, accent has a special role in this regard, as has been shown by Guiora and others.

Covert language prestige would have acted to consolidate group identity. In other words, common language would have communicated tribal membership. Accents would have evolved in order to mark that group membership and to indicate the outsider. Thus evolution would have selected for the inhibiting factor in order to mark in-group identity. The atrophying of language acquisition skills at puberty coordinates, clearly, with mating, and thus with family and clan formation. Language would have articulated the borders of cultural identity over and against the identity of other cultures. And accent would have solidified as a sentry device.

It is interesting to note that this also coordinates with maturation, the transition to adulthood, which is marked by the suppression of the interest in word play and rhyme, as Freud noted in his studies of humor and wit. It is worth quoting again the relevant passage:

> Playing with words and thoughts…would be the preliminary stage of humor. At a given moment, a critical or logical faculty puts an end to this playing. It is now rejected as nonsense or absurdity; criticism makes it impossible. It is now excluded…unless the maturing individual enters into a pleasurable mood that suspends the resistance, as it does in the joviality of the child.
>
> *(Freud, 1905, p. 144)*

This is the joviality of the child who delights in repetition and imitation, actions that engage language development. The acquisition of accent occurs during the period when ego boundaries are fluid, and it is aided by the delight in imitation, in adults, as well as in children. A colleague once told me that her daughter improved her French pronunciation while studying in France by imitating the accents and intonational patterns of female French university students. She was, in effect, making fun of the people she was speaking with, who, however, apparently did not notice that she was making fun of them. She did not suppress the childlike delight in imitation! And here, one can raise the question as to why imitators (and imposters) fascinate us. They perform for us the childlike joy of imitating, which we have outgrown. They are on the other side of the border of the fluidity of identity. The function of imitation and repetition in the construction of language and identity will be reexamined in the chapters on mimesis and mirror neurons.

This chapter has studied the dynamics of the formation of the ego, both individual and group, in the production of language. The following chapter will discuss research on neuro-psychoanalysis as it applies to the articulation of language and identity.

# References

Bates, E. et al. (1995). Individual differences and their implications for theories of language development. In P. Fletcher & B. MacWhinney (Eds.), *Handbook of child language* (pp. 96–151). Blackwell.

Forrester, M. (2015). *Early social interaction: A case comparison of developmental pragmatics and psychoanalytic theory.* Cambridge University Press.

Freud, S. (1905). Der Witz und seine Beziehung zum Unbewussten. Gesammelte Werke (Vol. 6, pp. 1–285). Imago. [English edition: Freud, S. (1953–1974). *Jokes and their relation to the unconscious. The standard edition of the complete psychological works of Sigmund Freud* (Vol. 8, pp. 1–236). Hogarth].

Freud, S. (1915). *Das Unbewusste. Gesammelte Werke* (Vol. 10, pp. 264–305). Imago. [English edition: Freud, S. (1953–1974). *The unconscious. The standard edition of the complete psychological works of Sigmund Freud* (Vol. 14, pp. 166–215). Hogarth].

Freud, S. (1923). *Das Ich und das Es*. In Freud, S. (1940). *Gesammelte Werke* (Vol. 13, pp. 235–289). Imago. [English edition: Freud, S. (1953–1974). *The ego and the id. The standard edition of the complete psychological works of Sigmund Freud* (Vol. 19, pp. 13–66). Hogarth].

Guiora, A. (1990). A psychological theory of second language pronunciation. *Leersderskenmerken: individuele erschillen in het leren van talen 37*(1), 15–23.

Guiora, A. (1991). The two faces of language ego. *Toegepaste taalwetenschap in artikelen 41*(3), 5–14.

Labov, W. (1972). *Sociolinguistic patterns*. University of Pennsylvania Press.

Lacan, J. (1966). Le stade du miroir comme formateur de la fonction du Je, telle qu'elle nous est révélée dans l'expérience psychanalytique. *Ecrits* (vol. 2, pp. 93–100). Editions du Seuil. [English edition: Lacan, J. (2006). *The mirror stage as formative of the I function. Ecrits* (vol. 2, pp. 75–81). W. W. Norton].

Marseille : qui est le mystérieux « Monsieur 13 août »? *Franceinfo*, 19 May 2019. https://www.francetvinfo.fr/faits-divers/marseille-mais-qui-est-le-mysterieux-monsieur-13-aout_3450745.html

Pietraszewski, D., & Schwartz, A. (2013). Evidence that accent is a dimension of social categorization, not a byproduct of perceptual salience, familiarity, or ease-of-processing. *Evolution and Human Behavior* 35, 43–50.

Wilson, A., & Weinstein, L. (1990). Language, thought, and interiorization: A Vygotskian and psychoanalytic perspective. *Contemporary Psychoanalysis 26*(1), 24–39.

# 7
# NEURO-PSYCHOANALYSIS

The research conducted in the field of neuro-psychoanalysis will aid in the description of the tripartite structure of language, consciousness, and identity formation. It will be argued that consciousness is engaged in and through language, and that consciousness is above all consciousness of self. The expression of language, fundamentally an act of self-consciousness in the dynamic of identity formation, is here situated within the field of neurolinguistic research.

The research of Kaplan-Solms and Solms is invaluable for integrating the findings of psychoanalysis into those of cognitive linguistics and neuroscience, especially in the context of embodied cognition. Solms holds that "we cannot know the body independently of its realization in the perceptual systems of the mind" (Solms, 1996, p. 339). He bases his research on the liminal stage within the "Perception-Consciousness System" (*Wahrnehmungs-Bewusstsein: w-bw*), first formulated by Freud, and located within the brain's posterior cortex, which mediates between the preconscious and conscious states. Its function is to progressively articulate consciousness. But Solms notes that,

> by the time the stimulus from the periphery reaches the cortex, it has already undergone a significant number of transformations at the subcortical level…we may equate this system…with the sensory receptors themselves, together with all the ganglia and nuclei with which they are connected during their passage along the spinal cord and cranial nerves, through the modality-specific nuclei of the brain stem and thalamus, toward the cortex…even at the level of external perception, our 'immediate acts of consciousness' have a long and complicated history.
>
> *(340)*

This constitutes the literal and overdetermined embodiment of language and consciousness. Similarly, in *Incognito: The Secret Lives of the Brain*, David Eagleman observes that

> a typical neuron makes about ten thousand connections to neighboring neurons. Given the billions of neurons, this means there are as many connections in a single cubic centimeter of brain tissue as there are stars in the Milky Way galaxy.
>
> *(Eagleman, 2011, pp. 1–2)*

This embodiment is a multivalent and syntagmatic process: "Perceptual consciousness always and only arises within an ongoing process of association" (Solms, 1996, p. 341), and the primary cortical zones form the nucleus of the ego, which is, in psychoanalytic terms, "a mental projection of the surface of the body" (342). And these connectivities operate epigenetically, as heritable changes in gene expression (active versus inactive genes) that do not involve changes to the underlying DNA sequence—a change in phenotype without a change in genotype.

Solms makes an important connection to the auditory sphere in the construction of identity, as was discussed in the previous chapter, but most importantly, the studies conducted by Solms situate this in the context of neurological research. Solms says, "The audioverbal modality is more closely bound up with self-consciousness than is the visuospatial modality, which is more closely bound up with object consciousness" (349). Thus one sees the vital function of language, spoken language—i.e., language spoken to another person—in the process of identity formation. He continues:

> During the process of language development, speech is perfected through the auditory modality, by critically listening to oneself and modifying one's own vocalizations until they match the vocalizations of significant others. In this respect one treats an aspect of one's own self as though it were an external object. This applies far less to one's visual image of oneself…the internalization of this attribute of speech makes it uniquely suitable for the purposes of self-reflective thought.
>
> *(349)*

One sees here an auditory instantiation of the mirror stage, most effectively described by Lacan. But here, it involves an audioverbal asymptotic relationship.

The "vocalizations of significant others" is a judicious term that indicates an extension of authority beyond the parental component to those whom one has invested with judgmental capacity and authority: "auditory self-reflection and critical comparisons between one's own speech and the speech of one's own parents…this feature of speech…lays the structural bedrock for the superego" (359).

The child imitates the form and content of the speech of the parents (and by extension authority figures). Thus "the child gradually develops the capacity to critically observe its own behavior on the basis of a running internal commentary" (359). This internal commentary would eventually constitute the behavioral standards of the individual. But Solms also reminds the reader of the contradictory nature of the voice of the superego: It says, "you ought to be like this…you may not be like this". The child is supposed to emulate the parent, and love the parent, but not love the way the parent loves. The child cannot have the libidinal object choice of the parent—this would violate the incest taboo, one that is foundational in the formation of human culture.

Similarly, Ana Marià Rizzuto, in her study of language in the clinical situation, notes that

> the patient's specific limitations with regard to participating in the analytic conversation…are motivated…by the reawakening of the affective experiences encountered in the course of speech acquisition and use under parental guidance…in brief, words have undergone a long developmental history of emotional accumulation of meaning (Rizzuto, 2002, p. 1326). She adds: To the conscious sense of the meaning of a word, analysts must add the motional and unconscious sense stemming from its having been used in particular contexts, with particular objects in specific affective moments.
>
> *(1327)*

Speech acquisition "under parental guidance" is a most important phenomenon. Rizzuto adds:

> In activating the language function and in offering words, the adult provides the child with an inner tool for transforming internal and external perceptions into conscious awareness while simultaneously offering an object to be libidinally cathected and identified within the constitution of his ego. The speaking and spoken to object becomes also an internal object. The word itself is an internalization.
>
> *(1332)*

She cites Freud, from *The Ego and the Id* (1923): "In essence a word is after all the mnemic residue of a word that has been heard" (1332).

In this context, she discusses the embryo's response to the mother's voice: "Upon birth, the baby prefers his mother's voice to others and recognizes it, suggesting its internalization" (1332). Moreover,

> the child registers the affective prosodic components of speech, acquires a sensitivity for the maternal language and, by 2 months, prefers that

language to any another. Finally, the child accepts as linguistic only those stimuli that are part of the mother tongue.

*(1333)*

And she adds: "The ego may, in fact, be regarded as a vocal-auditory structure" (1335).

Solms locates the ego's mediating functions in the brain's medial frontal region (Solms, 1996, p. 356). He bases much of his research on that of the Soviet neuropsychologist A. R. Luria (1973), and also the work of Isakower (1939), who was among the first to explore further the function of the auditory sphere in identity formation. The prefrontal brain region is commonly referred to as the locus of "executive functions" of planning, judgment, and behavioral control, especially concerning language. Solms says that

> the central role which language plays in the transformation of freely mobile energy into bound energy…the prefrontal region is, in one respect, just a further mnemic system…what is structuralized in the prefrontal system is neither a modality-specific aspect of perceptual reality, nor a concrete 'thing presentation', but rather a purely symbolic 'word presentation'.

*(357)*

These presentations are then subject to the "sequential nature of frontal syntheses" and enter into "the predicative and propositional structure of language", where cognitive structures organize them in terms of "first this, then that" and "if this, then that" sequences (358). This is a transcription into words and then into "a system of logico-grammatical rules…transcribed into successive, sequential programs…the structure for propositional speech" (362). But one sees here that this is not in the nature of language, but the instantiation in language of cognitive processes of sequentialization and dependency. This constitutes the function of secondary revision, a process that emerges when one recalls the dream, and that imposes a (more) logical structure on the dream narrative. But these "logico-grammatical rules" are suspended in dream, where one finds a "regressive process" that prefers "simultaneous forms of synthesis" (358). This corresponds to some of the first observations made by Freud on symbolism in dreamwork: that it is, to a large degree, the locus of cognitive dissonance, or, more accurately, it is a precognitive locus that comfortably expresses simultaneous antitheses, contradictions, nominal realism, rebuses, etc.

In his article on consciousness from 1997, Solms holds that mental processes are themselves unconscious, and that "consciousness is not merely a portion of mental activity; rather, it is a reflection of mental activity, or a perception of mental activity (which is itself unconscious)" (Solms, 1997, p. 684). He says of the Kantian maxim that the external world is unknowable to us—all that is knowable are the representations of that external world—that it is so, as well, with subjective internal experience: "The same limitations apply to our knowledge of our own mental processes" (688). These are mediated, filtered, arranged, and rearranged, in the prefrontal region by the ego, by our sense of self. He sees consciousness as an emergent phenomenon, and he is far from the first person to hold such a view. The title of the article should rather be "how consciousness works", because he never says what it is, nor does he say where the experience of being aware of something comes from. For Solms, consciousness arises from a coordination of various neurological activities, but is not locatable in any one of them. His perspective can be easily augmented by the inclusion of the theory of consciousness and language of the present inquiry.

Kaplan-Solms and Solms coauthored the book *Clinical Studies in Neuro-Psychoanalysis. Introduction to a Depth Neuropsychology* (2000). They hold that psychoanalysis "arose out of the mind-body problem", out of the question: "How is subjective awareness—consciousness—produced by the anatomical structures and physiological functions of the brain"? (Kaplan-Solms, & Solms, 2000, p. 4). For 19th century Austrian thought in general, there is no mind–body dichotomy, no soul or spirit in the body: Mental activity is a neurological phenomenon. The authors show how Freud the Austrian neurologist, starting in 1877, explored the nervous systems of animals and fish, up to the human "spinal cord and brainstem to the cerebral cortex…to the functions of the brain as a whole, until he finally reached the prototypical problem of human neuropsychology: the cerebral localization of language" (4). Involved in this was the discovery of neuroses (especially hysteria, i.e., conversion disorder) "for which no demonstrable lesion of the nervous system could be found…for the clinical symptomatology" (14). It is important to note that for Freud, the neuroses were "non-localizable physiological disorders" (15). They hold that Freud paved the way for the "dynamic school of behavioral neurology" (24).

As said, Kaplan-Solms and Solms base a lot of their research on the work of Luria, who worked closely with Vygotsky, especially his *Basic Problems of Neurolinguistics* (1976). Thus they see dreaming as "akin to psychosis in its functional organization…normal dreaming and psychotic illness can also be linked at the anatomical, physiological, and chemical levels" (56). They observe that "the technique of free association was specifically developed for the elucidation of the internal structure of functions that are obscured by resistances" (62). This is a valuable observation for illuminating the genesis of language as a process of "deep mining" of unconscious thoughts that then become "processed" and structured into coherent articulation via the process of secondary revision.

They study Freud's early work on aphasia and observe something that

> Freud had already recognized in 1891—namely, that 'the word' is produced by a complex functional system, with a number of component parts, linked (among other things) with the four primary modalities of

language: visual, auditory, kinesthetic, and motor. Each of these primary elements has a different cerebral representation.

*(89)*

Thus they conclude that the word "is a complex neuropsychological entity—comprised of numerous component parts" (90–91).

Freud does, however, privilege the auditory above the other sensory inputs. As already discussed, in the *Ego and the Id*, he held that verbal residues are derived primarily from auditory perceptions, so that the preconscious system has a special sensory source. The visualization of word-presentations are secondary products of reading, and the word is above all a memory residue of a word heard (Freud, 1923, p. 247).

In his monograph on aphasia, Freud resisted the notion of language centers and posited instead an interconnectivity that corresponds to current research in cognitive science. Physiologically, one finds in the brain connecting fibers, and psychologically, one finds networks of associations:

"The paraphasia observed in aphasic patients does not differ from the incorrect use and the distortion of words that healthy persons can observe in themselves in states of fatigue, or divided attention, or under the influence of disturbing affects" (Freud, 1891, pp. 13–14). This shows the interconnectivity of neurological connections and provides, as well, a physiological context for the mechanism of overdetermination.

He says of the word, that "it is a complex representation that proves to be constituted of auditory, visual and kinesthetic elements". He specifies:

> We learn to speak by associating a 'word sound image' with a 'word innervation feeling (*Wortinnervationsgefühl*)'. When we have spoken, we come into the possession of a 'representation of the movement of language' (*Sprachbewegungsvorstellung*), i.e., of a centripetal feeling from the organs of speech. The motor aspect of the 'word' is therefore doubly determined.

*(75)*

He adds:

> The word then is a complex representation consisting of collected images; in other words, the word corresponds to a complex process of associations informed by collected images of visual, acoustic, and kinesthetic origin. The word achieves its meaning through a connection with the representation of an object, at least if we restrict our observations to substantives. The representation of an object is, in turn, a complex of associations composed of the most varied visual, auditory, tactile, kinesthetic, and other impressions. Philosophy has shown us that the idea of the object

> contains this alone, and that the appearance of a 'thing', whose various 'properties' are conveyed by sense impressions, only comes about when we, while gathering up the sense impressions that we get from an object, add to those the possibility of a large chain of impressions in the same chain of associations.
>
> *(79–80)*

He then refers the reader to Chapter 3 of the *Logic* of John Stuart Mill. (It is interesting that psychoanalysis, which is based on a dualistic view of the mind, one divided into latent and manifest levels, should support a perspective from British empiricism, the philosophy that led to American behaviorism.)

He then goes on to cite cases of "optic aphasia", where patients cannot correctly name an object that they see—they engage in misnomers, but correctly recall the name when touching the object in question with their eyes closed. Freud concludes that "the speech apparatus was thus intact; it reacted erroneously via optical associations, but correctly via tactile ones" (82). This serves as another example of embodied cognition, especially the embodiment of language, in its interrelation with vision and touch. He concludes:

> The visual area of the cortex is the most important one for the association of symbols, as visual memories usually play the primary role in the association of objects. If these are not possible, the speech area can still receive impulses from the rest of the cortex, namely tactile, gustatory, and other associations, and can nonetheless be stimulated to produce speech.
>
> *(86)*

He also observes that

> word representations in a series of associations are better recalled than individual ones, and that words are better recalled the more extensive the associations are…words that have the narrowest meaning, i.e., ones that can be gleaned from few and specific object associations, are the ones most readily lost.
>
> *(90)*

Kaplan-Solms and Solms discuss a case of a patient exhibiting a subdural hematoma causing Wernicke's aphasia, i.e., damage to the area largely associated with language processing and understanding. The patient demonstrated an inability to retain audioverbal material in working memory (consciousness). She had gaps in her consciousness and experienced a sense of estrangement from herself, at times forgetting her own name, and also exhibiting a loss of memory for words, which eventually turned into a loss of memory for objects.

She complained of "an inability to think" (Kaplan-Solms & Solms, 2000, p. 108). Their analysis: She was unable to attach words to her thoughts, resulting in an inability to *bring her thoughts to consciousness* (and to keep them there). This immediately evoked "our metapsychological understanding of the relationship between words and things" (108). They observe that Freud, in the *Outline of Psychoanalysis* (1940) addresses how

> internal processes in the ego may also acquire the quality of consciousness. This is the work of the function of speech, which brings material in the ego into a firm connection with mnemic residues of visual, but more particularly of auditory, perceptions.
>
> *(162)*

The patient, Mrs. K, was "unable to attach words to her thoughts, and, therefore, was unable to render her thoughts conscious" (109). Her perceptual system, however, was intact.

In the psychoanalytic model, repression comes from the disconnection between unconscious mental processes and audioverbal traces—repressed thoughts are denied access to language, and thus to consciousness: "So when we say that speech associations bring ego processes to consciousness, what we really mean is that audioverbal associations perform this function" (112), the authors assert, and they add that "reflexive consciousness…is activated by way of 'word presentations' (i.e., audioverbal associations)" (112). They also extend this to a view of repression resulting from the withdrawal of the executive functions, which constitute, and are piloted by, the ego; the primary task of the ego is to control the subject in order to adapt to the demands of external reality. And this is a process of transition from preconscious to conscious modes of thought. Freud held that "the inside of the ego, which comprises above all the thought processes, has the quality of being preconscious". He added that "connection with mnemic residues of speech" is not "a necessary precondition for the preconscious state" (Freud, 1940, p. 162). But it is a precondition for the conscious state.

In *Incognito: The Secret Lives of the Brain*, David Eagleman posits that

> consciousness is probably not an all-or-nothing quality, but comes in degrees…I suggest than an animal's degree of consciousness will parallel its intellectual flexibility. The more subroutines an animal possesses, the more it will require a CEO to lead the organization.
>
> *(Eagleman, 2011, p. 143)*

He adds: "Consciousness is the long-term planner, the CEO of the company", while most of the daily functions are run by other parts of the brain, more or less automatically, and to which one has no access (70). The managerial metaphors here are quite interesting and, as cultural preconceptions, are a case in point for the theories of metaphor of Lakoff and Johnson (1980) (see Chapter 12).

Kaplan-Solms and Solms point out that the inferior parietal region of the left cerebral hemisphere is a region of convergence of information from various sensory inputs. This is the site of conversion to higher-order abstractions and "logico-grammatical concepts" (Kaplan-Solms & Solms, 2000, p. 145), and it is greatly facilitated by the function of language. The ego is the operator here in the management of the association of ideas. Associative linking forms the basis for the process of symbolization. The associative linking function is "the essential basis for the process of symbolization…whereby one idea stands for another in an associative chain, or by means of which the properties of one idea are transferred onto those of another" (147). This resembles a sketch of the processes of condensation and displacement (metaphor and metonymy).

The authors emphasize that "the fundamental mental mechanisms that underlie the surface phenomenology of human personality, motivation, and emotion are indeed inaccessible to simple behavioral observation due to the dynamic resistances that Freud described" (151). They transition to the phenomenon of the repression of the awareness of illness and discuss the following examples of constructed cognitive unawareness: anosognosia (denial of a disability or illness); anosodiaphoria (indifference to illness), and neglect syndrome, where patients act as if portions of their world do not exist. They cite the research of Ramachandran (1994), who shows that in patients who engage in the denial of paralysis, the information of the paralysis is still being continually recorded in the brain; it was able to be recalled in separate experiments, thus the denial did not erase the memory. So at a deeper level, the patient had the memory but repressed it. Ramachandran was convinced "of the reality of the repression phenomena that form the cornerstone of classical psychoanalytic theory" (Ramachandran, 1994, p. 324).

Ramachandran has a section of his study entitled "Neurology, Freud, and the Inner Ear", in which he says of anosognosia (the denial of paralysis), that "this disease provides an experimental approach to certain hitherto mysterious aspects of human nature such as the denial or repression of unpleasant memories or unpleasant facts about oneself" (317). He adds: "What is especially fascinating about anosognosia, on the other hand, is that the very notion of a 'person' or 'self' is called into question" (318). In his research, Ramachandran questions a patient about her paralyzed left hand. She denies that it is paralyzed. When he points to it, she says that it is not hers; it must be part of another person's body. He notes that her cognitive repression

> begins with rather simple denial of paralysis, but when her paralysis becomes increasingly obvious to her with repeated questioning, she is pushed into a corner and the only way she can rationalize the failure of

her arm to perform is to progress into the even more full-blown delusion that the arm belongs to her son! (This is analogous to what Freud might call projection.) What we are seeing here on a compressed time scale, is an amplified version of the same kinds of delusions and rationalizations that all of us engage in some time or the other.

*(320)*

He notes that patients exhibit this form of denial, "even though their intelligence, clarity of thought, and mentation are relatively unaffected in every other domain except for matters concerning the left hand"! (320). He asks, "Is the denial of paralysis mainly at the semantic/verbal level or does it run deeper? If it is mainly semantic, then is it possible that the patient is subconsciously aware that he/she is in fact paralyzed"? (320).

Ramachadran then conducted a fascinating experiment to answer this question. He decided to try a caloric (temperature) stimulation test on this patient. After she had repeated several times that she was not paralyzed, and that her arm belonged to her son, he administered 10 ml of ice-cold water into her left ear and waited until nystagmus appeared. Nystagmus is an involuntary rhythmic side-to-side, up and down, or circular motion of the eyes. It affects the inner ear balance mechanisms (vestibular mechanisms), or the back part of the brain (brainstem or cerebellum). The result was that the patient emerged from the denial syndrome and admitted that her arm had been paralyzed for a long time. When the caloric effect wore off, eight hours later, she reverted back to the denial syndrome and also repressed from memory the admission of paralysis that she had made earlier (324). This experiment points to the role of the auditory sphere in the articulation of identity, but it also involves the function of the superego as a regulatory voice of conscience, a form of self-monitoring. The patient had "heard herself" in dialog with authorial voices.

Kaplan-Solms and Solms discuss other cases of anosognosia (denial of a disability or illness) that demonstrate the same mechanisms of denial and repression. Here again, one can relate this to the mirror stage, where the infant experiences a disconnect between the experience of its own body and the mirror image of that body. They posit that the body is first experienced as something alien to the self. The authors invoke Freud's observation that the initial infantile reaction to the birth trauma—to the separation from the mother and into self and world—is one of resentment. This corresponds to the mirror stage: "The most primitive attitude in all of us towards the external object world— with all its frustrations and privations—is one of hatred"; the experience of the embodied self is a moment of ambivalence, of love and resentment. The body is perceived as "a constant source of unpredictable, unwanted stimulation… we experience a wish to be rid of it and left in peace—to be allowed to return to the blissful state that existed before the painful caesura of birth" (Kaplan-Solms & Solms, 2000, p. 198).

Another patient suffered an aneurysm that weakened his left hand, which was also subject to twitching paroxysms. He started hating his left hand and extended that to everyone in the hospital. He treated the left hand "as if it were part of external reality" (191). He desired to have it amputated and replaced by an artificial one—that way it would not be him. His hand became interchangeable with the hospital, which he treated as a "neglectful mother" (193). One sees a condensation between hand and hospital—both were alien and threatening. Thus he engaged in projection, and the hospital was responsible for the aneurysm that his body produced.

It is also important to view psychosomatic disorders from a psychosocial perspective. Research has shown an unconscious scanning of illegitimate and legitimate symptoms on the part of the patient. These would be the symptoms that the society in question considers to be acceptable. The group of symptoms scanned unconsciously is referred to as the "symptom pool". Shorter, in a study on psychosomatic illness, holds that "the unconscious mind…will therefore strive to present symptoms that always seem, to the surrounding culture, legitimate evidence of organic disease" (Shorter, 1993, p. x). And Ghazali notes: "As culture changes, so will the frequency of certain psychosomatic symptoms" (Ghazali, 2022). This demonstrates the involvement of a wide network of neurological connections in the conversion disorder that coordinate physical, psychological, and social input. The patient here would be mediating, unconsciously, the conversion via a self-image in dialogue with the social sphere.

An important conclusion to be taken from this research concerns the instability, ambivalence, and literally self-contradictory nature of ego and identity formation. Identity is constructed in and through language, as is consciousness itself, and the process of identity formation is a continually dynamic, ongoing process of embodiment and disembodiment, of introjection, rejection, and projection. These processes are either unconscious or preconscious in origin. This means that the articulation of speech itself is continually destabilized by these underlying contradictions. This is the door to speech errors.

In all cases, but especially the pathological ones, there is an intrusion of primary processes from unconscious to preconscious and into consciousness. This is a progression from dreamwork to consciousness, involving an exemption from mutual contradiction (cognitive dissonance), timelessness (conflation of tempora), and the replacement of external reality by psychic reality (208). Freud showed how humor can be produced by the transgression of primary process modes into secondary process ones during the transition from unconscious to conscious modes of thought. The expression of mutual exclusivity in humor is a prime example, and one is reminded of the maxim that the unconscious has no problem expressing simultaneous antithesis. It is also important to emphasize that displacement and condensation are pan-psychic devices and find expression in dreams and in waking consciousness.

The authors see the ventromedial frontal cortex as the site for the performance of "the fundamental economic transformation that inhibits the primary process of the mind" (230). This is the locus of the secondary process and the structuralization of the ego, which consists in sequential connections (as opposed to simultaneous ones in the posterior cerebral cortices). The sequentializations were initially formed under the verbalizations of the adults who interact with the child. They observe:

> The child uses this internalized set of connections to gradually differentiate, organize, and gain control over its thinking and actions. Following a critical period in the development of the prefrontal tissue, which occurs around the fifth year of life, these abstract, sequential codes—which psychologists describe as 'inner speech'—become firmly structuralized, and the child thereby achieves a very secure form of mental control over its own thinking and behavior.
>
> *(232)*

Here, inner speech dialogues with the speech of parental authority. Again, this is the voice of conscience.

Inner speech has been a controversial topic in linguistics, ever since Chomsky asserted that language is first and foremost inner monologue. He proposed that "language use is largely to oneself: 'inner speech' for adults, monologue for children" (Chomsky, 2002, p. 77). It is important to emphasize, however, that this is not properly inner speech, for as Pinker and Jackendoff have shown, inner speech is not yet fully articulated language. It still involves the "thinking in pictures", the imagistic cognition described by Freud. They assert:

> For one thing, the fragmentary snatches of inner speech that run through a person's mind are likely to be quite different from the well-formed sentences that motivate Chomsky's theories of linguistic competence. Other than in preparation for speaking and writing, interior monologues do not seem to consist of fully grammatical sequences of words complete with functional morphemes, such as *The teachers asked what attitudes about each other the students had noticed*, but rather of snatches of incomplete phrases. Whatever mechanism underlies inner speech—presumably the phonological loop that makes up a major component of working memory – it is not subject matter of any familiar theory of grammatical competence.
>
> *(Pinker & Jackendoff, 2005, p. 224)*

They add that

> a system for 'talking to oneself' would not need phonology or phonetics tuned to the properties of the human vocal tract; it would not need linear

order or case or agreement, and it would not need mechanisms for topic and focus, all of which presuppose that information has to be coded into a serial, perceptible signal for the benefit of listeners who currently lack the information and have to integrate it piecemeal with what they know.

*(224)*

In addition, they hold that

the innate aspect of the language faculty is for *learning* language from the community, not for *inventing* language. One cannot have inner speech without having words, and words above all are learned. (To be sure, people invent new words from time to time, but this is not the major source of their vocabulary.)

*(225)*

They do not deny, however,

that inner speech enhances thought and that this enhancement has been a major influence on the growth of civilization. But given that inner speech depends on having outer speech, acquired in a communicative situation, we are inclined to think that if anything is a by-product (or 'spandrel') here, it is inner speech. The primary adaptation is communication, with enhanced thought as an additional benefit.

*(225)*

Thus the structuralization of thought into language leaves the sphere of inner speech. Kaplan-Solms and Solms believe that "after this happens, …the whole of the child's mental life is…uniquely suited to reflexive functioning" (Kaplan-Solms & Solms, 2000, p. 232). The child shifts from an atemporal visual and spatial way of thinking to a verbal and sequential one, via "the internalization and structuralization of the parental voice" (232), which, according to the authors, enables the child to examine itself using the formal properties of language. The child then begins to plan sequential activities. Physiologically, this is expressed in the way that the prefrontal region "influences the rate, sequence, and pattern of neuronal firing throughout the cerebral cortex" (232–233). The prefrontal region "appears to perform the fundamental economic transformation that inhibits the primary process of the mind" (237).

This could be qualified a bit. It is clearly true that the inhibiting of primary processes is necessary for functioning in human culture. But this inhibiting is complete only during strictly controlled conscious attention. Otherwise, primary processes are continually "firing" and entering into preconsciousness. Moreover, the parental voice is not one of syntax alone. It is also the haunting voice of admonition. But it is true, however, that children model their construction of syntax on auditory input.

In *The Outline of Psychoanalysis*, Freud says that we know two things about that which we call our psyche: first, its bodily organ and location (*Schauplatz*), i.e., the brain or nervous system, and second, our acts of consciousness that we receive immediately. These are the two endpoints, and everything that lies between is unknown to us (Freud, 1940, p. 67). He adds that mental life (*Seelenleben*) is the functioning of an apparatus to which we attribute spatial extension and composition from numerous pieces.

Kaplan-Solms and Solms offer, however, a judicious caveat: "It would be a serious mistake to conclude...that the subjective mental contents that we experience...actually reside in these structuralized neuronal connections" (Kaplan-Solms & Solms, 2000, p. 260). Nor can our "conscious perceptual experiences...actually be found in the unimodal cortical zones. One will never find a thought inside a piece of tissue" (260). They posit instead the "lawful relationship" that exists between the nervous system and acts of consciousness in the form of "dynamic localizations" (260). Nonetheless, they do posit general locations for perception and memory:

> Whereas the external world is...represented as a series of things in the posterior zones of the right cerebral hemisphere, it is re-represented by a series of words in the corresponding zones of the left hemisphere... in the left-hemisphere mnemic [memory] systems, reality is represented primarily in terms of its audioverbal rather than visuospatial qualities.
> 
> *(262)*

This is an audioverbal and symbolic re-representation of both internal and external perceptual information that subsequently becomes verbalized. Words "tender the thought processes occurring in the depths of the ego *conscious*" (263). Words then translate from primary to secondary processes. The authors observe that "the activatory and mnemic connections between deep brain systems and the cortex...provide the anatomical and physiological basis for the whole mode of psychic functioning that Freud designated as 'primary process'" (268). They continue: "The ascending activating system, together with its limbic connections...is the anatomical and physiological correlate of the mental agency that in psychoanalysis is described as the 'id'" (268). Then a translation occurs, and "once thinking is attached to speech, it is structured by a fixed set of logico-grammatical rules" (263). It should be emphasized that this process is at once mental and lingual, a formalizing that falls into place in the transition to consciousness.

Solms also states elsewhere that the id can be located in the reticular activating system of the brain stem, together with its diencephalic, limbic, and cortical connections (Solms, 1996, p. 353).

It is also important to emphasize that this is a transitional phenomenon, not an on-or-off toggle switch. One cannot really speak of borders along the transitions from unconscious to preconscious to conscious states. The areas of transition can best be compared with the transitions in color perception, e.g., from green to blue in color, where hues blend into another, and one cannot properly say where green stops and blue begins. Moreover, there is a continual upwelling of perceptual information from unconsciousness to consciousness. In other words, "all the aphasias, apraxias, and agnosias may be interpreted as localized regressions from secondary to primary processes" (273). This is the playing field of speech errors, which Freud saw as the key to understanding the nature of language.

The executive and inhibitory functions of the mind are in the frontal lobes of the brain, particularly in the prefrontal region, which "represents the deepest layer of structuralization of perceptual information" (270). This is the locus of the ego and of language in their primary role as mediator among various mental forces. The authors assign a special symbolic function to language in this process: "What is structuralized in the prefrontal region is neither a unimodal aspect of perceptual reality nor a concrete 'thing-presentation', but, rather, a purely symbolic 'word-presentation'" (273). In this context, they revisit the Kantian maxim that the external world is unknowable to us, and they also configure it in a way befitting a poststructuralist Lacanian analysis:

> The symbolic transcriptions provide an especially powerful shield against stimuli, because they organize the infinite diversity of real external things into a fixed lexicon of categories. Thus, every possible experience of a particular type is reduced to a single word. In a very concrete sense, it can therefore be said that words protect us against things.
>
> *(279)*

Thus the lingualizing process is a psychological one that puts things in an order acceptable to the ego. The process of secondary revision would be applicable and active here. This is the "special role of speech in the dynamic functions of the ego" (273).

The neuro-psychoanalytic work on projective identification is important in this context, and Greatrex, in "Projective Identification: How Does It Work"?, has made a valuable contribution. The concept of projective identification places projection in an interactive context between self and non-self. In the normal defense mechanism of projection, one denies the presence of one's own uncomfortable feelings and instead attributes them to another person. In projective identification, feelings repressed from consciousness become projected in order to elicit those same feelings in the person upon whom the feelings are projected. The other introjects the projected qualities, and a cycle occurs of reciprocal projection, introjection, re-projection, and so on. Projective identification is an important process for the evolution, development, and processing of language within the framework of theory of mind (ToM).

Greatrex discusses projective identification as it is involved in the construction of self, and as it emerges in the transition from unconscious emotional systems to conscious ones. This involves research on mirror neurons, reflective thought, the repetition compulsion (*Wiederholungszwang*), and language. Projective identification begins in the infant's neurological propensity for imitation, intuition, and suggestibility, and also in the operation of mirror neurons (184). Greatrex speaks of "ludic circuits" in the mammalian brain "that generate joyous and social engagement, such as play and laughter", and that do not need "to be read out in the higher cortical memory areas" (Greatrex, 2002, p. 184).

The amygdala, which is the center of visceral fears and anxieties, can help us understand the etiology of fear and anxiety: "The learned fear response occurs quickly, because speed is more important than accuracy for survival. The response can bypass the neocortex (and is therefore unconscious) and can last indefinitely" (185). This repeated response to an emotion in a preorganized fashion "is actually similar to the classical Freudian concept of the repetition compulsion, which invokes libidinal and aggressive drives" (185). Analysis has shown that the more painful the experience, the more likely the patient is to place it in a context where it can be compulsively repeated. There is a strong resistance to attempts to enter into an organized response to the repeated trauma and to get beyond it. The repetition compulsion is learning-resistant. (185).

Freud describes the repetition compulsion (*Wiederholungszwang*) in *Beyond the Pleasure Principle* (*Jenseits des Lustprinzips*) (1920). He observed a child with a toy on a string, who would throw the toy away and then reel it back in, repeatedly. The child would exclaim *fort* (forth/away) and *da* (here) in doing so. Disturbed by the coming and going of his mother, the child tried to master the situation symbolically by staging the actions of coming and going *in a way that he could control*. This is known as the *fort/da* problem, and is connected to the birth trauma—the initial separation from the mother and the necessity of the acceptance of individuation.

Working with the research performed by LeDoux (1996), Greatrex contrasts emotional memory with the memory of an emotion, in other words, an unmediated automatic response to an earlier trauma with a conscious memory of that trauma:

> When we remember explicitly, we are generally in a self-reflective state in which we 'look at' a memory, using both intellectual and emotional capacities. Therefore, our conscious memory of a deep emotional event is flavored with the original feeling experience but remains a description of the event.
>
> *(186)*

Emotional memory is triggered by amygdala networks, those of the limbic system (186), and these, as unconscious phenomena, are reorganized in the process of description, in the entry into language; the mediation by language involves defense mechanisms: "Change that is mostly cognitively driven may not involve unconscious affect categories and may remain superficial…no reorganization takes place by mere superimposition, since the latter is merely a defense" (187). He adds: "Our affective procedural memories constitute the affective core of our personality that most defines who we are" (186).

The human brain is quite different from that of other primates, in that it develops to a great extent postnatally, an adaptation that evolved slowly and enabled safe passage through the narrow birth canal (but also immense labor pain). This produced the brain as a plastic organ that developed in the context of social interaction and cognition. Greatrex observes that the human brain "is a very open system that is 'soft assembled' and not 'hard wired'" (187). He places this in a current "socio-bio-evolutionary perspective", in which the adult symbolic and reflective mind evolved rapidly since the advent of homo sapiens, "because the genetic substrate of immature brains requires ongoing tuning by social interaction in order to evolve mature capacities" (187).

Greatrex also makes the observation, as an aside, that "play appears to be a central organizer that allows complex systems to emerge from simpler ones" (187). We have a subsymbolic (and presymbolic) communicative capacity that moves us to instantly imitate the other, to match their emotional state, and unconsciously so. This is the foundation of ToM. It is a trait selected by evolution that triggers the human revolution. And when we imitate, we do so in mind and body. The other occupies the self, as we engage in gestural imitation, especial facial imitation, hence the importance of the concept of projective identification. Greatrex invokes Freud as among the first to note this: "It is a very remarkable thing that the unconscious of one human can react upon the other without passing through consciousness". Greatrex terms this "affect contagion" (Greatrex, 2002, p. 188). With maturation, a sense of autonomous self emerges, and a capacity at self-regulation, but the nonvolitional spontaneous subsymbolic process of matching continues, at an unconscious level (intuition and suggestibility are involved here). This perspective has been supported by the work on mirror neurons (189).

Greatrex cites the work by Rizzolatti and Arbib (1998) that sees the mirror neuron system as phylogenetically fundamental for speech and earlier forms of intentional communication (190). He holds that there is an involuntary human mirroring action that becomes controlled voluntarily as the infant matures; this is "a developmental milestone" (190). If an observer finds another's action interesting, the premotor system exhibits a brief "prefix" of that movement, which is recognized by the actor–interlocutor, who in turn, recognizes an intention in the other individual. This establishes a "primitive dialogue" that forms "the core of language" (190). Greatrex points out that, in the analyst–analysand context, "what we have difficulty tolerating in the other is matched by what we disavow in ourselves" (191). We see here that this forms the core of language and the core of identity formation, which is a dialogic one.

This chapter has studied the research on neuro-psychoanalysis in the understanding of the tripartite structure of language, consciousness, and identity formation. As self/non-self interaction is fundamental to the construction of identity, and especially to the formation of the "language ego", it must involve imitation, self-mirroring, and repetition. These are discussed in the subsequent chapters on mimesis and mirror neurons.

## References

Chomsky, N. (2002). *On nature and language*. Cambridge University Press.
Eagleman, D. (2011). *Incognito: The secret lives of the brain*. Pantheon.
Freud, S. (1891). *Zur Auffassung der Aphasien*. Deuticke. [English edition: Freud, S. (1953). *On aphasia: A critical study*. International Universities Press].
Freud, S. (1920). *Jenseits des Lustprinzips. Gesammelte Werke* (Vol. 13, pp. 1–71). Imago. [English edition: Freud, S. (1953–1974). *Beyond the pleasure principle. The standard edition of the complete psychological works of Sigmund Freud* (Vol. 18, pp. 7–67). Hogarth].
Freud, S. (1923). *Das Ich und das Es. Gesammelte Werke* (Vol. 13, pp. 235–289). Imago. [English edition: Freud, S. (1953–1974). *The ego and the id. The standard edition of the complete psychological works of Sigmund Freud* (Vol. 19, pp. 1–66). Hogarth].
Freud, S. (1940). *Abriss der Psychoanalyse. Gesammelte Werke* (Vol. 17, pp. 63–140). [English edition: Freud, S. (1953–1974). *An outline of psychoanalysis. The standard edition of the complete psychological works of Sigmund Freud* (Vol. 23, pp. 144–207). Hogarth].
Ghazali, L. (2022). *A psychoanalysis of psychosomatic disorders and cultural influences*. Unpublished paper, The University of Richmond.
Greatrex, T. (2002). Projective identification: How does it work? *Neuropsychoanalysis* 4(2), 183–193.
Isakower, O. (1939). On the exceptional position of the auditory sphere. *International Journal of Psycho-Analysis* 20, 340–348.
Kaplan-Solms, K. & Solms, M. (2000). *Clinical studies in neuro-psychoanalysis. Introduction to a depth neuropsychology*. Karnac.
Lakoff, G. & Johnson, M. (1980). *Metaphors we live by*. University of Chicago Press.
Luria, A. (1973). *The working brain. An introduction to neuropsychology*. Basic Books.
Pinker, S., & Jackendoff, R. (2005). The faculty of language: What's special about it? *Cognition* 95, 201–236.
Ramachandran, V. (1994). Phantom limbs, neglect syndromes, repressed memories, and Freudian psychology. *International Review of Neurobiology* 37, 291–333.
Rizzolatti, G., & Arbib, M. (1998). Language within our grasp. *Trends in Neurosciences* 21, 188–194.
Rizzuto, A. (2002). Speech events, language development and the clinical situation. *International Journal of Psycho-Analysis* 83, 1325–1343.
Shorter, E. (1993). *From paralysis to fatigue: A history of psychosomatic illness in the modern era*. Free Press.
Solms, M. (1996). Towards an anatomy of the unconscious. *Journal of Clinical Psychoanalysis* 5, 331–367.
Solms, M. (1997). What is consciousness? *Journal of the American Psychoanalytic Association* 45(3), 681–703.
Vygotsky, L. (1976). *Basic problems of neurolinguistics*. De Gruyter.

# 8
# LANGUAGE AND MIMESIS

In his fascinating study: *How Language Began. Gesture and Speech in Human Evolution*, David McNeill offers a model of language development that unifies speech and gesture and locates them at an original point for language. This is a unity that produces meaning in an interactive dynamic. He speaks of the "equiprimordiality" of speech and gesture and claims that animals "have not taken the step that led to language, evolving a unit that is both sound production and gesture integrally" (McNeill, 2012, p. 69). This would coordinate with the observation that animals do not symbolize, nor engage in higher-order recursivity. This expands the perspective on the fundamental differences between animal and human communication.

He accesses the theories of George Herbert Mead (1863–1931), in Mead's most famous publication *Mind, Self, and Society from the Standpoint of a Social Behaviorist* (1974), specifically the idea that the human brain produced an embodiment of speech in gesture, one that is symbiotic and codetermined, i.e., communication consists in a symbiosis of speech and gesture. McNeill connects this with recent research on mirror neurons and configures the human capacity to imitate, and also to see one's own actions as imitable, as the bases for communicative language. Mead held that "a gesture is meaningful when it evokes the same response in the one making it as it evokes in the one receiving it" (McNeill, 2012, p. 70). McNeill qualifies this further and posits that the meaningfulness of gesture occurs when one views one's own actions as if they were those of someone else. This is not a schizophrenic confusion of self and non-self, it is simply the capacity for metacognition, although McNeill does not address it as such. McNeill also claims that this is not theory of mind (ToM), but it seems that it has to be, because of the necessary interactivity involved in the mirroring process of viewing another's actions as if they were your own.

DOI: 10.4324/9781003180197-9

He invokes the concept of "Mead's loop", which refers to a theory of mirror neurons, based partly on the work of Mead, that sees two stages in their development. The first is to view the actions of others as if they were your own, the second is viewing one's own actions as a spectator, i.e., as if they were the actions of someone else.

For McNeill, this equiprimordiality constitutes the "growth point hypothesis" (GP), which unifies language and gesture; they are two kinds of semiosis (symbolizing activities), and he underscores the unconscious nature of this process: "A gesture is an unwitting, non-goal-directed action orchestrated by speaker-created significances, having features of manifest expressiveness" (4). He also sees gesture as primarily, but not exclusively, manual. It is always there, he claims, even when not used: "It may even surface in some other part of the body, the feet for example" (19). This observation accesses psychoanalytic work on conversion and conversion disorder, the process of displacing the mental to the physical, and this also combines well with the theory of embodied cognition. One should add that facial gestures also fit into this model. He adds that people blind from birth still gesture, and they do so even to others who they know are blind. He also notes that people born without limbs have the feeling that they gesture. Moreover, memory loss interrupts speech and gesture, too; gesture does not fill in the gaps. Speech and gesture are thus inseparable, because "they are bound together by the requirements of idea unit formation" (13).

This supplies a model for viewing conversion disorder (hysteria) as a form of language. John Forrester, in *Language and the Origins of Psychoanalysis*, states that

> the difference between a neurological and a neurotic symptom is that the latter's location in the body is determined by the specific structure of a system of thoughts, whose expression in the body is often bound up with a verbal turn of phrase.

The organ of the body is not diseased, but the idea of the organ "is the line of crystallization of the neurosis". Thus, "the expression of words in the body amounts to a displacement of the proper locus of words" (Forrester, 1980, pp. 3–4). This is the conversion from language to body, in effect, a kinetic pun. One sees here a fusion of word, thought, and body. It is a message, a pun, and, most importantly, a fusion of word, psyche, and soma.

As has been stated previously, the transition from unconscious to consciousness involves a translation, a word formation. Freud and Breuer conceived of repression as the loss of the capacity to verbalize the problem, which causes its conversion into the symptom, the symbolic language. Similarly, Forrester says that "repression consists in depriving ideas of their word-presentations" (6), and adds that "the language of the symptom is characterized by its relative imperviousness to discursive change" (132). Forrester notes that the aphasic who repeats the same thing cannot substitute one word for another, nor one set of words for another set of words.

For McNeill, GP is the dynamic nexus of language, a dialectic. It is the "initial pulse" (McNeill, 2012, p. 19) of thinking while speaking, and also for speaking. Speech tends to categorize the imagery component in gesture and bring it into the system of language: "Syntax stabilizes the dialectic" between gesture and speech (76). Thus syntax is the establishment of sequential conventions for ease of communication, for "shareability" (76). Sequential syntax develops in the parameters of interactive language, both gesture and speech.

In the equally fascinating *Why We Gesture. The Surprising Role of Hand Movements in Communication*, McNeill specifies that "to orchestrate speech is why we gesture" (McNeill, 2016, p. 3), as does a conductor in arranging order and timing. He observes again that the prerequisite for language and gesture to be fully operational "was awareness of self as agent…not merely responding to others but awareness of being in public gave self-aware agency its foundational role" (124). He calls this a "self-response". Thus, for the purposes of this study, the realization that one can be imitated is a recursive metacognitive moment. McNeill holds that the gesture–speech unity emerges in children at age three to four, enabled by "the emergence of self-aware agency", which "means the condition of being aware of oneself as an agent" (154). It is not clear, however, that children are self-aware at this age. It seems rather that speech remains egocentric at that age. McNeill holds that "for an individual speaker, embedded in context, his/her cognitive Being is a gesture-speech unity" (187).

McNeill reiterates the ineluctability of the process of conversion in the gesture–speech dynamic: "At the origin, language was a unity of gesture and speech. If for some reason it is repressed, the inner gesture, imagery in actional form, remains and leaks out through some other part of the body" (187). The element of repression aligns perfectly with the psychoanalytic account of conversion—the repression of linguistic articulation causes the idea to become embodied, and here, in the form of word play or allusion. Concerning the idea of a gesture–speech equiprimordiality, one could counterargue that there are people and cultures that do not gesture when speaking, but in McNeill's model, there would still be an embodiment of language expressed in less obvious ways.

He also adds that the actions of gesture and speech "are thus intimately tied to metaphoricity. Mead's loop made metaphoricity obligatory, the 'experience' of one thing…in the form of something else…when the orchestration of actions of the vocal tract and hands was undertaken by something other than those actions" (119–120). He adds: "This is the semiotic of metaphoricity, one thing (voice) gaining significance in terms of something else that it is not" (120). This is the moment of metaphor as the action of comparing two things that stand in no contiguous relation. He insists upon "the semiotic opposition of gestures to linguistic form that constitutes the dynamic in GPs" (191).

Michael Tomasello's *The Cultural Origins of Human Cognition* places the transmission of language in a mimetic context. He argues that the complexity of human culture derives largely from social and cultural transmission, not from genetics, and that cultural transmission is speedy in comparison with genetic changes. The conduit for this is largely learning from parents (Tomasello, 1999, pp. 3–4). Cultural innovations are cumulative in human culture, but much less so in animal culture. They are cumulative due to theory of mind—humans can understand other humans "as beings *like themselves* who have intentional and mental lives like their own" (5). They are able "to 'identify' with their conspecifics" (10). ToM offers a structure for understanding how humans can intuit, for instance, why another person is using a certain tool in a certain way. This constitutes the concept of cultural inheritance (52), which happens when an organism does not learn or discover something on its own, but when "one organism adopts another's behavior or perspective on some third entity" (52). The human faculty of imitation facilitates this. Tomasello sees children as conservative imitators. From age one to three, "they generally imitate exactly the relational structure of the constructions they are learning from mature language users…young people are virtual 'imitation machines'" (159).

He maintains that "the capacity to understand conspecifics as intentional/mental agents like the self" is innate in *homo sapiens*. It is "the major cognitive characteristic distinguishing modern from premodern human beings" (54). Children born into this matrix pickup on verbal and nonverbal social signals. Those who are isolated do not, and do not develop language. They are not born into the symbolic matrix, where they learn that a given object does not have a fixed meaning, but a contextual one: "One and the same place may be construed as the coast, the shore, the beach, or the sand—all depending on the communicative goals of the speaker" (9). Tomasello adds: "Linguistic symbols thus free human cognition from the immediate perceptual situation… by enabling multiple simultaneous representations of each and every, indeed all possible, perceptual situations" (9). This is also the skill that enables metaphorical extension (see below).

This perspective can be easily coordinated with the model described earlier that places the generation of language in the framework of ego psychology, of the interactive mirroring and reciprocal identification between self and non-self.

Tomasello argues that non-human primates cannot attribute motivation and cause to events, nor to others. For example, if a given chimp invents a novel way to perform a task, say extracting termites from a nest with a stick, other chimps will not imitate the exact method used by the first chimp. They would see that it is possible, and then go about doing it their own way, with much trial and error. They "would not be focused on the innovator's behavioral techniques…the novel strategy would simply die out with the inventor" (39). A human, by contrast, would imitate the process and innovate upon it, thus scaffolding or "ratcheting" the procedure. He offers the interesting observation that "we know others' intentional states as well as we know our own, and in some cases better" (71). This is interesting from a psychoanalytic standpoint, as self-awareness can be blocked by defense mechanisms.

He maintains that humans understand symbolic reference interactively with other humans. To develop this skill, children must put themselves in the place of the adult and must use a symbol toward the adult in the same way the adult used it toward them (105). He calls this "role reversal imitation" (105). This means that children not only imitate the adult, but they also must see themselves in the eyes of that adult. They become aware of themselves as the object of the symbolic gesture. This is a recognition of self as mediated by the gaze of the other, in which they see themselves being seen and take on the role of the observer of themselves. This clearly coordinates with the theory of the mirror stage. This would be level-one reflection, a kind of quotative imitation. In fact, the symbol is born in this mirrored interchange: "The result of this process of role-reversal imitation is a linguistic symbol: a communicative device understood intersubjectively from both sides of the interaction" (106). This is a very astute observation: The learning of the context-free referent, i.e., the symbol, is acquired in the process of role-reversal imitation.

This raises the question of the function of consciousness and recursivity in this context. He sees role-reversal imitation as enabling "reflective meta-discourse" (190). He says, "Children internalize the discourse in which adults instruct them or regulate their behavior...and this leads them to examine and reflect on their own thoughts and beliefs in the same way the adult has been doing" (191). He holds that, between ages five and seven, children develop discursive metacognition: "They begin to actively monitor the social impression they are making on other people" (192). Thus it is no coincidence that they begin to use subordinate clause recursivity at this stage: e.g., "she thinks that I think". It is also here that they begin to use metalinguistic skills to talk about language. He thinks that this is the result of "adults using reflective meta-discourse with children" (192). They internalize the "voice" of another person. Now this clearly coordinates with the auditory function in the construction of "the language ego", as Guiora terms it. This is the "thou shalt", the parental voice that Freud describes, in which adults are continually monitoring the speech of children, and saying, e.g., "Don't be impolite".

Tomasello refers to the work of Karmiloff-Smith (1992), in which she says that "representational redescription" is what distinguishes human cognition from that of other species. Humans "re-present knowledge to themselves" in the learning process (194). The proposition that this arises through the internalization of the speech of adults is most interesting and fruitful for the perspectives of this study. It can place the capacity for self-reflection, i.e., consciousness, in a psychoanalytic perspective. Here, consciousness and conscience are coterminous. This can also illuminate the homophony in French, for instance, between *conscience* (consciousness) and *conscience* (conscience).

Earlier, the possibility was discussed that this arose in the need to protect oneself, and also in the activity of hunting. But one sees here that it may have arisen as well from the power of the parental voice in a psychoanalytic context. Tomasello maintains that "it results from an individual taking an outsider's perspective on its own behavior and cognition...as if they were another person looking at it" (196). And the proto-outsider would be the voice of parental authority.

For Tomasello, self/non-self mirroring and reversal is the garden of human language, the context from which it emerges. Humans acquire language by understanding usage contextually. To the hypothetical question as to whether or not someone who grew up in isolation could invent a private language, he answers no, because "there would be no way to constitute their intersubjectivity, and there would be no communicative motivation or opportunity for taking different perspectives on things" (133).

He maintains that children never learn words out of context. When they learn, e.g., "ball", the ball is always doing something. Language is, at this stage, concrete, and episodic. He subscribes to the "verb island" hypothesis, in which children learn verbs episodically and organize constructions around individual verbs. They have not generalized to patterns across verbs: "There are no other hidden principles, parameters, linguistic categories, or schemas that generate sentences" (139). Language, and perception, for that matter, are item-specific. He holds that adult idioms operate this way, as well.

He makes a consequential argument about the stage when children can generalize, and focuses on ditransitives, e.g.: "He gave her the wrench". He holds that "the construction, as an abstract structure, is itself a symbol, carrying meaning to some degree independently of any of the words involved" (141). There is no generating structure here, but a conventional one, agreed upon, and thus generalizable. Once the structure is successfully communicated, i.e., once the listener intuits the meaning of the novel utterance (ditransitive, passive, etc.) and uses it with others, it becomes generalized and context-free. ToM enables the listener to intuit the meaning through intonation, inuendo, etc. He notes that children have trouble doing passive transformations. They repeat the active and passive sentences but cannot transform easily (145). This underscores the episodic condition of the early acquisition of language.

Tomasello assigns an executive function to cultural transmission: "The stories told by a culture...are a major part of the way it views itself, and so comes to shape the cognition of its individual members as well" (158). Social and cultural processes "turn basic cognitive skills into extremely complex and sophisticated cognitive skills" (189). And he asks why these skills take so long to emerge ontogenetically. He thinks that it is due to the dependence on "real-life social interaction over a several-year period" (198).

**132** Language and mimesis

Social cognition and ToM have changed "in fundamental ways the *process of evolution*" (201), in that humans have shaped that process through their cooperation. New generations learn the cultural habitus and interact with that habitus "almost totally through the mediating lenses of preexisting cultural artifacts" (202). This would correspond to the psychoanalytic concept of the collective unconscious (*kollektives Unbewusstes*), as the mediation would proceed in a largely unconscious manner. He asserts: "The social conventions that comprise a natural language can only be created in certain kinds of social interaction, and some linguistic constructions can only be created after others have first been established" (211).

Tomasello offers an astute explanation of the imaginative and metonymic generation of the future tense. The idea of going somewhere (present) constitutes movement toward a future goal. It thus rendered, e.g., "I am going to send it" (43). The idea of reaching a destination, combined with another verb (send), created the future tense. Thus the idea of an anticipated action determined the grammaticality. In other words, the grammaticality was induced by an aspect (metonymy/displacement) of the action. The same is true of "I will it to happen" (43). Postponed in time, it renders "It will happen" (cf. French *je vais aller; nous allons y aller,* etc.).

Merlin Donald, in "Mimesis and the Executive Suite: Missing Links in Language Evolution", believes that mimesis precedes language: It "establishes the fundamentals of intentional expression in hominids, without which language would not have had an opportunity to evolve, since there would have been no existing communicative environment on which natural selection could act" (Donald, 1998, p. 60).

Donald offers solid arguments for a mimetic foundation for language. He shows the insufficiency of the modular model favored by universal grammarians. He terms this the "Cartesian school", a high prestige term that tends to mask the problems of Chomsky's *Cartesian Linguistics.* It might better be termed the school of Chomsky's uncommon reading of Descartes. He also offers the more judicious term of the "non-continuity stance" to describe the parthenogenesis of language in the UG paradigm. On the other side, there is the "neuro-biological approach", which is an appropriate term, as cognitive neuroscience generally views continuity in evolution. The *fiat lingua* perspective is, in his perspective, improbable, as evolution "must practice the art of the possible and can select only from raw material already in existence" (45). Language thus arises from a complex and interconnected basis.

There is no single language module in this perspective, instead a domain-general network, "a system of interconnected modules, each of which performs a specific cognitive operation" (45). He terms this "the executive processes of the mind" (46), organized by an "executive suite". The work of Lakoff and

Johnson (see Chapter 12) can illuminate the metaphoricity of this locution, which seems to be informed by the models of business and hotel management studies.

Nonetheless, Donald does not deny some modularity in language processing, he simply does not see a single totalizing language module. And he has a very important point: "Language does not self-install". Again, we are bound to metaphor in describing the theoretical, and most of our metaphors relate to current culture. Self-installation is an ineluctable computer metaphor, but a productive one, as language does not proceed like a downloaded program that, once opened, populates the device.

Regarding the fact that people isolated from birth do not invent language, he says, "One might imagine that, given an event-structure to describe, a preprogrammed, fully equipped language acquisition device would dive into the task of labelling and describing the world" (50). He claims that a fully preprogrammed language module would self-trigger "simply by being exposed to the episodic event-structure of the world, just as the visual system triggers vision, simply by being exposed to normal levels of patterned light" (50). This is not the case with language. Language capacity "depends on complex epigenetic programming that does not take place without extensive cultural interaction" (50). Epigenetics is the study of heritable phenotype changes that do not involve alterations in the DNA sequence. Thus this is not a preprogrammed unfolding, but an interactive model involving a complex of neural networks interfacing with the environment.

The critical/sensitive period, in this model, could simply be seen as a period for establishing vital neural networks. If these are not developed while the brain is growing, the brain will establish other neural networks. The capacity left out of development would then require extensive post-facto remodeling, which, as has been attested to, is a most difficult undertaking.

Donald describes the "executive suite", which consists of many components, including metacognition, imitation, self-recognition, multitasking, highly developed memory, mind reading (ToM), and symbolic invention. These are all skills that humans possess to a much higher degree than do apes. Of these skills, he foregrounds metacognition, which humans excel at, imitation (we imitate far better than apes—we are the best at aping), multitasking (another current metaphor, imperative for complex communication), memory recall, self-reminding ("autocuing"), self-recognition (we are better at it than apes), and something he calls "purposive rehearsal". He observes that "human children endlessly rehearse and refine their own actions...purposive rehearsal requires the individual brain to evaluate its own outputs and conceive of idealized actions as a template for judging outcomes" (55). This is a form of "intentional representation; the act is used to represent itself" (55). Here, the child is developing the capacity for recursion (metacognition) and representation. This also relates to psychoanalytic accounts of play and repetition, especially the repetition compulsion.

Donald emphasizes that

> even protolanguage could not have evolved before the central executive apparatus had reached a certain point. Intentional communication demands a great deal of executive management. The moment to moment difficulty of acquiring and managing language in the real world is very high, because the cultural environment that encompasses language is constantly changing, and in need of rapid updating. Moreover, human speakers often carry out several complex operations at once.
>
> (57)

He adds that "language is really a gigantic meta-task, requiring the coordination of an entire hierarchy of subtasks and sub-subtasks, regulated from working memory" (57).

Donald then moves to the primacy of imitation in the enabling of language. He holds that early hominid culture displays advances that would have been dependent upon imitation, but not necessarily language, such as advanced tool development, the use of fire, hunting, the division of labor, etc. This is a *mimetic culture*, one that "establishes the fundamentals of intentional expression in hominids, without which language would not have had an opportunity to evolve, since there would have been no existing communicative environment on which natural selection could act" (60). And it would have been the basis for a dissemination of practical skills and would have evolved along with the need for disambiguation. He offers some examples of mimetic behavior such as pointing, games, pantomime, and gesture. He does not discuss the presence of ritual in his configuration of mimesis, but it seems to be implicit in his model that mimesis would establish ritual.

Clearly, the compulsion to repeat would of necessity contribute to this process. It facilitates the organization of culture and the defining of one culture off from another. Donald holds that mimesis is "a profound instinct in humans to imitate the group". And he observes the strength of mimesis: "The threat of social ostracism is so profound that it can drive individuals to suicide" (64). Since mimesis precedes the acquisition of language both ontogenetically (in child development) and phylogenetically (in human evolution), one can hold that one is dealing, fundamentally, with *a mimetic instinct*, not a language instinct.

The following chapter integrates research on mirror neurons into the analysis of the mimetic faculty and coordinates these with research on embodied cognition, especially as it relates to the embodiment of the matrix of language and consciousness.

## References

Donald, M. (1998). Mimesis and the executive suite: Missing links in language evolution. In Hurford, J. R. et al. (Eds.), *Approaches to the evolution of language: Social and cognitive bases* (pp. 44–67). Cambridge University Press.

Forrester, J. (1980). *Language and the origins of psychoanalysis*. Columbia University Press.

Karmiloff-Smith, A. (1992). *Beyond modularity. A developmental perspective on cognitive science*. MIT Press.

McNeill, D. (2012). *How language began. Gesture and speech in human evolution*. Cambridge University Press.

McNeill, D. (2016). *Why we gesture. The surprising role of hand movements in communication*. Cambridge University Press.

Mead, G. (1974). *Mind, self, and society from the standpoint of a social behaviorist*. University of Chicago Press.

Tomasello, M. (1999). *The cultural origins of human cognition*. Harvard University Press.

# 9
# LANGUAGE AND MIRROR NEURONS

The recent research on mirror neurons is most valuable for the development of a psychoanalytic linguistics in the context of the production of language via identity/ego formation, especially as concerns embodied cognition and the psychoanalytic notion that the ego is above all a *bodily* ego. The anthology *New Frontiers in Mirror Neurons Research* (Ferrari & Rizzolatti, 2015) is especially important in this regard. In the chapter "On Gesture and Speech", by Gentilucci et al., the authors present findings indicating that the neural circuit controlling gestures and speech "probably evolved from a circuit that controls arm and mouth movements involved in ingestion". This supports "the gestural theory of the origin of speech". They think that "manual gestures are linked to mouth movements used for syllable emission. Gestures and words are also related to each other" (Gentilucci et al., 2015). The motivation to communicate involved a transference from gestures to words, "inducing modification in voice parameters". One can introduce here a bridge to orality, to oral incorporation and the oral phase in the psychoanalytic model, which lasts through the first year of age. This would involve the symbolic ingestion of the other, based initially on the dynamics of breastfeeding.

The authors reiterate that vowels can be broadly described according to how wide the mouth is open in pronouncing them. There are open vowels such as /a/ and closed ones such as /i/. In examining the connection between mouth opening and manual grasping, the authors posit that "specific internal mouth postures assumed for pronunciation of vowels may affect the control of grasping". They cite experiments to test this hypothesis, where "participants reached to grasp differently sized objects while pronouncing different vowels, that is, /a/, /ɔ/, and /i/. Pronouncing /a/ produced an increase in finger-opening parameters, whereas pronouncing /i/ produced a decrease.

Pronouncing /ɔ/ produced an intermediate opening". /ɔ/ is a mid-back vowel, thus of intermediate location.

They cite a behavioral study, conducted in Italian, in which participants were presented with the words: *ciao, no,* and *stop. (Ciao* can indicate "hello" or "goodbye" in Italian.) They were asked to perform various tasks of word pronunciation and gesture. One of the tasks was to pronounce the word and execute the gesture afterward, and then pronounce the word and execute the gesture at the same time. The study showed that voice spectra parameters increased when the word was pronounced simultaneously with the gesture.

In a similar experiment, one of the same words (*ciao, no, stop*) was read as a printed word, then pronounced by an actor, then mimed by an actor, and finally, pronounced by an actor who mimed the gesture at the same time. The participants were asked to pronounce the words after each presentation. Their voice spectra were widest after the last condition—the actor miming and pronouncing simultaneously.

It should be noted that the experiments were performed in Italian, a language known for its large gestural component. As someone who grew up in an italophone household, I tend to gesticulate a lot when speaking Italian. I also gesticulate in English, French, and German, but considerably less. There are clearly cultures in which gesturing while speaking is less common than it is in Italian.

*New Frontiers in Mirror Neurons Research* includes "Epigenetic Regulation of Mirror Neuron Development, and Related Evolutionary Hypotheses", by Tramacere et al. The authors illuminate the role of mimesis in the evolution of facial expressions. They observe that

> results from behavioral and neurophysiological research suggest that mirror neurons encoding mouth actions in the premotor cortex in macaques and humans, probably involved in imitation of facial expressions, could have been stabilized during phylogeny. The nearly automatic imitative responses of primate newborns to the affiliative gestures of the experimenter in fact lead us to hypothesize a process of genetic assimilation or Baldwin effect for which the sensorimotor matching between perception of others' facial expressions and one's own facial movements became linked to the genetic sequences and rapidly expressed, although they still preserve a degree of plasticity.
>
> *(Tramacere et al., 2015)*

The Baldwin effect concerns phenotype interaction with genotype in natural selection. Here, the sensorimotor matching of facial expressions would have created neural pathways that would have entered into a feedback loop between automatic response and response to that response, which would have resulted in a snowballing of modes of facial interaction. It should be noted, however, that this would have had to be based upon a mimetic instinct. "Concerning the evolution of plasticity that is behaviorally induced, such as that associated with hand mirror neurons in primates", the authors hold that

> whenever sensorimotor training produces such a profound change, increasing the complexity of cerebral substrates involved in a specific task and allowing the subjects to perform new cognitive abilities, then these changes could constitute an additional source of new variability in evolution.

The authors add that

> the view of mirror neuron development via an epigenetic perspective states that the evolution of neurons that respond both to the observation and the execution of mouth and hand actions is partly the result of the stabilization of environmentally induced phenotypic traits through genetic assimilation or the Baldwin effect.

The article "Schizophrenia, Bodily Selves, and Embodied Simulation", by Gallese and Ferri (2015), offers a transition from the mimetic model to the phenomenon of the embodied self. Again, one is reminded of Freud's assertion that the ego is above all a bodily ego. The authors begin with a discussion of the experience of one's own body as "a source of power for action", which is a sense of one's own body "that is enactive in nature and enables the formation of the most primitive concept of the self, the bodily self". This is "an action-capable agentive entity" that "rests on the workings of the motor system. Our body is experienced as the set of all the motor potentialities that define the horizon of our interaction with the world". This horizon would also demarcate the boundaries of self and ego. Decentered as it is in the state of nursling dependency, "such a primitive sense of the self as a self-propelled, mobile, bodily self is thought to be antecedent to the distinction between sense of agency and sense of ownership".

Clearly, this coordinates well with Lacan's notion of the mirror stage: The authors observe that "the motor experience of one's own body, even at a covert level, allows an implicit and pre-reflective bodily self-knowledge to emerge, leading to a self–other distinction". The subsequent reflective moment, i.e., the moment of recursive metacognition, would then enable the differential of self and other. This would be an embodied simulation. They add: "The constitution of the self is intrinsically related to the constitution of the other as a self. This starting point is highly consistent with the reciprocity linking self and other, as conceived by the model of embodied simulation". Schizophrenics, on the other hand, "do not inhabit their body, in the sense of using the body as a medium for relating to the world". Thus the matrix of embodied self and embodied cognition is the foundation of self-awareness and subsequent self/non-self-awareness. The absence of this in the schizophrenic constitutes the moment of the confusion of self and other, often exhibited in the illusion, with schizophrenics, that someone else is occupying one's body.

In "The Paradigmatic Body: Embodied Simulation, Intersubjectivity, the Bodily Self, and Language", Gallese and Cuccio see the evolution of human language as "an exaptation of functional sensorimotor processes, which put them into the service of human linguistic competence". They also use the terms "neural exploitation" and "neural reuse". They emphasize that "reading or listening to a sentence describing a hand action activates the motor representation of the same action…motor activation has also been observed during the comprehension of abstract and figurative use of language such as metaphors and idioms".

"Thus, symbolic relationships are by definition characterized by reflexiveness", they add. This is clearly a long-standing theory in the research on the capacity to symbolize, but here, it is couched in the context of research in physiology and neurology. They add that "symbols are defined through other symbols", here accessing the line of research on signification that began with Saussure. They go on to specify that "this level of reflexiveness is pre-theoretical; it emerges in the linguistic activity of each speaker and leads to a form of linguistic awareness of a practical character." They then speak of an "epilinguistic quality…the natural tendency of speakers to reflect on their own language—a tendency made possible by the distinctive quality of language being able to speak of itself".

This is an excellent, if terse, explanation. The reflexive capacity, as discussed above, would begin in the practical (pre-theoretical) stage of imagining oneself in a situation. This would be adaptive and not limited to humans. In higher-order organisms, to be aware of one's vulnerability would be an adaptive advantage. The shift to the theoretical would be reserved for humans, in the capacity to see the symbolic as supra-contextual. The authors say as much, when they criticize (ungenerously) the faculty of language in a narrow sense (FLN) and its expression in recursivity. They say that

> this perspective, in addition to suffering from the usual cognitivist solipsism, is exposed to comparative verification in the animal world. If the FLN marks human linguistic uniqueness in terms of syntactic recursivity, the latter must be entirely absent in the extra-human animal kingdom.
> *(Gallese & Cuccio, 2015, pp. 11–12)*

This is certainly not the case. One could qualify this by viewing the syntactic as both a linguistic and supra-linguistic phenomenon, i.e., the establishment of sequential behavior that also incorporates and operates upon the behavioral input.

Gallese, in "Finding the Body in the Brain. From Simulation Theory to Embodied Simulation" (2016), says that, for Chomsky and Descartes, "language is exclusively a tool that expresses a thought formed independently of language itself…language is a tool through which we manifest an autonomous thought that precedes language—a thought structured by logic but certainly not by language" (Gallese, 2016, p. 308). This clearly clashes with the models of language seen in the investigations of embodied cognition and mirror neurons. The title of the article is an ironic reversal of the age-old western notion of the mind–body dichotomy, a platonic and neoplatonic model that persists in the UG perspective. For Gallese, the mind is a biological and neurological entity. Not so for *Cartesian Linguistics*, which is based upon Descartes' *Meditationes de Prima Philosophia, in qua Dei existentia et animæ immortalitas demonstratur* (1641), which may be translated as "Meditations on the first philosophy, in which it is demonstrated that God exists, and that the human mind is distinct from the body" (Descartes (1641, 1647). This is a discussion that has little audience in the research conducted by the community of natural scientists.

Gallese and Cuccio mention Freud's status as the first to hold that the ego is above all a bodily ego:

> Sigmund Freud realized long before others how much the self is a bodily self. Freud also helped us to understand how little we know about who we are, particularly when aspiring to ground this knowledge solely on self-questioning rationality. What are the drives of which Freud spoke but a further manifestation of the double status of our flesh?
> *(Gallese & Cuccio, 2015, p. 19)*

They are referring to Freud's assertions in *The Ego and the Id* (1923); the notion of "the double status of our flesh" fits well into their analysis. As they state earlier in the article, "the motor experience of one's own body, even at a covert level, allows an implicit and pre-reflective bodily self-knowledge to emerge, leading to a self–other distinction". The locus of the "double status of our flesh" would be the liminal region where the pre-reflective becomes the reflective, and where "the constitution of the self is intrinsically related to the constitution of the other as a self". This is the point of the articulation of self *in and through language*.

They propose "that embodied simulation seems to be able to naturalize the notion of paradigm, thus naturalizing one of the processes that makes language reflexiveness possible, and thus contributing to 'creating' the human being". The paradigm is simply that found in the example of the Latin, *rosa rosae rosae rosam rosa*, the paradigm for the first declension feminine nouns. The authors hold that pattern recognition and duplication involve metacognition and recursion, made possible by the dynamics of reflexiveness. In other words, meditation on language makes the analysis of language possible. For them, embodied simulation "allows one to go beyond the body while remaining anchored to it". We are moving here toward a notion of the involvement of secondary processes in the articulation of language, processes that must also include secondary revision. In psychoanalytic terms, this would be the emergence of "formal language" in the transition from preconscious to conscious modes of thought. This is not, however, the original point for language. It is a secondary process imposed upon language in its incubation, and in its emergent manifestations.

The authors say as much in emphasizing "the neural bases of our capacity to be attuned to the intentional relations of others". They hold that "at a basic level, our interpersonal interactions do not make explicit use of propositional attitudes. This basic level consists of embodied simulation processes that enable the constitution of a shared meaningful interpersonal space".

The cognitive scientist Philip Lieberman has offered a neurological model of overdetermination and embodied cognition most relevant for the psychoanalytic model. It also involves a physio-neurological mirroring of perception.

Lieberman has done extensive work on the embodiment of language within the basal ganglia, which are a group of subcortical nuclei located at the base of the cerebrum. They are connected to several functions, including motor activity, coordination eye movements, and cognition. Lieberman notes that damage to the basal ganglia effects producing and understanding syntax. He also found that lack of oxygen has a similar effect on basal ganglia and speech production and understanding. In *Eve Spoke*, he cites the data concerning climbers on Mt. Everest who, at 24,000 ft., experienced a 50% decrease in the speed of thinking and speaking. He concludes: "the parts of the human brain that control speech also play a part in thinking" (Lieberman, 1998, p. 3).

He holds that general cognitive processes of automatization code the rules of language, syntax, math, logic, etc., in a basal ganglia cortex highway. These take the form of matrisomes, groups of motor neurons that control the muscles used when performing rote tasks unconsciously:

> It is probable that we form cortical cognitive matrisomes, populations of neurons that code the semantic referents of words and syntax of a language as we learn it. The cognitive matrisomes would be formed by the process of automatization that we know takes place in motor cortex as we learn to tie our shoes, shift gears, and perform an array of learned tasks.
> *(Lieberman, 2013, p. 59)*

His model of language is the "functional language system" (FLS), which is "overlaid on sensorimotor systems that originally evolved to do other things and continue to do them now" (1). The brain is not organized by modules, which he terms "a set of petty bureaucrats each of which controls a behavior and won't have anything to do with one another" (2). The FLS "is a distributed rather than a strictly hierarchical system" (Lieberman, 2000, p. 6), thus facilitating the embodiment of language, especially the conversion of psyche into soma. He says of the functional language system: "The FLS integrates activity in many parts of the human brain, including the subcortical cerebellum, thalamus, motor cortex, premotor cortex, prefrontal regions, and sensory cortex" (159).

Lieberman observes: "Studies show that children acquire language after suffering brain damage which destroys the neuroanatomical structures that usually regulate language. Other structures take on the task through a general process of neural plasticity" (11).

He cites PET scan experiments showing that when we think of the concepts associated with a word, we activate the corresponding neural circuits in the brain. Thinking of the name of a hand tool activates the primary motor cortex, and thinking of the name of an animal activates visual cortex areas associated with shapes and colors. There is a process of neurological encoding of meaning here, in a quite promiscuous manner, that is not self-evident and clearly not modular (63). The visual perception of an object is nothing like a snapshot that gets stored in a single location in the brain. Various aspects of the object are instead stored in "a distributed cortical system" (66) that is also modified by learning. And here, one sees an optimal playing field for the conversion of psyche to soma, in normal activity, and also in conversion disorders. He specifies that "the neural bases of human language are not localized in a specific part of the brain" (81).

The basal ganglia "appear to sequence automatized syntactic processes" (159). He adds:

> Imaging data suggest that the neural representation of the "meaning" of a word enlists the cortical regions that are activated in the perception of the colors, shapes, and other properties of the objects and actions coded in a word, such as the motor activity that may define a word through its function (e.g. hand movements for a hammer). In this light, the meaning of the sentence: *The boy was running* reduces to an internal image of a boy running…contrary to traditional, formal linguistic theory, predicate logic does not characterize the neural bases of human semantic knowledge.
>
> *(159)*

Lieberman reiterates that the language production and processing is nonalgorithmic and consists in massive interconnectivity (161).

He adds that "verbal working memory appears to be instantiated in the human brain by a dynamic distributed network that recruits neural 'computational' resources in response to task demands such as syntactic complexity and sentence length" (Lieberman, 2000, p. 81). Thus "subcortical circuits involving basal ganglia are key elements of the human brain's functional language system, regulating speech, comprehension of syntax, and certain aspects of cognition" (123).

Liebermann cites data indicating that children learn syntax associatively "by deriving a prototype by means of associative mechanisms", and adds that "many linguists and philosophers also short-change the power of associative learning" (162). In that vein, Bates and Dick, in "Beyond Phrenology: Brain and Language in the Next Millennium" (2000), observe that language function is spread throughout the brain.

James R. Hurford, in *The Origins of Language: A Slim Guide*, has offered a quite reasonable survey of these issues by juxtaposing them with data from anthropological research, taking the reader briskly from homo erectus to the present. Hurford argues that language is a learned skill, rather than an innate instinct. The human capacity for language is based on the FLS and distributed across many subsystems of the brain, many of which link directly to the subcortical basal ganglia (2014).

Similarly, Rizzuto notes: "The speech apparatus is thus a very unique anatomical structure because even though it has anatomical features, these are not utilized exclusively for speech". She notes that the pathways leading to the speech apparatus "are shared with sensory functions of the organs that bring sensory information to the cortex from all the senses and, also, sensory input from all muscles involved in any of the speech functions" (Rizzuto, 1993, p. 116).

She adds: "The ever expanding network of associations makes it theoretically possible that nothing that has been experienced is ever representationally lost, and might be capable of becoming psychically available" (120). This can be seen as corresponding to Freud's assertion that there is no chronology in the unconscious. Memory traces can be evoked irrespective of temporality.

This is a "distributed" network, i.e., a rhizomic one, as opposed to the modular arborescent one of UG. In *The Unpredictable Species*, Lieberman says of the modular configuration of brain activity as espoused by Pinker: "Your car's shop manual provides a better guide to understanding how your brain works than books such as Steven Pinker's 1998 *How the Mind Works*" (Lieberman, 2013, p. 4). For example, if your car does not start, the manual does not refer you to a central organ solely responsible for starting the car, but instead to the battery, voltage regulator, starter, generator, spark plugs, distributor, etc. It links you to a panoply of parts that codetermine starting the car. Each performs a local operation, but dependent upon collaboration with other parts. Is there an element in the automobile that is only found in the automobile, and nowhere else in the production of material goods? No. What then is the unique essence of the automobile? Well, it is the automobile itself. The unique combination of parts. One could extend the car metaphor further to characterize the unique essence of language. It is language itself.

He sees the impulse to locate dedicated areas in the brain as a kind of neo-phrenology: "Phrenology lives on today in studies that purport to identify the brain's center of religious belief, pornography, and everything in between" (8). He subscribes instead, with Gould, to the concept of "brain design by Rube Goldberg" (25).

He says that modular theories of the organization of the brain "do not differ in principle from the 'faculties' of the brain that nineteenth-century phrenologists mapped onto skulls" (Lieberman, 2000, p. 8). He explains that modular mechanical and electronic design was developed in order to do quick repairs. These consist in local dedicated circuit boards that can be popped in and out. Again, one sees the influence of technology on the metaphors for perception and cognition.

Has an amusing hypothesis: the UGD: the universal grammar of driving, i.e., an organ of the human brain that programs people to know how to drive, complete with the multitude of parameters necessary for engaging all responses to vehicular situations (Lieberman, 2013, pp. 162–163). If one has never driven, the toggle switch for doing so is still there, it just has not been turned on. He thinks that UG is even more extreme than the silly driving example, because it claims

> that the brain of every 'normal' human being who ever was, lives today, or will ever be, contains an identical store of knowledge that enables him or her to rapidly and effortlessly acquire any language that has ever existed, exists, or will occur.
>
> *(163)*

UG "enables a child to 'acquire' any language without tedious processes such as associative learning, imitation or any form of learning" (163–164).

He says, "Chomsky's model of the brain still seems to be based on the digital computers that were being developed at MIT when he first developed his linguistic theories in the mid-1950s" (99). He observes elsewhere: "Cognitive scientists have attempted to understand mind-brain relations using modular theories that owe more to IBM than to Charles Darwin" (Lieberman, 2000, p. 159).

He summarizes: "The algorithmic methods that characterize most formal linguistic studies are not appropriate tools if we wish to understand better the mind-brain relations that govern linguistic ability" (159). He adds: "algorithmic descriptions of linguistic phenomena are perfectly valid tools so long as they are not equated with the mental operations carried out by the human brain" (161).

In this perspective, one can see UG as a modern attempt to find the original language, a quest that has been going on since antiquity (Bonfiglio, 2010). The search for the primal language continues. Lieberman observes: "Time and effort have been wasted in the linguistic quest to discover the 'true' set of algorithms that describe linguistic 'competence'" (161). While there is no such true set of algorithms, the psychoanalytic mechanisms described in this study (displacement, condensation, overdetermination, repetition, secondary revision, ego formation, and others) aid greatly in illuminating the processes that constitute the matrix of language and thought.

Lane et al. (2015), in their study of how the visual cortex responds to syntactic movement, offer evidence suggesting that the occipital lobe—the visual cortex located at the back of the brain—participates in language processing. They report fMRI results showing that in those who are congenitally blind, the visual cortex is more active during linguistic than nonlinguistic comprehension. They find "that these occipital areas respond more to sentences with syntactic movement but do not respond to the difficulty of math equations" and "conclude that regions within the visual cortex of blind adults are involved in syntactic processing" (Lane et al., p. 12859). Their study demonstrates the high plasticity of the human brain, which improvises connections as a function of input. In the case of the congenitally blind, a part of the visual cortex becomes repurposed for language processing.

They believe it "unlikely that occipital cortex is evolutionarily adapted… for representing syntactic structure" and "suggest that language-specific adaptations are not required for a brain area to participate in syntactic processing" (12865). But they wonder how to reconcile this with "the fact that language is uniquely human? On the one hand, it could be argued that language is a cultural, rather than biological, adaptation, and there are no brain networks that are innately specialized for language processing". But, at the same time, they also astutely qualify this with the recognition that "there is evidence that evolution enabled the human brain for language". In order to balance the cultural and the biological, they propose that

> one possibility is that biological adaptations are only needed to initiate language acquisition…during the course of development, the capacities of these specialized regions may spread to nonspecialized cortical areas. In blindness, this process of colonization expands into occipital territory. On this view, small evolutionary adaptations have cascading effects when combined with uniquely human experience.
>
> *(12865)*

One sees here no clear divide between the cultural and the biological. Both "sides" do hold that the brain is language-ready, but is ready in the way that we are born ready to learn to walk or born ready to learn to ride a bicycle?

This chapter has studied embodied cognition, mirroring, and their engagement in neurological structures, especially basal ganglia, and it has demonstrated their psycho-physiological presence in the networking of language. The following chapter investigates the concept of grammar as it applies to the research done in this study up to this point.

## References

Bates, E., & Dick, F. (2000). Beyond phrenology: Brain and language in the next millennium. *Brain and Language* 71, 18–21.

Bonfiglio, T. (2010). *Mother tongues and nations: The invention of the native speaker.* De Gruyter.

Des-Cartes, R. (1641). *Meditationes de prima philosophia, in qua Dei existentia, & animæ humanæ à corpore distinctio, demonstratur.* Parisiis. Apud Michaelem Soby.

Descartes, R. (1647). *Les méditations métaphysiques de René Descartes.* Camusat.

Ferrari, P. & Rizzolatti, G. (Eds.) (2015). *New frontiers in mirror neurons research.* Published to Oxford Scholarship Online.

Gallese, V. (2016). Finding the body in the brain. From simulation theory to embodied simulation. In B. McLaughlin & H. Kornblith (Eds.), *Goldman and his critics* (pp. 297–314). Wiley.

Gallese, V., & Cuccio, V. (2015). The paradigmatic body: Embodied simulation, intersubjectivity, the bodily self, and language. In T. Metzinger & J. Windt (Eds.), *Open mind* (pp. 1–23). MIND Group.

Gallese, V., & Ferri, F. (2015). Schizophrenia, bodily selves, and embodied simulation. In P. Ferrari & G. Rizzolatti (Eds.), *New frontiers in mirror neurons research.* Published to Oxford Scholarship Online.

Gentilucci, M. et al. (2015). On gesture and speech. In P. Ferrari & G. Rizzolatti (Eds.), *New frontiers in mirror neurons research.* Published to Oxford Scholarship Online.

Hurford, J. (2014). *The origins of language: A slim guide.* Oxford University Press.

Lane, C. et al. (2015). "Visual" cortex of congenitally blind adults responds to syntactic movement. *The Journal of Neuroscience* 35(37), 12859–12868.

Lieberman, P. (1998). *Eve spoke: Human language and human evolution.* W. W. Norton.

Lieberman, P. (2000). *Human language and our reptilian brain.* Harvard University Press.

Lieberman, P. (2013). *The unpredictable species.* Princeton University Press.

Rizzuto, A.-M. (1993). Freud's speech apparatus and spontaneous speech. *The International Journal of Psychoanalysis,* 74(1), 113–127.

Tramacere, A. et al. (2015). Epigenetic regulation of mirror neuron development, and related evolutionary hypotheses. In P. Ferrari & G. Rizzolatti (Eds.), *New frontiers in mirror neurons research.* Published to Oxford Scholarship Online.

# 10
# WHAT IS GRAMMAR?

In 2002, Noam Chomsky published "An Interview on Minimalism", in which he discusses the apparent progress from the early generative grammar paradigm to the minimalist one. His summations offer a radical departure from the initial tenets of universal grammar (UG):

> Well, the right answer is that there aren't any constructions anyway, no passive, no raising: There is just the option of dislocating something somewhere else under certain conditions, and in certain cases it gives you what is traditionally called the passive and in other cases it gives you a question and so on, but the grammatical constructions are left as artifacts...so the early generative grammar had a very traditional flair. There is a section on the Passive in German, and another section on the VP in Japanese, and so on...what happened in the Pisa discussions was that the whole framework was turned upside down. So, from that point of view, there is nothing left of the whole traditional approach to the structure of language, other than taxonomic artifacts, and that's a radical change, and it was a very liberating one.
> 
> *(Chomsky, 2002, pp. 94–95)*

This radical retrenchment provides a safe space for grammar, which has receded from the front lines of linguistic generalization, where universalizing models became deconstructed in the face of the immense complexity of human language. He adds:

> If you had asked me ten years ago, I would have said government is a unifying concept, X-bar theory is a unifying concept, the head parameter

is an obvious parameter, ECP, etc., but now none of these looks obvious. X-bar theory, I think, is probably wrong, government maybe does not exist.

*(151)*

This reveals a condensation of the initial paradigm, which has been pared down to simply recursion and merge, but the initial displacement into a model borrowed from the mechanics of information science remains intact. This is an abstract and idealizing model "liberated" from the illogic of language and the stress of dealing with its complexities. And it becomes housed prehistorically by the assertion that "there is no real evidence for use of language prior to maybe 50,000 years ago or so" (149).

One sees here that the concept of the rules of language is a notoriously mobile one. The terms "syntax" and "grammar" are generally used to refer to those rules. Grammar is normally understood as a set of structural rules that dictate the construction of sentences, clauses, phrases, and words in a language, while syntax refers to the arrangement of words and phrases in the construction of sentences. In the discourse of language, however, the terms are often used interchangeably. Where syntax/grammar originates, however, is a hotly debated topic. Did this arise independently of other aspects of language? Of other mental functions?

Generally speaking, there are two camps: one that sees grammar as producing speech, and one that sees speech as producing grammar. In the former position, the rules and principles are there a priori, and speech becomes the surface articulation of those rules. In the latter position, speech develops patterns and customary usages, and these become codified into grammar and syntax. And for the former position, it is generally held that there is a "universal grammar" (UG), a separate language organ that resulted from a prehistoric genetic mutation in humans.

James McGilvray has provided scholarship with one of the most thoroughly original justifications of the theory of universal grammar. In 2017, he contributed the chapter "On the History of Universal Grammar" to *The Oxford Handbook of Universal Grammar*. It is an unequivocally laudatory description of UG, in which he claims that Chomsky's goal is to "construct a science of language" (McGilvray, 2017, p. 77), as if none had been attempted before. He defines UG as: "the hidden but scientifically discoverable innate component of the human mind/brain that allows a neonate's mind with minimal input to develop a computational/derivational system that yields an unbounded number of hierarchically structured conceptual complexes characteristic of a human language" (77). There are a lot of unexplained assumptions here, e.g. that the component is innate, computational, unbounded, and hierarchical, and the chapter as a whole is replete with some quite astounding assertions.

First of all, the chapter falls into a binary dichotomy between nature and nurture. The author says that the premise of Chomsky's *Cartesian Linguistics* was that "internalist and nativist assumptions lead to good natural sciences of mind; externalist and anti-nativist ones do not" (78). This is quite interesting, in that it separates the empirical and directly observable from a good natural science of language. Seeing language as one of the discrete parts of the mind that have "internal growth agendas" (78) falls, however, into good natural science. He claims that Chomsky chose Descartes, because he thinks that Descartes provided the best early modern description of natural science methodology, especially constructing theories of hidden phenomena (85).

He offers a characterization of natural science methodology guaranteed to stun the natural scientist. "Natural sciences are postulated formal theories of hidden phenomena" (79), we are told, that "typically deal with phenomena out of reach of direct observation" (79). This sets up a top-down and deductive model that starts with a presupposition instead of using an inductive model that operates from observable data, because, of course, observable data are not essential to good natural science. And language is no exception. He excludes from the natural science of language "complex organism behavior, including and especially human linguistic behavior. We easily deal with it with our native folk psychology, or what sometimes goes by the title 'theory of mind'. But it is out of reach of natural science" (80). So linguistic behavior is folk psychology, and we need to exclude it from scientific inquiry: "One must abandon common sense intuitions about language, sentences, words, and meaning in order to understand what a natural science of language says" (79).

And all this is because "linguistic action/use is out of the reach of the methods of natural science", but "the language system is not" (80). The language system, which produces languages, while being independent of them, is a formalist construct that reduces "the apparent complexities of individual languages" to "a small number of principles that provide infinite range from finite means" (80). So we cannot grasp linguistic action—it is out of the reach of our methods—but we can grasp the hidden innate program for language.

This reflects a progressive backpedaling of the original proposals for UG, as they confronted counterevidence from a host of languages that did not fit into the paradigm. The retreat began in the 1980s with the principles and parameters program, which simplified the requirements for the language algorithm, and continued into the minimalist format proposed in this century (80). Minimalism began with "the introduction of a single syntactic/compositional recursive operation Merge" (81). Thus "UG could be the recursive operation Merge, period", which is "unique to humans" (82). With the simplification down to Merge,

> accounting for the evolution of UG and language and accommodation to biology is now easy: All one must account for is the introduction of

Merge, and that can be seen as the result of a single saltational event in a single breeding hominin.

*(83)*

This enables real natural science linguists "to make sense of why nothing seems to have changed for the last 50,000 years or so" (83). This is a wonderful example of reasoning backward. We posit an invisible prehistoric language organ that appeared all of a sudden and then claim that it has not changed, even though no one has seen it. What has really not changed, however, is the nuclear program of UG over the past 60 years. It has merely painted itself into a minimalist corner.

While we have no evidence of an innate language organ, we are told that there is "lack of evidence for a gradualist and kludgy alternative" (82). The kludgy state of things, however, is the condition of natural languages. He says that "no adequate natural science of language has, or likely can, deal with the uses to which a specific person puts what his computational system provides" (sic) (88). One wonders if an adequate natural science of language can deal with the syntactic error "has…deal" in this sentence that substitutes an infinitive for a past participle.

The obsessional insistence on a metalinguistic language algorithm generates here a world that we are not familiar with: "Thanks to the success of Chomsky's internalist and nativist science of the mind, there are fewer empiricist linguists now than there used to be" (33). The opposite is clearly the case, as applied linguistics has grown considerably over the past decades. Nonetheless, we are told that "there is no science of creative language use, only of an isolated generative system that makes creative use by people possible" (92).

McGilvray's assertions more closely resemble metaphysical speculation than natural or social science inquiry.

Is this inflexible extremist retrenchment the final cry before the collapse of the system? McGilvray's assertions here are much more radical than those found in his "Introduction for Cybereditions" to *Cartesian Linguistics* (CL) of 2002, where he is actually quite generous to empiricism and does not exclude empirical and non-nativist inquiry a priori from natural science. For decades now, there has been a continual stream of evidence from *the natural and social sciences* problematizing the notion of an ontological essence to language. This seems to have caused a desperate recalcitrance on the part of some fervent disciples, instead of a more urbane and liberal collaboration.

Pinker and Jackendoff (2005) have offered a recent assessment and qualification of the theory of universal grammar in the article "The faculty of language: What's special about it"? They critique the notion that a faculty of language can be separated from the usages of language. Such a distinction, they note, would problematize the relation between language and mathematics. They note:

> Recursive language is a human universal or near-universal, emerging reliably and spontaneously in ontogeny. But recursive number cognition is not. The majority of human cultures, like all animal species, do not have recursive number systems (or at least did not until recent incursions of Western civilization), but instead quantify objects using a system for estimating analogue amounts and a system for categorizing a finite number of small numerosities.
>
> *(Pinker & Jackendoff, 2005, p. 230)*

"Numerosity" is used here in the sense of "quantity". For instance, the Pirahã quantify in terms limited to one, two, three, a lot, a little. A few/a lot are used to estimate analog amounts. Similarly, the authors note that

> there are domains of human concepts which are probably unlearnable without language. For example, the notion of a "week" depends on counting time periods that cannot all be perceived at once; we doubt that such a concept could be developed or learned without the mediation of language. More striking is the possibility that numbers themselves (beyond those that can be subitized) are parasitic on language—that they depend on learning the sequence of number words, the syntax of number phrases, or both. Vast domains of human understanding, including the supernatural and sacred, the specifics of folk and formal science, human-specific kinship systems (such as the distinction between cross- and parallel cousins), and formal social roles (such as "justice of the peace" and "treasurer"), can be acquired only with the help of language.
>
> *(206)*

These observations help situate grammar in the paradigm of interconnectivity put forth in the current study. Language and cognition are, in short, inseparable. The matrix of language and cognition extends far beyond the paradigm of formal logic.

And they add:

> Moreover, functional morphemes such as articles, auxiliaries, and affixes are also part of the lexicon (since each involves a pairing between a sound and some other information, both of which are specific to the particular language), yet the information they encode (case, agreement, finiteness, voice, and so on) is continuous with the information encoded by syntax. Such words are not used, and presumably could not be acquired, in isolation from some syntactic context. And as functional morphemes go, so go verbs, since verbs encode similar kinds of grammatical and semantic information, have similarly close linguistic, psychological,

> and neurological ties to syntax, and, at least in part, require syntactic analysis to be acquired. So other than acquiring the names for salient things, it is hard to see how words can be carved away from the narrow language faculty and relegated to a generic mechanism that learns facts from people's intentions.
>
> *(213–214)*

The narrow language faculty (FLN) consists of the nucleus of recursion and merge, the miraculous big bang that released an infinity of linguistic combinations. This study has shown how, viewed from preliterate and adult nonliterate language processing and metalinguistic knowledge, "word" is itself a relative concept, and not a linguistic given. Fully operational language functioning preceded literacy by millennia. The authors add:

> Another hallmark of words is that their meanings are defined not just by the relation of the word to a concept but by the relation of the word to other words in the lexicon, forming organized sets such as superordinates, antonyms, meronyms (parts), and avoiding true synonyms.
>
> *(214)*

They argue against the idea that the nucleus of language consists only of recursion, which they limit to phrase structure, "in which a noun phrase, for example, can contain a noun phrase, or a sentence can contain a sentence" (216). Otherwise,

> languages are full of devices like pronouns and articles, which help signal which information the speaker expects to be old or new to the hearer; quantifiers, tense and aspect markers, complementizers, and auxiliaries, which express temporal and logical relations; restrictive and appositive modification (as in relative clauses); and grammatical distinctions among questions, imperatives, statements, and other kinds of illocutionary force, signaled by phrase order, morphology, or intonation;

and they add that "none of it involves recursion per se" (215–216).

They follow this up with a positive assessment of the work of Daniel Everett (see below):

> Indeed, at least one language seems to rely entirely on these devices, forgoing use of the recursive power of syntax entirely. Based on 30 years of fieldwork on the Amazonian language Pirahã, Everett (2004) claims that this language lacks any evidence of recursion. All semantic relations conveyed by clausal or NP embedding in more familiar languages, such as conditionality, intention, relative clauses, reports of speech and

mental states, and recursive possession (my father's brother's uncle), are conveyed in Pirahã by means of monoclausal constructions connected paratactically (i.e. without embedding). However, Pirahã very clearly has phonology, morphology, syntax, and sentences, and is undoubtedly a human language, qualitatively different from anything found in animals.
(216)

The authors "support the notion that language evolved piecemeal in the human lineage under the influence of natural selection, with the selected genes having pleiotropic effects that incrementally improved multiple components" (218). (Pleiotropy occurs when one gene influences two or more seemingly unrelated phenotypic traits.) They add:

> Though Chomsky denies the truism that language is "properly regarded as a system for communication", he provides no compelling reasons to doubt it, nor does he explain what a communication system would have to look like for it to be more "usable" or less "dysfunctional" than human languages.
> (224)

They are alluding here to the assertion made by Chomsky in *The Minimalist Program*:

> Language design as such appears to be in many respects "dysfunctional", yielding properties that are not well adapted to the function language is called upon to perform…what we seem to discover are some intriguing and unexpected features of language design…unusual among biological systems of the natural world.
> (Chomsky, 1995, p. 162)

The question of utility here would instantiate a very narrow language faculty for understanding how rituals work. In gastronomy, for instance, one does not normally ask what the utility is of all the intricate steps in complex recipes. One does not normally say that the intricate preparation for Lasagna Bolognese, for instance, is silly—just go fry a hamburger and eat it. On the contrary, complex recipes are celebrated as expressions of creative and sophisticated culinary artistry. They are complex repetitions and displacements (spinoffs) of in-group ritual practices, a form of covert prestige, and they *communicate those rituals and that prestige*. Human sexuality may be used as another example. It exhibits the oddest manner of rituals, contradictions, diversions, avoidances, postponements, simulacra, fetishizing, fixations, obsessions, repressions, suppressions, etc. Does this mean that it did not develop for the purpose of reproduction? Or that it is an ineffective method for population growth?

Robert Bellah, in *Religion in Human Evolution*, discusses play as the platform for ritual and proposes the existence of a play instinct. This is play for play's sake, an action without any ulterior goal in mind. Bella thinks that "ritual is the primordial form of serious play in human evolutionary history" (Bellah, 2011, p. 92).

John McWhorter makes an interesting observation in this regard: "There are few better examples than Fula of West Africa of how astoundingly baroque, arbitrary, and utterly useless to communication a language's grammar can become over the millennia and yet be passed on intact to innocent children" (McWhorter, 2001, p. 188). Fula has 16 genders. McWhorter's comments on the baroque aspects of grammar help us understand the function of language as ritual. Once in place, these arbitrary elements in language serve to condense, displace, overdetermine, and repeat the intricacies of social interaction and group formation. And this phenomenon is true of evolution in general, in its biological and psychological manifestations. As Stephen Gould has pointed out, evolution "is a quirky mass of imperfections, working well enough (often admirably); a jury-rigged set of adaptations built of curious parts made available by past histories in different contexts" (Gould, 1985, p. 54).

Human oral anatomy is a case in point. Human speech was greatly facilitated by the evolution of the supralaryngeal vocal tract (SVT), which made it possible to produce more speech sounds, but the enlargement of the oral cavity also made it easier to choke. Thus, the advantage of communication outweighed the risk of choking to death. Also, when humans started cooking—roughly around 500,000 years ago—our teeth got smaller, creating the parabolic dental arcade, which left more room for oral articulation. Humans can hear only up to 15 different nonspeech sounds per second, but 20–30 speech sounds per second (Kenneally, 2007, p. 150).

It is "fitting" to discuss briefly the folklore surrounding the phrase "survival of the fittest". Darwin never used the word "fittest" in *On the Origin of Species* (1859). One finds, instead, "best fitted" numerous times. At that time, the word carried connotations of "fitting in well", and had not yet shifted to mean "strong" or "powerful". Darwin did use the phrase "survival of the fittest" in the subsequent *The Descent of Man* (1860), but there, as well, having the sense of an optimal fitting in an accidental and overdetermined nature.

Pinker and Jackendoff say something quite similar pertaining to language: "Modern language is a tuning up of evolutionary earlier systems resembling pidgins". They say of the four major syntactic mechanisms for encoding meaning—phrase structure, linear order, agreement, and case—that they "can be thought of as incremental improvements, each of which makes the system more reliable. There is a progression of functionality" and not a progression toward perfection (227). This makes sense, as languages can cycle through stages of synthesis and analysis, developing inflectional morphemes, losing them, developing new ones, losing those, etc.

The authors recommend that "most of the technical accomplishments of the preceding 25 years of research in the Chomskyan paradigm must be torn down, and proposals from long-abandoned 1950s-era formulations and from long-criticized 1970s-era rivals must be rehabilitated" (220–221).

As an aside here, but an important one, there is a recent phenomenon in German that calls into question the integrity of the passive transformation. It concerns the passive use of the present active participle, which is formed by adding -d- to the infinitive. For instance, *kochen* "to boil" + d = *kochend* "boiling".

The perfect participle of weak verbs such as *kochen* is formed with the prefix -*ge*- and the suffix -*t*- framing the verb stem. In the case of *kochen*, the stem is -*koch*-. This will yield *gekocht* "boiled". Both the active and the perfect participle are used as adjectives. Thus:

| Das | kochende | Wasser |
| The | boiling | water |
| Das | gekochte | Wasser |
| The | boiled | water |

However, the present active participle is also used in the following construction:

| Das | zu kochende | Wasser |
| The | to boiling | water |

"The water to be boiled"

Other examples include:

| die | nicht | zu vergessende |
| The | not | to forgetting |

"The not to be forgotten"

As in, e.g.,

| Die | nicht | zu vergessende | Verabredung |
| The | not | to forgetting | appointment |

"The not to be forgotten appointment"

Since verbs beginning with the prefix *ver*- do not add the perfective prefix *ge*-, there is a near homophony between *vergessend* "forgetting" and *vergessen* "forgotten":

| Der | vergessene | Termin | |
| The | forgotten | deadline | |
| Der | sich selbst | vergessende | Mann |
| The | himself | forgetting | man |

"The man forgetful of himself"

For the examples with *kochen*, there is the fixed phrase *bereit zum Kochen*, meaning "ready to boil", but here, the verb is used as a noun. "Ready for the boiling" would be a close translation.

All one needs to do is delete the *-m-* from *zum* and add the *-d-* participle ending, and one has a passive use of an active present participle.

Here, the speaker does not demonstrate a clear concept of active/passive. The position of the verb as an adjective preceding the noun can go in either direction, depending on the context. Here, grammar and morphology are overridden by context, and also by the phonetic similarity between present and perfect participle. In the case of *gekocht* and *kochend*, the similarity is partial; in the case of *vergessen* and *vergessend*, there is near homophony.

This demonstrates the power of associative perception, of overdetermination; it can override established grammar conventions and become perfectly idiomatic.

The work of Ronald Langacker, in *Cognitive Grammar: A Basic Introduction*, can aid in integrating grammar and syntax into a psychoanalytic model. Langacker holds that "grammar is not only an integral part of cognition, but also a key to understanding it" (Langacker, 2008, p. 4). In his theory of cognitive grammar (CG), syntax is not an autonomous phenomenon, but instead an aspect of grammar, which he views as symbolic in nature—a pairing between a semantic structure and a phonological structure. CG resists "the imposition of boundaries between language and other psychological phenomena", e.g., "perception, memory, cognition" (8). Since language "is neither self-contained nor well-defined, a complete formal description (a 'generative grammar' in the classical sense) is held to be impossible" (10). His view of CG is, indeed, minimalist, but not in any reductionistic sense; he holds that language only needs semantic, phonological, and symbolic structures (15).

Concerning lexical items, he observes that lexicon is the set of fixed expressions in a language, not the set of words in a language, because the expression goes beyond the word; e.g., "moonless night", or the neologism "dollarless" (16). As stated earlier, during the phases of language acquisition, the expression, indeed the concept of a word, goes beyond "the word" itself and persists in the nonliterate adult's segmentation and processing of words as entire expressions.

He proposes a taxonomy of language that recruits four cognitive processes: association, automatization, schematization, and categorization. Association entails psychological connections, an overdetermined matrix of interconnectivity. It is "the association between a semantic and a phonological structure that defines a symbolic relationship" (16). And here, one sees the basic condensation (metaphor) involved in associating a sound with a meaning. In automatization, things become habitual: "Through repetition or rehearsal, a complex structure is thoroughly mastered" (16). This can be connected to the mastering evident in the repetition compulsion, in which language can be seen as the expression of a desire to establish a connection. In the discussion of the repetition compulsion, the child's mastering efforts were responses to a disconnection—the absence of the mother—and a desire to compensate for the absence. Schematization concerns the abstraction of, e.g., a lexical item from the instantiations of its usage, as the word "ring", which can signify in varied contexts. In categorization, these become elaborated into their subdivisions: a finger ring, a smoke ring, etc.

This taxonomy is useful for explaining idioms, which UG has a hard time accounting for, because it separates grammar from lexicon and describes grammar as a set of distinct categories that discrete words are plugged into. But the overdetermination of language, especially lexicality, is not compatible with this separation. The associations of a word precede its placement near other words, and this can indeed explain syntactic drift. We associate through condensation and displacement, and this determines syntax as a product of automatization: syntax is habit, convention, and this is especially the case in metaphorical and idiomatic expressions, e.g., Jill *kept an eye* on her brother. In responding to a linguist who had criticized some of his theories, Langacker said, "Calling me a stubborn ostrich was presumably not an attempt at biological classification" (41). Language production and processing are continually jumping categories, as is evident in anticipations and perseverations.

One of Langacker's section titles reads: "Are meanings in the head"? He subsequently quips, "It's hard to imagine where else they might be". This reminds me of an article I read as an undergrad in a philosophy course. The title of the article was: "Why the Mind Is in the Head" (McCulloch, 1965). I also had a hard time imagining where else it could be. In opposition to a "dictionary view" of semantics, CG proposes "encyclopedic semantics", in which "a lexical meaning resides in a particular way of accessing an open-ended body of knowledge pertaining to a certain type of entity". He represents this with

> a series of concentric circles, indicating that the knowledge components have varying degrees of centrality…for any given lexical meaning, certain specifications are so central that they are virtually always activated whenever the expression is used, while others are activated les consistently and others are so peripheral that they are accessed only in special contexts…a lexical meaning is neither totally free nor totally fixed.

And it is "both linguistically and psychologically realistic" (Langacker, 2008, p. 39). Now this works well with dream images in condensation that radiate outward from a nuclear center and constitute the phenomenon of overdetermination.

CG posits no discrete boundary between semantics (compositionally determined meaning) and pragmatics (contextual interpretation). It sees no modular view of language and no semantic representations that in themselves have "any kind of independent cognitive status" (41). Again, meaning is extrapolated from interconnections among linguistic representations, always, for this study, with a preconscious element.

Langacker offers the following interpretation of the famous sentence: "Colorless green ideas sleep furiously" (Chomsky, 1957, p. 15): "Uninteresting new ideas remain dormant and resist all efforts to make them catch on" (Langacker, 2008, p. 190). (There have been other attempts to interpret this poetically.) Generativists see this as proof of autonomous innate grammar and syntax, which can produce nonsense utterances within the structural rules of a given language. In other words, the structure slots are there first, and they can be filled with nonsense. But this is not the case: The learned pattern dominates through repetition. Moreover, unconscious sense is often conscious nonsense, and this is determined by the structural dynamics of displacement, condensation, overdetermination, and secondary revision. I can offer another interpretation of the sentence in question: Environmental thoughts that are green in political conviction, but not literally in color, make us toss and turn at night.

There is no innate grammar or syntax, but there is, within a given language, a natural grammar. It consists in the combinations established by repetition, and these are coarticulated by the mechanisms of condensation and displacement that associate elements within the phonology of the language in question. These would be the constructions that "sound right" to the L1 speaker.

Langacker does not discuss recursivity, but instead constituency, which he sees as "one manifestation of hierarchical organization, evident in virtually every realm of human functioning" (207). But clearly, this form of repetitive subordinate nesting into categories, subcategories, sub-sub categories, etc., is an instantiation of recursion. But these hierarchies are not impermeable, and rhizomic cross-pollination is certainly possible. In addition, the same item can be found in several different categories. The important thing is that these hierarchical structures need to be memorized, e.g., army, division, brigade, battalion, company, and platoon. I forget these, as they have no utility for me. But on the other hand, I readily reproduce president, provost, dean, associate dean, and chair. These are recalled mental imprints, not recursions created on the spot. Langacker says that the constituent hierarchies found in the UG tree diagrams "emerge from other phenomena and represent just one of the configurations that symbolic assemblies can assume" (207).

In elegant simplicity, Kenneally (2007) said that language is not a thing. Langacker says the same, but from the approach of cognitive metaphor: "Actually, there is no such thing as 'a language'…a very general metaphor, applied to language in many ways, construes linguistic entities as physical entities" (215). And he supplies these metaphors, some of them unappetizing: We can pick up a language "like our clothes pick up cat hairs"; we can acquire it, "the way we might acquire an art collection", etc. Language is metaphorically configured as a container with compartments; we can "know a language", as if it were a set of facts, an object, or a person. (216). It "resides" in the brain, as if it were a tenant, or a residence. I suggest that a more apt metaphor would be an itinerant one: language is homeless in the brain, settling in convenient niches, repurposing structures for residential needs, e.g., sleeping under a bridge (metaphorically), and co-opting other niches and structures.

Langacker strongly rejects language models based on

> such powerful icons as formal logic, computer programming, and Chomsky's archetypal conception of a 'generative' grammar (a precise and explicit set of symbol-manipulating rules that enumerate all and only the well-formed sentences of a language)…these expectations are inappropriate for natural language, which is not a self-contained or well-defined formal system. I likewise reject the metaphor that likens mind to a digital computer and language to a program that it runs. CG is more at home in the 'connectionist' ('neural network') world of dynamic systems, parallel processing, distributed representations…
>
> *(10)*

One could add to this a question: Why has it been acceptable, even taken as self-evident, to try to fit language into the structure of formal logic and computer programming, but not to try to fit it into the structure of psychoanalysis and the dynamics of the human unconscious?

Language is "something people do rather than something they have" (216). It is dynamic, and also an abstraction from idiolect to dialect, to sociolect, etc., a generalization that overrides individual differences. He sees "talking… as a socioculturally grounded cognitive activity" (216) and observes that the "acquisition [of language] is never really completed" (218), i.e., it is an asymptotic endeavor. Moreover, as this model is based on usage, the traditional formalist distinction between competence and performance is irrelevant; language production and processing engage general cognitive functions, and not the instinctual actions and reactions of a language organ.

In discussing discourse, he says, "A discourse comprises a series of usage events", and these can include "signals, such as gestures and body language (conceivably even pheromones)" (457). This is the expression's full contextual understanding: "All linguistic elements are both prospective and retrospective" (461). Thus they involve anticipations and perseverations in their embodiment: "The brain, however, is the nexus of a nervous system that runs throughout the body" (500). Langacker's understanding of language fits tidily into the psychoanalytic model. Language is embodied in the nervous system, and thus enables the conversion of psych into soma.

One sees here a configuration of grammar that consists in symbolic relationships among semantic and phonological structures, where syntax is a product of repetition and, ergo, habit. Language consists in a continual and preconscious processing via perceptions, anticipations, and perseverations involving condensation, displacement, repetition, and overdetermination that associate elements within the semantics and phonology of the language in question. Chomsky's assertions cited at the beginning of this chapter—that there are no constructions anyway: no passive, no raising, etc., and that there is just the option of dislocating something somewhere else under certain conditions—offer a casino model of the production of language, where the (micro)chips fall as they may. The psychoanalytic model proposed in this study offers a more structured account of language production: language as a psychological phenomenon, in the largest sense of the word.

The following chapter situates the evolution of language in a psychoanalytic perspective, with an emphasis on the nature of grammar.

## References

Bellah, R. (2011). *Religion in human evolution.* Harvard University Press.
Chomsky, N. (1957). *Syntactic structures.* Mouton.
Chomsky, N. (1995). *The minimalist program. Current studies in linguistics.* MIT Press.
Chomsky, N. (2002). An interview on minimalism. In N. Chomsky, et al. (Ed.), *On nature and language* (pp. 92–161). Cambridge University Press.
Gould, S. (1985). *The flamingo's smile: Reflections in natural history.* W. W. Norton.
Kenneally, C. (2007). *The first word.* Viking.
Langacker, R. (2008). *Cognitive grammar: A basic introduction.* Oxford University Press.
McCulloch, W. (1965). Why the mind is in the head. In W. McCulloch (Ed.), *Embodiments of mind* (pp. 72–87). MIT Press.
McGilvray, J. (2002). Introduction for cybereditions. In N. Chomsky (Ed.), *Cartesian linguistics. A chapter in the history of rationalist thought.* Cybereditions Corporation.
McGilvray, J. (2017). On the history of universal grammar. In I. Roberts (Ed.), *The Oxford handbook of universal grammar.* Oxford University Press.
McWhorter, J. (2001). *The power of Babel.* Henry Holt.
Pinker, S., & Jackendoff, R. (2005). The faculty of language: What's special about it? *Cognition* 95, 201–236.

# 11
# THE EVOLUTION OF LANGUAGE IN A PSYCHOANALYTIC PERSPECTIVE

Daniel Everett, in the fascinating work *How Language Began: The Story of Humanity's Greatest Invention*, observes, and correctly, that for a mutation to spread, it must give the organism a survival advantage in the environmental niche (Everett, 2017, p. 31). In this context, he claims that a mutation for syntax would probably not provide a survival advantage, because there are plenty of languages with simple syntax, and they have survived well (31). Also, what use would it have been to speak complexly if there were no interlocutors around who could understand? (31). Additionally, for quick communication, simple sentences are more effective than more complex ones. Everett holds that language existed before grammar; grammar is thus an add-on (77). I propose that morphological complexity would have proceeded in increments, each marking distinctions in group formation and distinction from other groups. Thus it would have evolved as do rituals in general and, as do rituals, they would have expressed the psychological elements of group cohesion. These consist in matrices of symbolic interconnectivity, in which the utility is the symbolic structure itself.

Everett also holds that practically no one is studying language as a whole (15). Grammar is but a minor feature of language, in his opinion, and he sees it as "at best only a small part of any language…there are tongues that have very little grammar and others in which it is extremely complex" (16).

As stated earlier, Everett is noted for having completed extensive study of the Pirahã language of Brazil, and he observes that there are languages like Pirahã, e.g., Riau (Indonesia), that do not have hierarchical grammar. Their grammars "are little more than words arranged like beads on a string rather than structures as chunks within chunks" (105). The beads on a string constitute associative sequences that operate as do normal human conversations

DOI: 10.4324/9781003180197-12

in their twists and turns. It is human intelligence that enables the decoding and intuition of meaning. He notes: "Animals need instincts because they lack flexible cognition" (106). As stated earlier, the crux of "flexible cognition" is the capacity to symbolize, as Everett points out below.

Everett posits the following scenario: A homo erectus may have screamed "shamalamadingdong as he saw a sabre-toothed cat run by him only a hundred yards away. He was in all likelihood gesticulating, screaming, and engaging his entire body to communicate what he had seen" (239). And gesticulating wildly. Eventually, the early human intonated and emphasized one morpheme over another, e.g., shamalamaDINGdong. This spread by imitation, the emphasized elements became isolated, and ecce the birth of grammar and syntax. He proposes that the early humans would have been gesticulating at the same time (239–240).

This description of the development of intonation corresponds to the motivated word segmentations discussed in Freud's analysis of verbal parapraxes, where one segment is emphasized over another. It is relevant to note that in the parapraxis, the emphasis on one segment is overdetermined by homophonic connection to highly charged psychological elements, with little attention to morpho-syllabic integrity. The segment gains meaning post-facto when a motivated emphasis becomes placed upon it via the homophonic correspondences.

Everett says that "the core of language is the symbol, a combination of a culturally agreed upon form with a culturally developed meaning" (291). He proposes that

> the symbol may have resulted from associating two objects by mistake, such as a tree root confused with a serpent, or simply by regular association of one thing in the world with another object or event, as Pavlov's dog learned to associate food with the ringing of the bell. Once this connection was made, humans began to use their symbols, each one learning from the other.
>
> *(291)*

Folklore says that the stimulus Pavlov used was a bell, but this is not clear in the data supplied in Pavlov's experiment. Pavlov had noted, however, that the dog had started salivating at the sight of the assistant who had brought it food previously, even though the assistant carried no food at that time. Everett's account of the origin of the symbolic function differs from that of Solms (1996), who places the symbolic moment in the child's internalization of parental speech. While the content differs, the structure is similar, as it involves the process of condensation (metaphor), an association of "one thing in the world with another object or event", which had previously been unconnected. This would be another perspective on the origin of metaphor, and thus of the human symbolic function. It is important to note that, in the psychoanalytic perspective, condensation (and displacement) are ineluctable cognitive processes that are operating both in sleep and wakefulness. One can, indeed, construct metaphors: This is obvious. But the cognitive networking is continual. Kövecses refers to this as "our unconscious meaning-making activity" (Kövecses, 2006, p. 327).

In *The Symbolic Species. The Co-evolution of Language and the Brain*, Terrence Deacon argues convincingly that the ability to symbolize is the original point for language. He sees "the computational demands of symbolization" as "the indirect source of the selection pressures that initiated and drove the prolonged evolution of an entire suite of capacities and propensities that now constitute our language 'instinct'" (Deacon, 1997, p. 340). And here, the use of quotation marks is an ironic indicator that qualifies the status of language as an instinct. The skill at symbolizing, recognizing, and recombining symbols would have led to grammaticalization, and thus to syntax.

Deacon relies on Pierce's understanding of icon, index, and symbol: Icons are based on similarity between the sign and what it refers to; indices are based on contiguity (or causality) in space or time; and symbols have no basis other than convention. Thus a map refers iconically to the territory that it covers, smoke refers indexically to the fire, and a red light refers symbolically to the need to stop.

He holds that symbolic communication in humans arose around 2 million years ago, but that it was "multimodal", i.e., it included both gesture and speech, and that eventually, speech dominated. The placing of the symbolic function at 2 million years ago coincides nicely with the emergence of *homo erectus*, whose skills at tool making, sailing, coordinated hunting methods, and group organization would have been facilitated by the engagement of the human symbolic function.

The evolution of language along with the symbolic function took place in a codeterminative interaction with the environment: "Languages are social and cultural entities that have evolved with respect to the forces of selection imposed by human users" (110). Similar to the evolution of computers to be user-friendly, to adapt to the needs of humans, "language structures may simply reflect the selection pressures that have shaped their reproduction" (111). Languages evolved to be user-friendly to children, beginning with syllables, rhyme, and allomorphy. And eventually, "languages evolve so as to embody in their syntax the most frequently guessed patterns" (122). Deacon encourages us to "think of languages a bit as we think of viruses" (112), i.e., they mutated, and the optimal forms for their distribution were the ones that succeeded. Language is thus a phenotype.

The progression from forms based on syllable and rhyme to formal structures would be similar to the development of literature from poetry to narrative verse, and then to narrative prose. Verse, rhyme, and meter are the best mnemonic devices for the oral communication of large chunks of text. Prose narrative spread with literacy and the invention of the printing press.

Networks of symbolic and acoustic reference lie at the basis of language, and these interact at the phonetic, morphemic, and lexical levels. Deacon says,

> The symbolic basis of word meaning is mediated, additionally, by the elicitation of other words (at various levels of awareness). Even if we do not consciously experience the elicitation of other words, evidence that they are activated comes from priming and interference effects that show up in word association tests.
>
> *(64)*

And he adds: "The content words that combine in sentences are almost invariably metonymically related to one another" (306). This understanding of the formation of symbolic language corresponds to the psychoanalytic mechanisms of overdetermination and displacement.

Concerning the poverty of stimulus argument, Deacon holds that children merely learn language patterns and then extend them. They learn an incomplete pidgin, which they complement, filling in the blanks with similar patterns that they have learned:

> Early recognition of global representational relationships…and an inability to track local word-association patterns, lead young children to initially treat many phrases as unanalyzed wholes…subsequent maturation of learning abilities enables children to later pick up the word-association patterns buried within phrases that previously escaped their notice.
>
> *(139)*

It should be noted that this only applies to preliterate children, who then become literate. It is not the maturation of learning abilities that enables this transition, but instead the entry into writing, as is evidenced in the examination of metalinguistic knowledge among adult illiterates.

Deacon's discussion of Saussure, however, is in need of some qualification. He claims that Saussure made "the assumption that a one-to-one mapping of words onto objects and vice versa is the basis for meaning and reference" (69). Deacon, however, sees the reverse of this, saying, "The correspondence between words and objects is a secondary relationship, subordinate to a web of associative relationships of a quite different sort" (70). This is certainly correct but the problem is that Saussure did indeed see meaning as a relationship between a concept and a sound-image, and not as an accurate recording of an objective thing out there (the Kantian thing in itself), thus moving the theater of meaning inside the mind. In an endopsychic space, signification would be subject to myriad associative relationships. That is where, according to Saussure, signs obtain their meaning only in relation to other signs, and not in a relation between the mind and external reality. Deacon eventually winds up saying as much himself: "Because symbols do not directly refer to things in the world, but indirectly refer to them by virtue of referring to other symbols, they are implicitly combinatorial entities…occupying determinate positions in an organized system of other symbols" (99).

Deacon contextualizes this in a multivalent perspective on language and cognition. He emphasizes that the prefrontal cortex—disproportionately large in humans—, which is the seat of the "executive function", i.e., the organizing of complex behavior and the conceptualizing of the future, is "not a single homogeneous structure with a single function. No prefrontal area receives direct input from primary sensory or motor modalities". Similarly, "intelligence is not a unitary brain function, and language isn't walled off from other cognitive functions" (269). He adds:

> Even the minutest divisions of cognitive function we hope to explain at the psychological level are ultimately products of the functioning of a whole brain…if there was ever a structure for which it makes sense to argue that the function of the whole is not the sum of the functions of its parts, the brain is that structure.
> 
> *(287)*

The question is: What are the basic cognitive functions that language is not "walled-off" against? These must operate along the matrix of syllable and morpheme, and these constitute *the alternative logic of language*. We must continually remember that "language is not processed by some general learning capacity, but by quite heterogenous cognitive subsystems, none of which is a language processor by design" (298).

Deacon emphasizes:

> Though breaking up language analytically into such complementary domains as syntax and semantics, noun and verb, production and comprehension, can provide useful categories for the linguist, and breaking it up according to sensory and motor functions seems easier from a global neuronal viewpoint, we should not expect that the brain's handling of language follows the logic of either of these categorical distinctions.
> 
> *(298)*

The foundational processes of syllable and morpheme in the generation of language were and are furthered by the mimetic and ludic function of human behavior. The aping capacities of the highest primate became co-opted in the development of language. Play involves repetition of base structures, as is evidenced in any game. This must have been facilitated by the emergence of a behavior that took pleasure in repetition and imitation. This is a mimetic function, in which laughter becomes contagious. Hurford (2014) also devotes a lengthy discussion to mirror neurons and imitation, noting that laughing can be contagious, as can yawning. Deacon notes this, and proposes that "the enigmatic connection between laughter and humor may be a side effect of the adaptation for symbol learning" (Deacon, 1997, p. 420). This is an astute observation, as jokes and wit require higher-level symbolic reasoning and comprehension. This is especially the case in punning, and most certainly in the reversals found in ironic expression. He summarizes that "the shift of representation from one system of associations to another parallel but previously recognized one is common to both interpreting jokes and reconstructing symbolic relationships" (420). He states that "brain-language co-evolution has significantly restructured cognition from the top-down" (417). This is quite the opposite of UG theory. The restructuring of cognition "from the top-down" would proceed from the matrix of language and the continuum of unconscious–preconscious–consciousness.

He embarks upon an excursion into the nature of consciousness at the end of the book: "To be conscious of something is to experience a representation of it. The subjective experience of consciousness is always a consciousness of something" (448). He holds that "consciousness of iconic representations should differ from consciousness of indexical representations" (449). Yes, this would be clearly the case, because icons and indexes are quite different things, but the mechanism of metacognitive reflection would be the same. It is the light that illuminates indexicality and iconicity. He posits a hierarchy of consciousness, or perhaps more correctly, consciousnesses, with consciousness of symbolic relationships being the most complex. Deacon does, however, confuse consciousness with representation. Clearly animals can represent, since they have memory. Consciousness does not equal representation; one is conscious *of* a representation.

As has been stated earlier, this is the light of metacognition. Consciousness is always one step removed from thought: one step above that which is being thought about. He says that "it is the virtual, not actual, reference that symbols provide, which gives rise to this experience of self" (452). For this study, that which gives rise to the experience of self is the transcendent mechanism of consciousness itself.

James R. Hurford, in *The Origins of Language: A Slim Guide*, has made an interesting observation on the human capacity to symbolize. He accesses research on the emergence of clothing, which he places in an evolutionary perspective. Homo erectus began to shed fur about 1.8 million to 1 million years ago, and a viable explanation involves the necessity of cooling and respiration, which enabled our ancestors to run down game. This sounds odd at first glance, since many quadrupeds run much faster than humans. But because they respirate and cool through their mouths (their fur impedes cooling via the skin), they sprint very quickly and then tire. They are not long-distance sprinters. Humans engaged in persistence hunting, as do current hunter–gatherer cultures, where they simply jog for hours behind the animal until it is exhausted.

Now archaeological data indicates that modern humans started wearing clothes about 170,000 years ago. This is deduced from the presence of body lice in human remains. Body lice live in clothes (as opposed to hair lice) and are then transferred to the skin. The absence of body lice in earlier human remains indicates that they went naked. Hurford speculates that this was an instance of proto-fashion motivated by culture and not by climate, because anatomically modern humans were then confined to Africa. Clothes could have functioned as an indicator of status and would have instantiated an *early construction of identity via symbolic communication between self and other* (Hurford, 2014, p. 12).

Derek Bickerton, in *Adam's Tongue, How Humans Made Language, How Language Made Humans,* proposes that human language began when someone came back from the hunt, having found a large carcass, and imitated the sound of the animal. Thus imitation of something not present would have been the beginning of symbolic language (Bickerton, 2009, p. 160). (Linguistics often refers to this as "displacement", but clearly in a different sense than that of this study.) Humans were "actively carving out the niche of high-end scavenging, and this process in turn fed into the growth of protolanguage" (219), which would have occurred when they returned to camp and mimed the animal whose remains they had located. This would have taken place between 2 million and 1.6 million years ago. Bickerton also adds: "Chomsky believes that human thinking came first and enabled language. I believe that language came first and enabled human thinking" (190–191). He concludes: "Eventually, language and human cognition did coevolve, but first, the first words had to trigger the first concepts" (210). This gets trapped, however, in a chicken-or-egg impasse. I prefer to see language and thought as a reciprocally codeterminative entity. But Bickerton does propose that "until we could talk, we could not even think" (195). Now this fits well into the psychoanalytic paradigm, where the emergence of conscious language instantiates consciousness itself. One becomes conscious of something by its attachment to verbal residues. It is also important to note that the mimetic faculty is crucial to this development.

Bickerton thinks that the change proceeded from protolanguage (beads on a string) to language (hierarchy and merge), otherwise one could not communicate complex ideas. "Beads on a string won't support long and complex sentences…longer messages sent this way would take up so much time that the receiver (and maybe even the sender!) would have forgotten the beginning before the end was reached" (235–236). I am not convinced that hierarchy gets around this problem. People are continually forgetting the beginning of what they are saying, and what others are saying, as well, long before they get to the end of the idea. As stated earlier, long and complex sentences are not the way we talk, unless we rehearse our lines first. Our normal conversations are random sequences of what reminds us of what—associative interconnections within the matrix of displacement and condensation. It should be noted that, in order to facilitate careful, unequivocal communication, the associative connections that are continually occurring to the speaker (and listener) must be suppressed.

Kenneally points out that the word "language" is "used to describe too many different phenomena" (Kenneally, 2007, p. 10). The title of the first section of her work is "Language is Not a Thing", in majuscule (15)—a wonderfully succinct statement—instead, it is "a bitsy pile of stuff" (289). When we speak of language, we always speak only of one or more of its aspects, but not of its totality. If we try to generalize to the totality of language, the generalization conceals more than it reveals, in that it excludes a multitude of other aspects of language. Language cannot be reduced to one fundamental thing. This is clearly the mistake made in prescriptivist proclamations about right and wrong, or good and bad language, but also in attempts to essentialize language, i.e., to reduce it to an original point, or a single drive or biological determination. Even Darwin, whose theories can be seen as the major turning point to a bio-materialist understanding of human behavior, held that language is not a true instinct (Darwin, 1871, p. 58).

On literacy, Kenneally observes that

> writing cannot be considered the bare bones of speech, for it is something else entirely. Writing is static, structured by the conventions of punctuation and the use of space. The kinds of sentences that occur in writing bear only an indirect relationship to the more free-flowing and complex structures of speech…and writing is only six thousand years old.
>
> *(Kenneally, 2007, p. 5)*

And as we have seen, writing is also an imposition upon language, and restricting study to written language alone can also hamper linguistic research itself. She quotes from Stephen J. Gould in the article "Evolution: The Pleasures of Pluralism" (1997):

> Reading and writing are now highly adaptive for humans, but the mental machinery for these crucial capacities must have originated as spandrels that were co-opted later, for the brain reached its current size and conformation tens of thousands of years before any human invented reading and writing.
>
> *(55)*

The term "spandrel" has its origins in architecture and is used to describe the space left open when an arch is installed within a rectangular frame, which leaves openings on the top left and right of the rectangle. Spandrels are a byproduct of arch design and became co-opted later as a space for decoration. Gould is largely credited with popularizing the term in evolution to describe a spinoff from an evolutionary change, a byproduct that was not initially part of the process of natural selection that favored the change. Gould sees reading and writing as spandrels, and even language as a whole. Some recent usages of the term "offline" bear the same concept, i.e. an element external to the operating program.

Gould's argument, as Kenneally sees it, is that there is no language organ, and language was not specifically selected. It is simply a complex of spandrels, and, as Kenneally would say, not a thing:

> At some point in the past, Gould believed, our brains evolved to a level of complexity that would enable us to reason our way through certain situations, and at that level we had the structures for language already in place. In a sense, language simply 'happens' when you have a machine complex enough to accommodate it. So rather than language being selected, we lucked into it.
>
> *(55)*

And this would have codetermined progressive changes in the vocal anatomy that facilitated verbal communication. Clearly, this would not have happened all of a sudden. The pathways connecting these spandrels could have evolved over time. And the crucial aspect here is the ludic faculty. The spandrel is the spinoff that the language user–architect integrates into their speech.

Kenneally compares this to the evolution of the eye, a popular analogy among gradualists. The delicately complex organ did not emerge in a spontaneous miracle of ocular parthenogenesis. It evolved in gradual tiny steps, with certainly numerous missteps along the way that did not help the organism see better, and that were thusly eliminated. The advantageous tiny changes would have each been preserved by natural selection and passed on (59–60).

The article "A Pessimistic Estimate of the Time Required for an Eye to Evolve" (Nilsson & Pelger, 1994) offers a viable scenario. One begins with a mutation: a patch of light-sensitive cells on the skin of an organism. Sensitivity to light would have had an adaptive advantage in spatial orientation. Postulating subsequent permutations of the mutation that would have effected an increase of 1% in light sensitivity, they calculated 1,829 evolutionary steps from the initial skin patch to an eye, taking 364,000 years in total. Animals with modern eyes were already in existence 550 million years ago.

Kenneally refers to the work of Simon Kirby, in the article "Culture and Biology in the Origins of Linguistic Structure" (2017). Kirby has been doing computer modeling of language evolution. Kenneally paraphrases Kirby, saying that he thinks that "agents basically learn to speak on the basis of having seen other populations speak before them". He sees language acquisition as a form of iterated learning, in which speakers learn by imitating what they see and hear. His computational models show that it is possible for "linguistic structure to emerge out of nothing", according to Kenneally (232). This is clearly an overstatement. An automobile, for instance, emerges from an assembly of multiple parts, not *ex nihilo*. The model that Kirby proposes does indeed seem more plausible than the parthenogenetic view of the appearance of language proposed by many generativists. Kirby's model is very effective for depicting language evolution, as speakers cannot visualize the entirety of their language. They engage in inductive reasoning and infer the whole. Thus a structure evolves; it is not programmed a priori.

Kenneally proposes a model for language as a kind of virus. In this model, language evolves as do all organisms. It has its own agency, somehow parasitic, in that it depends on humans for its continued existence. Language mutates, combines, and recombines, just as do the genes that we inherit, say, from our parents. The mutations would be scattershot, just as those in nature, with usage, utility, and niche determining their continuation. She also cites the work of Luc Steels, a researcher who works for The Sony Corporation in Paris. Steels studies how linguistic structure emerges from the spontaneous interaction of individual robots in "an absence of central planning" (240). Kenneally holds that "human language ability is an emergent adaptive system that is created by a basic cognitive mechanism rather than by a genetically endowed language module" (241). She holds that "there was no one moment at which humans became definably human, just as language did not appear suddenly from the ether" (Kenneally, 2007, p. 202).

Thus language proceeds as do social structures in general. If you populate a new housing development, social structures will just emerge out of the interactions of individuals. One may also make an analogy with sports. Baseball, for example, did not suddenly appear in the form that it is found in now. A proto-sport of stick and ball (or stone) gradually evolved into the current complicated structure, step by step. I know of no arguments that hold that there was already a blueprint for baseball in the human brain.

Calvin and Bickerton think that the idea that complicated social life created language is backward—it is language that made social life enormously complicated: "Social life plus protolanguage was like a muscle-building machine for the brain. And above it all was the attraction of having as a mate someone who got words out…quickly, clearly, and appropriately" (Calvin & Bickerton, 2000, p. 201). This is a nicely concise illustration of the dynamics of language evolution in the matrix of social organization and sexual selection. The only problem is that they try to squeeze merge into this process, which is kind of like putting a square peg in a round hole, or better yet like nesting boxes inside boxes instead of describing a holistic interconnectivity. And again, the argument that language created complicated social life is one side of the chicken-or-egg theory. It has to be both together.

They offer an interesting illustration of the pressure of collaboration, one that recapitulates the theory of the primal horde of Darwin and Freud. They discuss primate sexuality, in which often "the largest and most aggressive male…virtually monopolizes the females in the group. Any male…who wants to break this monopoly has to choose a moment when the alpha male's attention is otherwise engaged" (124). This common mammalian phenomenon "ensures that only the toughest and brawniest pass on their genes to succeeding generations", with the result that some of the unlucky males "may go to their graves as virgins" (124–125). But for humans, strategies of circumvention can be found: "Smarter species are unlikely to put up with forced celibacy if they can find a way to escape it", and they do so by forming alliances against the dominant male (125). They add: "In species with bigger brains, the sexual tyranny of alpha males is typically circumvented". Thus "male-male alliances are formed", which provides "some indirect evidence that the motive for alliance formation is primarily the desire to spread one's genes…and that's how reciprocal altruism, father of the more selfless kind, was born" (125).

This coordinates very well with the psychoanalytic account of the band of brothers rebelling against the patriarch, as found in Freud's *Totem und Tabu* (*Totem and Taboo*), in which he offers a psychoanalytic interpretation of the fraternal rebellion. This is a continuation, in group form, of the oedipal rebellion against the father. He observes that "Darwin's primal horde has no account of the beginnings of totemism. All that we find there is a violent and jealous father who keeps all the females for himself and drives away his maturing sons as they grow up". He then says that, "with the aid of the celebration of the totem meal", we can account for how this came about:

> The most primitive kind of organization that we actually come across—one that still exists in certain tribes—consists of bands of males, composed of members with equal rights and subject to the restrictions of the totemic system, including inheritance through the mother…one day the brothers who had been driven out came together, killed and devoured their father, and so ended the patriarchal horde. United, they dared to do, successfully, what would have been impossible for them individually…the totem meal, which is perhaps humankind's earliest celebration, would thus be a repetition and a commemoration of this memorable and criminal deed, which was the beginning of so many things—of social organization, of moral restrictions and of religion.
> 
> *(Freud, 1913, p. 171)*

Freud follows this with the speculation that the brothers landed in a situation of sibling rivalry regarding the women of the clan. Though each one desired to have all the women for himself, as did the father, the social organization would have collapsed in a chaotic struggle. They then instituted the law against incest, and the social organization thus solidified (174).

Calvin and Bickerton expand this to account for "reciprocal altruism", which "contains the roots of many of the things we hold most dear—morality, democracy, and yes, even language (or at least syntax)" (Calvin & Bickerton, 2000, p. 126). The authors propose that this form of collaboration necessitated a consciousness of interdependent relationships and a systematic social planning: If I do this for you, you will do that for me. This requires recognition of debt and obligation. And it is here that the leap of faith to syntax is made. The authors see this as a syntactic relation of agent, theme, and goal, a model based on formal logic. The agent is the performer of the action, the theme is the receiver, and the goal is where the action is directed.

The argument that this constitutes protosyntax is quite interesting. Calvin and Bickerton speculate that this happened most likely 150,000 years ago (143), but clearly planning and reciprocal obligation would have been in place in human culture long before that. How could *erectus* have sailed without it? Language would have simply verbalized the perception of dependency and planning that had gradually emerged in human group-formation. Language uses what the mind has. To say that the understanding of dependent, reciprocal, and hierarchical relations created language would be like saying that the understanding of gravity created stone-throwing. Or better yet, a dedicated module for projectile propulsion. The authors observe that the transition from protolanguage to syntax was "the Great Leap Forward, the evolutionary Good Trick" (97).

One sees here a *psychoanalytic* moment in the development of the structures of in-group collaboration. Cognition of interdependent relationships would have crystallized in the matrix of a grammar/syntax of *language and behavior*. Solms spoke of "auditory self-reflection and critical comparisons between one's own speech and the speech of one's own parents" and held that "this feature of speech…lays the structural bedrock for the superego" (Solms, 1996, p. 359). This is a sociolinguistic structure emergent in the interactive dynamics of child and parent, both in ontogeny and phylogeny.

These interdependent relationships are, obviously, facilitated by language. As such, they become articulated in the structures of the principal psychoanalytic mechanisms, but especially those of condensation and displacement (metaphor and metonymy). The following chapter revisits the studies on metaphor made by Lakoff and Johnson (1980) and their relevance for a psychoanalytic understanding of language.

## References

Bickerton, D. (2009). *Adam's tongue: How humans made language, how language made humans.* Hill and Wang.

Calvin, W., & Bickerton, D. (2000). *Lingua ex machina. Reconciling Darwin and Chomsky with the human brain.* MIT Press.

Darwin, C. (1871). *The descent of man*. John Murray.
Deacon, T. (1997). *The symbolic species. The co-evolution of language and the brain*. W.W. Norton & Co.
Everett, D. (2017). *How language began*. Liveright.
Freud, S. (1913). *Totem und Tabu. Gesammelte Werke* (Vol. 9, pp. 3–206). Imago. [English edition: Freud, S. (1953–1974). *Totem and taboo. The standard edition of the complete psychological works of Sigmund Freud* (Vol. 13, pp. 1–161). Hogarth].
Gould, S. (1997). Evolution: The pleasures of pluralism. *The New York Review of Books* 44(11), 47–52.
Hurford, J. (2014). *The origins of language: A slim guide*. Oxford University Press.
Kenneally, C. (2007). *The first word*. Viking.
Kirby, S. (2017). Culture and biology in the origins of linguistic structure. *Psychonomic Bulletin Review* 24, 118–137.
Kövecses, Z. (2006). *Language, mind, and culture*. Oxford University Press.
Lakoff, G., & Johnson, M. (1980). *Metaphors we live by*. University of Chicago Press.
Nilsson, D., & Pelger, S. (1994). A pessimistic estimate of the time required for an eye to evolve. *Proceedings of the Royal Society of London B* 256, 53–58.
Solms, M. (1996). Towards an anatomy of the unconscious. *Journal of Clinical Psychoanalysis* 5, 331–367.

# 12
## METAPHOR AND PSYCHOANALYSIS

The work of Lakoff and Johnson, in *Metaphors We Live By*, highly recognized in the science of language for decades now as a major contribution to the understanding of cognitive metaphor, aligns well with the psychoanalytic account of language. The authors assert, and rightfully so, that "most of our ordinary conceptual system is metaphorical in nature" (Lakoff & Johnson, 1980, p. 4).

They hold that "human thought processes are largely metaphorical. This is what we mean when we say that the human conceptual system is metaphorically structured and defined" (6). In their view, cognition is not a referential connection between thought and object, as would be the case from a radical behaviorist standpoint, but instead, it is an approximate evaluation of a perception. One of the first examples they give is the understanding of time: "Thus we understand and experience time as the kind of thing that can be spent, wasted, budgeted, invested wisely or poorly, saved, or squandered. Time is money" (8). They note—and this is a very important observation—that metaphor is constructed by the ideologies of culture, e.g., time is money; we speak of "saving time". Such metaphors are not universal. They are examples of "structural metaphors that are basic to Western industrial societies" (66). And there is a symbiosis here: "Not only are they grounded in our physical and cultural experience; they also influence our experience and our actions" (68). Here, economics informs the cognitive apparatus for understanding time. This is clearly the dominant apparatus in our neo-capitalist era; the logic of neo-capitalism informs many metaphors. The authors see these as "structural metaphors, cases where one concept is metaphorically structured in terms of another" (14). They note the extensive use of spatial and orientational metaphors, such as "up and down" to indicate "happy and sad" (14–15). Status is also indicated spatially, as in: "That would be beneath me" (17).

DOI: 10.4324/9781003180197-13

Indeed, the authors generalize that "most of our fundamental concepts are organized in terms of one or more spatialization metaphors" (17). They offer the category of ontological metaphor, in which an abstract notion is treated as if it were a concrete object: "Our experiences with physical objects (especially our own bodies) provide the basis for an extraordinarily wide variety of ontological metaphors, that is, ways of viewing events, activities, emotions, ideas, etc., as entities and substances" (25). Here, the referent is granted objective status, e.g.: "Inflation is an entity: Inflation is lowering our standard of living" (26).

The metaphor "his mind snapped" (28) is quite transparent at first glance, but a bit of reflection reveals the imposition of the metaphor upon the referent. It is important to note that one views here a continuation of concretism in the use of language, despite Piaget's notion that concretism disappears in full adult operationality in language. This aligns well with the psychoanalytic view of the unconscious workings of language, as seen in dreamwork, and as these persist into conscious behavior. One sees concretism in the child's understanding of language, in dreamwork, and also in the construction of metaphor in the operational adult. The homology of metaphor/metonymy and condensation/displacement is evident in this research.

But most importantly, their work shows the ineluctability of metaphor:

> If you say, 'The odds are against us' or 'We'll have to take our chances', you would not be viewed as speaking metaphorically but as using the normal everyday language appropriate to the situation. Nevertheless, your way of talking about, conceiving, and even experiencing your situation would be metaphorically structured.
>
> *(51)*

It is important to emphasize that nonmetaphorical speech (if at all possible) can be seen as pedantic and boring. Not only is metaphorical and metonymic speech necessary, it is also preferred. We appreciate the clever trope in language, as well as the quip. This displays *a priori* the ludic basis of language, manipulated in its infancy, and appreciated in adulthood. The authors also offer one of the more amusing examples of metonymy: "The ham sandwich is waiting for his check" (35).

Kövecses, in *Language, Mind, and Culture*, is largely in agreement with Lakoff and Johnson, and he offers a useful description of metaphor and metonymy. Metonymy involves one single domain, a part for whole, while metaphor involves two distinct domains. "Love is a journey" would be metaphorical, as the two semantic domains are separate: [love] [journey]. Metonymy would be a relationship of contiguity or proximity, while metaphors are characterized by resemblance or correlations. Within-frame (in-frame) mappings constitute metonymy, and cross-frame mappings constitute metaphor. He holds that metaphor is "linguistic, conceptual, social-cultural, neural, and bodily at the same time" (Kövecses, 2006, p. 130). He adds that "abstract meanings are always constituted by figurative meanings...the comprehension of abstract meanings does, in fact, recruit metaphoric mappings" (204). He observes: "The most prevalent metaphor for rational thought is physical manipulation...in English, one can hammer out a solution, can have an incisive mind..." (221). Cutting seems to be a common metaphor—"sharp thinker, dull thinker", etc.

Lakoff and Johnson also observe that metaphors are continually requiring subsequent metaphors:

> But metaphors are not merely things to be seen beyond. In fact, one can see beyond them only by using other metaphors. It is as though the ability to comprehend experience through metaphor were a sense, like seeing or touching or hearing, with metaphors providing the only ways to perceive and experience much of the world. Metaphor is as much a part of our functioning as our sense of touch, and as precious.
> (Lakoff & Johnson, 1980, p. 239)

It is quite common for English speakers to view words of Latin origin as highly abstract, when, in fact, they are based on the most concrete of metaphors. "Subjective" comes from the Latin *sub* ("under") and *jacere/iacere* ("throw, hurl"), and the literal meaning is "thrown under". "Reject" means "throw again/back", "project" means "throw forth", etc. But the authors ask:

> Are there any concepts at all that are understood directly, without metaphor? If not, how can we understand anything at all? The prime candidates for concepts that are understood directly are the simple spatial concepts, such as up. Our spatial concept up arises out of our spatial experience.
>
> (56)

They offer an excellent taxonomy of metaphorical usage, most of the details of which are not necessary here, and a few examples will suffice. They have many subcategories, e.g., ideas as food: "Raw facts, half-baked ideas, warmed-over theories...food for thought" (46); love as electromagnetism: "The electricity between us. There were sparks. I was magnetically drawn to her" (47). There are structural metaphors, e.g., "rational argument is war" (61): "The point here is that not only our conception of an argument but the way we carry it out is grounded in our knowledge and experience of physical combat" (63). Thus physical combat structures our conception of argument.

They use the term "embattlement" frequently in analyzing how conversations turn into arguments. A speaker can offer an interpretation of an issue and then find it qualified by an interlocutor, who informs the speaker of exceptions to her/his perspective. The speaker, being curious, can then modify the perspective. One could ask where the battle is here, but that would ignore the sublimating aspect of the interchange. Hostility is diffused, sublimated, and deflected by rules of politeness. This is caused by the mechanism of the suppression of instincts, which is foundational in human culture, as Freud insisted in his work on malaise in human culture, *Das Unbehagen in der Kultur* (1930) (*Civilization and Its Discontents*). It is important to note that metaphorical extension is not caused by the insufficient expressive potential of language. In other words, metaphor does not arise because the speaker is consciously looking for another way to say something. Metaphor (and metonymy) emerges from the cognitive linguistic system of displacement, condensation, and overdetermination, embodied along the ineluctable networks of associations among psyche, body, and language.

The authors show the emotional basis of locutions that are seen to be objective and neutral.

They hold that all rational arguments "contain, in hidden form, the 'irrational' and 'unfair' tactics that rational arguments in their ideal form are supposed to transcend" (64), and they offer examples:

> It is plausible to assume that… (intimidation)
> Obviously,… It would be unscientific to fail to… (threat)
> As Descartes showed,… (authority)
> The work lacks the necessary rigor for… (insult)
> Your position is right as far as it goes,… (bargaining)
> In his stimulating paper,… (flattery).
>
> *(64)*

This mode of locution instantiates the psychoanalytic view that acculturation, the "civilizing" of the individual, is a process of containing, suppressing, sublimating, and diffusing aggressive instincts. These examples can be seen as illuminating the irrational basis of the apparently rational: hostility diffused and socialized through sublimation. And this is one of the main points to be gleaned from this study: that metaphors both express and conceal urges that are suppressed from formal discourse and displaced into more acceptable forms. The Latin verb *arguere*, the root of "argumentation", meant initially "to show or prove", but secondarily, "to accuse, blame, or denounce". It comes from the Proto-Italic ★argu, "bright", from the PIE root indicating "white". This is a notion of a clearing up, thus a noncombative processing of an underlying aggression.

The authors discuss the metaphorical understanding of causation and the fact that it necessitates an overdetermination, a polyvalent interconnectivity: "A proper understanding of causation requires that it be viewed as a cluster of other components" (70). They add: "Our successful functioning in the world involves the application of the concept of causation to ever new domains of activity—through intention, planning, drawing inferences, etc." (72). And here, they perform a wonderful rescue operation on the notion of definition: "Definitions for a concept are seen as characterizing the things that are inherent in the concept itself" (116). This is merely a form of naïve referentiality. There is nothing inherent in the concept; as with the symbol, it gains its significance by relation to and difference from other elements. They emphasize that "understanding takes place in terms of entire domains of experience and not in terms of isolated concepts" (117), and they add that "the concepts that occur in metaphorical definitions are those that correspond to natural kinds of experience" (118). They offer love as an example, which is a wonderful choice, as love is something we understand, but have great difficulty defining in any coherent way: "Our comprehension of love is metaphorical, and we understand it primarily in terms of concepts for other natural kinds of experience: journeys, madness, war, health, etc." (119).

They summarize:

> An account of how people understand their experiences requires a view of definition very different from the standard account...individual concepts are not defined in an isolated fashion, but rather in terms of their roles in natural kinds of experiences. Concepts are not defined solely in terms of inherent properties; instead, they are defined primarily in terms of interactional properties...definition is not a matter of giving some fixed set of necessary and sufficient conditions for the application of a concept...rather than being rigidly defined, concepts arising from our experience are open-ended.
> 
> *(125)*

These interactional properties emerge from the metonymic chains of associations that start to congeal in preconscious activity.

They emphasize that

> new metaphors have the power to create a new reality...if a new metaphor enters the conceptual system that we base our actions on, it will alter that conceptual system and the perceptions and actions that the system gives rise to. Much of cultural change arises from the introduction of new metaphorical concepts and the loss of old ones. For example, the Westernization of cultures throughout the world is partly a matter of introducing the time is money metaphor into those cultures.
>
> *(145)*

This is a valuable statement for the field of linguistic relativity. And clearly, one can "update" that with the more recent introduction of metaphors from information science into the lexicon. These have clearly informed the invention of universal grammar.

Another metaphoric configuration occurred during the early renaissance; the phrase "mother tongue" (*lingua materna*) entered into our cultural habitus along with an ideology of bodily and familial ownership of language (Bonfiglio, 2010). The fusion of concept and vocabulary in the phrases "mother tongue" and "native speaker" created an intractable ideology of L1 ownership, property, nationality, etc. It is important to note that the metaphor did not create the idea: They arose in symbiosis, as did language and thought in the first place.

The authors discuss the misconception that "metaphor is just a matter of language and can at best only describe reality", which they see as stemming "from the view that what is real is wholly external to, and independent of, how human beings conceptualize the world—as if the study of reality were just the study of the physical world" (Lakoff & Johnson, 1980, p. 146). This leads one to ask if the resistance to linguistic relativity may be a vestige of a naïve positivist empiricism. On the contrary, they hold that

> new metaphors, like conventional metaphors, can have the power to define reality. They do this through a coherent network of entailments that highlight some features of reality and hide others. The acceptance of the metaphor, which forces us to focus only on those aspects of our experience that it highlights, leads us to view the entailments of the metaphor as being true. Such 'truths' may be true, (158) of course, only relative to the reality defined by the metaphor.
>
> *(157–158)*

They add that "truth is always relative to a conceptual system that is defined in large part by metaphor" (159).

They criticize the objectivist view by saying that it ascribes to a context-free "disembodied meaning" (199). Thus there is a matrix of language, thought, and embodiment that represents experience to the subject. The resistance to this realization may be ascribed to a persistence of the supposed mind/body or soul/body dichotomy, the "ghost in the machine", which took a reasoning subject as independent of the container that the subject resides in. The perspective advocated by Lakoff and Johnson is grounded in the idea of embodied metaphoric cognition, i.e., that metaphors extend from the human body.

The eighteenth-century Italian philosopher Giambattista Vico, in *La nuova scienza* (1744), was among the first to situate metaphor as based, to a large degree, on metaphorical extensions from the human body. He examines some of these in the following passage. Clearly, some of the idioms of eighteenth-century Neapolitan Italian cited by Vico would have no current equivalent in English, and translations tend to omit them or modify them so as to make them idiomatic in current English. Here, they are rendered in their original signification:

The following merits observation: In all languages the greater part of the expressions surrounding inanimate things are formed by transpositions from the human body and its parts and from the human senses and passions. As *head* for top or beginning; *forehead, shoulders,* forward and backward; *eyes* of screws and windows; *mouth* for any opening; *lip* for the rim of a vase or other objects; the *tooth* of a plow, a rake, a saw, a comb; *beards* for roots; the *tongue* of an ocean; the *mouth* of a river or mountain; a *neck* of land; an *arm* of a river; a *hand* for a small number; the *breast* of a river or gulf; the *sides* of a corner;...*heart* for center (the Latins said *navel*); a *leg* or foot of land; *foot* for end; *plant* for base or fundament; the *flesh* or bone of fruit; a *vein* of water, rock, or mineral; wine as the *blood* of the vines; the *bowels* of the earth. Heaven or the sea *smiles*; the wind *whistles*; the waves *murmur*; a body *groans* under a great weight. The farmers of Latium said their fields *thirst, bear fruit, swell* with grain; and our own farmers speak of *plants making love, vines going mad, trees weeping.* Countless others can be gleaned from all languages. All of this is a consequence of the axiom that humans, in their ignorance, make themselves the measure of the universe. And as in the examples given, they have made of themselves an entire world. Just as rational metaphysics teaches that *homo intelligendo fit omnia* [humans become all things by understanding them], this imaginative metaphysics shows that *homo non intelligendo fit omnia* [humans become all things by not understanding them], and perhaps the latter is truer than the former, for when humans understand, they extend their minds to comprehend things, but when they do not understand, they make things out of their own selves, transform themselves into these things, and thus become them.

*(Vico, 1748, pp. 191–192)*

Vico's concluding phrases align well with the views of Lakoff and Johnson. The authors also critique the notion of abstract categories. A category is, for them, a transitional generalization dependent on many factors:

Categories (e.g., chair) are not rigidly fixed in terms of inherent properties of the objects themselves. What counts as an instance of a category depends on our purpose in using the category...such categories are not fixed but may be narrowed, expanded, or adjusted relative to our purposes and other contextual factors. Since the truth of a statement depends on whether the categories employed in the statement fit, the truth of a statement will always be relative to the way the category is understood for our purposes in a given context.

*(Lakoff & Johnson, 1980, p. 164)*

They often refer to what they are doing as a "theory of understanding", a nicely neutral term, instead of "epistemology". Understanding for them is collaborative, metaphorical, rhizomic, reticulate, and not fundamentally hierarchical or modular. (One may refer here to the rhizomic and arborescent distinction made by Deleuze and Guattari). They emphasize that

> metaphors are basically devices for understanding and have little to do with objective reality, if there is such a thing. The fact that our conceptual system is inherently metaphorical, the fact that we understand the world, think, and function in metaphorical terms, and the fact that metaphors cannot merely be understood but can be meaningful and true as well—these facts all suggest that an adequate account of meaning and truth can only be based on understanding.
>
> *(184)*

Between objectivism and subjectivism, they offer "an experientialist synthesis" (192), in which metaphor is "imaginative rationality" (192):

> Our views on conventional metaphor—that it pervades our conceptual system and is a primary mechanism for understanding—put us at odds with the contemporary views of language, meaning, truth, and understanding that dominate recent Anglo-American analytic philosophy and go unquestioned in much of modern linguistics.
>
> *(196)*

They are against the following assertions:

- a theory of meaning for natural language is based on a theory of truth, independent of the way people understand and use language
- meaning is objective and disembodied, independent of human understanding
- sentences are abstract objects with inherent structures
- the meaning of a sentence can be obtained from the meanings of its parts and the structure of the sentence (196)

To which they add, in capital letters:

- fitting the Words to the World without People or Human Understanding
- meaning Is Independent of Use
- linguistic Expressions Are Objects: The Premise of Objectivist Linguistics
- grammar Is Independent of Meaning and Understanding (200–205)

They see all of this as an example of Anglo-American analytic philosophy imposing itself on modern linguistics. They assert:

> This tradition is epitomized by the linguistics of Noam Chomsky, who has steadfastly maintained that grammar is a matter of pure form, independent of meaning or human understanding. Any aspect of language that involves human understanding is for Chomsky by definition outside the study of grammar in this sense. Chomsky's use of the term 'competence' as opposed to 'performance' is an attempt to define certain aspects of language as the only legitimate objects of what he considers scientific linguistics,

including "only matters of pure form and excluding all matters of human understanding and language use", which is "in no way dependent on the way people actually understand language" (205).

The authors "maintain that it is possible to give an account of truth and meaning only relative to the way people function in the world and understand it. We are simply in a different philosophical universe from such objectivists" (217). They do not wholly negate objectivism, they merely say that does not provide the proper configuration of language:

> Classical mathematics comprises an objectivist universe. It has entities that are clearly distinguished from one another, e.g., numbers…mathematical logic was developed as part of the enterprise of providing foundations for classical mathematics. Formal semantics also developed out of that enterprise.
>
> *(218)*

Classical mathematics and mathematical logic formed the preparation for formal semantics, which the authors call "objectivist models". These are "models appropriate to universes of discourse where there are distinct entities which have inherent properties and where there are fixed relationships among the entities" (218). They conclude that "objectivist philosophy provides an inadequate basis for the human sciences" (218).

Lakoff and Johnson situate ritual in a context that corresponds well to psychoanalytic theory:

> Religious rituals are typically metaphorical kinds of activities, which usually involve metonymies—real-world objects standing for entities in the world as defined by the conceptual system of the religion…the metaphors we live by, whether cultural or personal, are partially preserved in ritual. Cultural metaphors, and the values entailed by them, are propagated by ritual. Ritual forms an indispensable part of the experiential

basis for our cultural metaphorical systems. There can be no culture without ritual.

*(234)*

And as discussed, the "baroque" intricacies of grammar can be seen as a form of ritual.

In the 2003 edition, the authors summarize:

> Most of the key ideas in this book have been either sustained or developed further by recent empirical research in cognitive linguistics and in cognitive science generally. These key ideas are the following: Metaphors are fundamentally conceptual in nature; metaphorical language is secondary. Conceptual metaphors are grounded in everyday experience. Abstract thought is largely, though not entirely, metaphorical. Metaphorical thought is unavoidable, ubiquitous, and mostly unconscious. Abstract concepts have a literal core but are extended by metaphors, often by many mutually inconsistent metaphors. Abstract concepts are not complete without metaphors. For example, love is not love without metaphors of magic, attraction, madness, union, nurturance, and so on.
>
> *(Lakoff & Johnson, 2003, p. 272)*

Contradictory aspects of metaphor (mutual exclusivity) are very common. An example can be taken from the English words for being and existence: "To be" originates in an IE root meaning "to grow", and the imperfect form "was" is an IE root, meaning "to remain". One sees in the same verb opposing meanings of change and stability to characterize existential presence itself.

This study does take issue, however, with their assumption that metaphor is primarily conceptual, and secondarily linguistic. The psychoanalytic model proposes, instead, a codeterminative emergence of language and thought along the progression of unconscious—preconscious—consciousness.

While the authors do not refer to the work of the Princeton psychologist Julian Jaynes, their own work shows considerable similarity with *The Origins of Consciousness in the Breakdown of the Bicameral Mind* (1976), discussed above. The similarities between the theories of Jaynes and those of Lakoff and Johnson are indeed striking. Jaynes also holds that "metaphor is not a mere extra trick of language…it is the very constitutive ground of language" (Jaynes, 1976, p. 48), and he notes that many metaphors are constructed via extensions from the human body: "the head of an army, table, page, bed, ship, household, or nail, or of steam or water" (49). He asserts that "language is an organ of perception, not simply a means of communication" (50). Of special importance is his observation that root metaphors "become hidden in phonemic change, leaving the words to exist on their own" (51) and to present the illusion of independent referentiality.

He observes that the "tabula rasa" notion that consciousness copies experience itself presumes that consciousness "does something", of which he says, "even that is a metaphor. It is saying that consciousness is a person behaving in physical space who does things" (53). And he adds, "in what 'space' is the metaphorical 'doing' being done" (53)? These are observations remarkably similar to those found in Lakoff and Johnson's analysis of metaphor.

Jaynes uses the term "analog" to describe consciousness: "An analog is at every point generated by the thing it is an analog of. A map is a good example" (53). He adds: "Subjective conscious mind is an analog of what is called the real world. It is built up with a vocabulary or subjective field whose terms are all metaphors or analogs of behavior in the physical world" (55). He says of visual metaphors, e.g., "seeing" what somebody means, that "the mind-space to which they apply is a metaphor of actual space…and the adjectives to describe physical behavior in real space are analogically taken over to describe mental behavior in mind-space" (55). Jaynes describes metaphor as a transferring between the subsets of the metaphor and the subsets of the object of description, as in "the metaphor that the snow blankets the ground". There are nuances "about warmth, protection, and slumber until some period of awakening. These associations then automatically become the associations" (57) of the object described.

In *Philosophy in the Flesh. The Embodied Mind and Its Challenge to Western Thought*, Lakoff and Johnson revisit the question of consciousness and display ideas similar to those of psychoanalysis, without, however, directly addressing that science. In the second sentence of the opening page to the work, they say, "Thought is mostly unconscious" (Lakoff & Johnson, 1999, p. 3). They also hold that "reason is not completely conscious, but mostly unconscious" (4). They are clearly setting themselves against the question of a mind–body dichotomy. Their perspective is anti-Kantian and anti-idealist, and some of their assertions are indeed amusing: "There exists no Kantian radically autonomous person"; and equally: "There is no poststructuralist person" (5), i.e., there is neither the completely absolute nor the completely arbitrary. And they add: "There is no Chomskyan person, for whom language is pure syntax, pure form insulated from and independent of all meaning, context, perception, emotion, memory, attention, action, and the dynamic nature of communication" (6).

They offer an interesting resume of Chomsky's *Cartesian Linguistics*. For Descartes, there is a mind–body dichotomy and an autonomous disembodied reason. For Chomsky, language takes over from the role of reason in Descartes. Language is universal and innate, ecce UG. Syntax is seen as separate from meaning. They claim that for Chomsky, language must be independent of memory, attention, perception, motion and gesture, and culture (475). The mind creates language "from nothing external to itself" (475). This is the autonomous syntax module. It plays no part in gradualist evolution, as it cannot be shared with apes. Thus Chomsky makes it happen all at once about 80,000 years ago. As Catania noted, this assertion "was closer to creationism than any other part of psychological research" (Kenneally, 2007, p. 39). In this model, syntax becomes the essence of language, a creation of a spatialization that does not see itself as such.

They agree with the cognitive science understanding of the brain cited from several sources in this study: "There is no neural subnetwork in the brain that does not have neural input from other parts of the brain that do very different kinds of things" (480). There is no input-free module in the brain: "A grammar is not an abstract formal system, but a neural system" (499). And one recalls Kenneally's pithy summary that language is not a thing.

Oddly, Lakoff and Johnson speak at length of a "cognitive unconscious" without once mentioning psychoanalysis or Freud. For this study, the cognitive unconscious is constructed by the battery of psychoanalytic mechanisms: displacement, condensation, overdetermination, repetition, repression, secondary revision, etc.

The connection between the conceptual metaphor theory (CMT) of Lakoff and Johnson and the cognitive model of psychoanalysis has been well studied by Marianna Bolognesi and Roberto Bichisecchi in the article "Metaphors in Dreams: Where Cognitive Linguistics meets Psychoanalysis".

Bolognesi and Bichisecchi observe that "the most recent insights in cognitive semiotics and metaphor studies have also underlined the fact that the experiential bases of conceptual metaphors are not only subconscious, but also deeply rooted in personal, interpersonal, and cultural dynamics" (Bolognesi & Bichisecchi, 2014, p. 5). The authors seek to analyze metaphors from the perspective of dreamwork: "We believe that emotions are subconscious forces that provoke the emergence of specific metaphors in dreams" (6). They specify that "the metaphors that appear in dreams are indeed a form of communication whose main objective is to implicitly carry specific emotions by means of cross-domain conceptual mappings, and in this way communicating them to the dreamer" (7). Thus the generation of metaphor is embodied in the experience of the speaker and, as an embodied phenomenon, is not always the product of reflective meditation:

> Emotions that enter our mental life through our bodies can get shaped in the form of primary metaphors, i.e., some emotions are understood by our mind in terms of bodily reactions…we understand affection through the bodily experience of physical proximity, and therefore of physical warmth.
>
> *(8)*

They add: "In addition, there are conceptual metaphors that carry rather than explain emotions. In other words, conceptual metaphors that are not based directly on correlations in experience trigger emotional responses by comparing two apparently distant concepts" (8). They make use of the mirror neuron hypothesis in order to account for representation: Mirror neurons "map sensory representations of others' actions onto the observer's neural substrates... by reproducing the same underlying neural patterns inside their own mind". This is based upon "a previous experiential reference inside ourselves". They highlight "the self-referential quality of mirror neurons: In order to understand other people's actions, intentions, and emotions, we need to have a somehow similar experiential background that allows our neural system to mirror another person's behavior" (9). The inclusion of the neural system here helps to support an otherwise familiar hypothesis: that one has to assimilate the experiences of the other into the experiences of the self in order to arrive at a common understanding. This recalls Julian Jaynes's observation that understanding consists in the feeling of similarity. In this model, there is no abstract understanding a priori. The authors access this with their observation that "metaphors carry emotions" (10).

The authors believe that "the ultimate function of metaphors that appear in dreams is to keep a trace, in the mind of the dreamer, of emotions and personal experiences that are important specifically to the dreamer and contribute to shaping the dreamer's identity" (10). The authors offer an interesting, but sweeping statement: "It is a metaphor's destiny to confirm and consolidate the identity of the individual who produced it" (11). This is a wonderfully concise summation of the configuration of identity in a psychoanalytic perspective.

This chapter on the embodiment of metaphor recalls Freud's observation that the ego is above all a bodily ego, and that language is the medium for the expression of identity and the articulation of consciousness. But one also sees here that identity and consciousness proceed *via metaphorical extension from the human body*. Informed by the nuclear mechanisms of displacement and condensation, they emerge along the continuum of unconscious–preconscious–consciousness.

The idea that these mechanisms are fundamental to the articulation of identity can aid in the understanding of linguistic relativity, for language can configure the individual, social, and national self. This means that information threatening to the configuration of identity will meet with resistance, a resistance to the linguistic understanding of a "foreign" concept. In Chapter 13, those resistances are studied.

## References

Bolognesi, M., & Bichisecchi, R. (2013). Metaphors in dreams: Where cognitive linguistics meets psychoanalysis. *Language and Psychoanalysis* 3(1), 4–22.

Bonfiglio, T. (2010). *Mother tongues and nations: The invention of the native speaker.* De Gruyter.

Deleuze, G., & Guattari, F. (1980). *Mille plateaux. Capitalisme et schizophrénie* (vol. 2). Editions de minuit. [English edition: Deleuze, G., & Guattari, F. (1987). *A thousand plateaus. Capitalism and schizophrenia* (vol. 2). University of Minnesota Press].
Jaynes, J. (1976). *The origins of consciousness in the breakdown of the bicameral mind.* Houghton-Mifflin.
Kenneally, C. (2007). *The first word.* Viking.
Kövecses, Z. (2006). *Language, mind, and culture.* Oxford University Press.
Lakoff, G., & Johnson, M. (1980). *Metaphors we live by.* University of Chicago Press.
Vico, G. (1978). *La scienza nuova: giusta l'edizione del 1744* (vol. 1). Editori Laterza. [English edition: Vico, G. (1984). *The new science of Giambattista Vico.* Cornell University Press].

# 13
## PSYCHOANALYSIS AND LINGUISTIC RELATIVITY

What is being proposed here accesses a most contested issue: linguistic relativity, the idea that language determines or influences thought, which is commonly known as the Whorf hypothesis, named after Benjamin Lee Whorf, a fire prevention engineer who studied linguistics with Edward Sapir. It is also referred to as the Sapir–Whorf hypothesis (Whorf, 1964). The awkward terms "Whorfianism" and "Neo-Whorfianism" are also current. Whorf studied the native American Hopi language of the southwest and contrasted its grammar with that of the major European languages. He observed that the Hopi language expressed many phenomena, e.g., plurality, numeration, quantity, time, space, etc., quite differently than do the European languages. This led him to the conclusion that the Hopi and European worldviews were radically different, and that these worldviews were enabled by the different linguistic systems. While some of Whorf's assertions are quite problematic, there do remain, however, some aspects of language that lend themselves well to the arguments of linguistic relativity. As linguists continue to examine previously unrecorded languages, they find striking differences in ways of expressing, for instance, color, spatial orientation, gender, and even arithmetic (there are cultures very uninterested in counting), and experiments do show that the linguistic peculiarities are bound up with cognition.

One of the major respected apologists for linguistic relativism is the Israeli linguist Guy Deutscher, a research fellow at the University of Manchester. Deutscher's *Through the Language Glass: Why the World Looks Different in Other Languages* is an especially astute assessment of linguistic relativism. It should be noted that negative critiques of Whorf often overlook the factor of habituation in his theories. This is indicated in the title of one of his most discussed essays, "The Relation of Habitual Thought and Behavior to Language", and

DOI: 10.4324/9781003180197-14

it is important to emphasize that, for Whorf, it is the habits of language that reinforce our perception and cognition. And as is well known, habits can be difficult to break. Deutscher notes:

> No one (in his or her right mind) would argue nowadays that the structure of a language limits its speakers' understanding to those concepts and distinctions that happen to be already part of the linguistic system. Rather, serious researchers have looked for the consequences of the habitual use from an early age of certain ways of expression.
> *(Deutscher, 2010, p. 156)*

He notes "the dominant view among linguists and cognitive scientists today" that "the influence of language on thought can be considered significant only if … one language can be shown to prevent its speakers from solving a logical problem that is easily solved by speakers of another language" (234), of which he says, "How many daily decisions do we make on the basis of abstract deductive reasoning, compared with those guided by gut feeling, intuition emotions, impulse … how many wars have been fought over disagreements in set theory?" (235). One could add to this the question raised in Chapter 5 on the scientific principles of falsifiability: How many of our daily disagreements are fought over falsifiability criteria (Popper, 1934)?

The ideas of Charles Taylor, in *The Language Animal: The Full Shape of the Human Linguistic Capacity*, relate well to this discussion. Taylor offers a generous discussion of the Sapir–Whorf hypothesis, of which he says,

> The claim could just be that different ways of formulating some scene or state of affairs which belong to different languages (Hopi and English, for instance) draw attention to different features and relations, and that this can influence the way people react to that situation, or what they will spontaneously notice in it or what they tend to remember afterward.
> *(Taylor, 2016, pp. 321–322)*

He adds that "differences in lexicon and grammar require that we pay attention to different things". They "may force us to encode certain features in describing a given situation" (323). And he is clearly on the mark in saying that

> the crucial site where the Sapir-Whorf hypothesis applies is in the area of contemporary cultural differences…between people who are equally 'modern'…it is clear that their diverse understandings of human meanings, ethical ideals, and aspirations to self-transformation are frequently opaque to each other. And this even within the same society, let alone differences with societies which are geographically and historically more distant.
> *(327)*

Taylor offers a parallel between "different ways of encoding the same external reality", as in the case of color terms, and "different human realities" (328), e.g.: religious, political, and ethical.

He adds:

> The linguistic capacity is essentially more than an intellectual one; it is embodied: in enacted meanings, in artistic portrayals, in metaphors which draw on embodied experience, and also in…the ubiquity of 'body language'—tone of voice, emphasis, expressive gesture, stances of intimacy, of aloofness.
>
> *(333)*

And he makes a very astute observation: "Our language straddles the boundary between 'mind' and body" (333). It is interesting that he puts the word "mind" in quotation marks.

Psychoanalytic perspectives are largely absent from discussions of linguistic relativity. They can be very useful in illuminating the psychological attachment to meaning that can suppress intercultural and interlinguistic understanding. In American English, one finds semantic shifts in terms that once shared common meanings with related terms in European languages. Gradually, these terms slipped along their chain of associations and have acquired uncommon meanings that ally with American ideologies. Of special interest are the terms: tipping, exceptionalism, liberal, red, and English. These alterations of word-concepts function as acts of dissimulation that resist criticism, and in the alterations, one finds psychoanalytic dreamwork mechanisms, especially condensation, displacement, inversion, and denial (Bonfiglio, 2017).

The practice of "tipping" is a case in point, as in the common American restaurant "tip". The *Oxford English Dictionary* defines a tip as "a small present of money given to an inferior, esp. to a servant or employee of another for a service rendered or expected; a gratuity, a douceur", and dates the appearance of the noun to 1755. This is, of course, not the situation in the United States, where the income of restaurant servers depends more on gratuities than on wages, and the thing called the tip increases the check by 20%. In the area I live, the standard wage for servers is $2.14/h, representing about 20% of total income. The remainder is gotten via gratuities; thus customers pay most of the server's salary on behalf of the employer. Benefits are rare, and job security is minimal. Servers working on a given evening will receive about $10 from the owner (which is taxed) and are expected to seek the rest from customers. If customers are directly paying the server's salary, why is this called a tip? It is because the use of the term masks the exploitative economic conditions of the employees and makes the exploitation seem to be an act of generosity. It is a casino-like situation without a dependable wage that liberates the proprietor from all social responsibility.

Consumers do not want to be reminded of inequality and exploitation. The innocuous term "tip" and the gentility associated with the "gratuity" enable the customers' amnesia. The practice not only distracts attention from inequality and exploitation, it renarrates them onto a different stage, one where the server entertains a kind and appreciative audience. The term "tip" is anchored in the matrix of American language, thought, and ideology. It habituates Americans not to see exploitative working conditions. And the habituation can make it difficult to see otherwise in other economies. One often hears Americans ask, "Why don't the French tip"? when the reverse is the case. Americans do not tip in restaurants; they pay salaries. The French tip, on occasion, and depending on circumstance. In restaurants, the tip is usually a euro or two. Now the American usage is a semantic extension of the term "tip" to cover an unpleasant economic reality that one would rather not be reminded of. This is the function of metonymies in the psychoanalytic context; they move laterally along the chain of syntagmatic substitutions in order to avoid the stressful meaning, shifting along the semantic field to a safe place.

The term "American exceptionalism" also underwent a semantic shift, and here for ideological reasons, as well. The term "exceptionalism" originates in the Latin *excipere*, literally "to take out". This is readily visible in the phrase "to make an exception", which conveys the original meaning of the term "exceptional" in the sense of "out of the ordinary", "extraordinary", etc. The Romance languages preserve the original meaning of an anomaly, while American English has shifted the meaning from an anomaly to an instance of excellence. The term "exceptional" entered into political currency with the work of Alexis de Tocqueville, in *De la démocratie en Amérique*:

> The situation of the Americans is thus completely exceptional, and it is quite believable that no democratic people will ever get there. Their totally puritanical origin, their uniquely commercial habits, even the country they live in, which seems to divert their intelligence from the studies of science, literature, and the arts; the proximity to Europe, which enables them to completely neglect these studies without relapsing into barbarism; a thousand particular causes, of which I have only come to know the major ones, have, in a unique way, fixed the American spirit in the midst of purely material things…let us stop viewing all democratic nations with the model of the American people, and let us try envisaging them according to their own characteristics.
> 
> (De Tocqueville, 1840, p. 40)

"American exceptionalism" indicates the anomalous situation of the United States and an economic system that no modern industrialized nation is interested in having. Its healthcare "system", unlivable minimum wage, ridiculously high college tuition, ghettos, highly lopsided distribution of wealth, insufficient public transportation, lack of social programs—one could continue almost indefinitely—are the envy of no first-world nation. One can mask this reality by sliding the signifier "exceptionalism" from "anomaly" to "excellence". In doing so, one represses awareness of the socioeconomic problems and replaces it with an image of superiority. Article after article in national journals speaks of either maintaining or regaining American exceptionalism, as in an example from the *New York Times*, in which the author asked,

> Is America exceptional among nations? Are we, as a country and a people and a culture, set apart and better than others? Are we, indeed, the 'shining city upon a hill' that Ronald Reagan described? Are we 'chosen by God and commissioned by history to be a model to the world' as George W. Bush said?
>
> (Blow, 2011)

The author's words reflect the desire to understand exceptionalism as greatness and not anomaly, and this is quite understandable from a psychological standpoint. For instance, imagine the reaction of an American high school student to the following two statements, each taken in isolation:

- you are no longer the best student in school
- no one wants to be like you

It is quite clear which statement would be less threatening to hear. And if one had the option of sliding the signifier one way or another and repressing one of the meanings, it is clear which meaning one would obliterate. Such is the case in the United States, which represses the meanings of anomaly in the term "exceptionalism". This repression is a defense mechanism enabled by the semantic reduction of the term, which also reduces the field of discourse and thought.

Another excellent example in this regard is the employment of the terms "liberal" and "liberalism" in the United States, where their political meanings have also undergone semantic reduction and, in some cases, a reversal of meaning. In the international political polarity of left wing/progressive and right wing/conservative, liberalism has been normally aligned on the right. The word originates in the Latin *liber*, "free", and indicates, in the theater of political economy, a privileging of the individual and the freeplay of individual liberties, a limitation of the power of the state to limit those liberties, and general tolerance.

The *Merriam-Webster Unabridged Dictionary* has a surprisingly traditional definition of liberalism: "a theory in economics emphasizing individual freedom from restraint especially by government regulation in all economic activity and usually based upon free competition, the self-regulating market, and the gold standard ...called also economic liberalism".

It is quite odd that these definitions clash radically with the popular understanding of liberalism in the United States. Most Americans would be quite perplexed on reading them. If someone were to offer such definitions, the assessment would most likely be laughed off outright. The term "liberal" and its derivatives migrated along the chain of associations until it wound up at the opposite end of the American political spectrum. Initially meaning "conservative", it now means "anticonservative". Such a semantic reversal is not uncommon in historical linguistics. For instance, the Indo-European root for the English word "black" actually signified "to shine" or "to burn brightly". Its meaning slid incrementally along the path of things associated with fire, e.g., ashes, and the meaning eventually reversed from light to dark. "Liberal" slid along the line of social issues, indicating permissiveness and tolerance of difference, until the economic basis was eclipsed.

The confusion of the term "liberal" has recently generated the term "neoliberal", in order to illuminate the conservative economic ideology. But "neoliberal" has a weak presence in the vernacular and often elicits confusion, if not cognitive resistance, as the listener is habituated to read "liberal" as left wing, and this habituation acts as a wonderful decoy from imperative issues. This is an inversion that leaves the dominant model unmarked.

Among the semantic shifts in American political vocabulary, one of the most delightful involves the color red. It is also one of the most improbable. The color red has a long history of association with left-wing workers' liberation movements. This became iconic in the late nineteenth century. The flag of the Paris Commune was red. The flag of the Soviet Union was also red, with a hammer and sickle, but it reverted oddly to the white/blue/red colors of Tsarist Russia after the establishment of the Russian Federation in 1991. The flag of China is still red, as is the flag of Vietnam. The fear of left-wing (communist and socialist) activity in the United States, which persisted throughout the twentieth century, generated the terms "red menace", "red scare", "red tide", "red tactics", and many other permutations. The association of the color red with leftism was so common that it produced the nickname "pinko".

This is no longer the case. "Red" now means Republican. One normally points to the year 2000 as the starting point for this "red shift". During the presidential campaign of that year, a cable news network decided to use blue to represent states voting Democrat and red to represent those voting Republican. Thus Texas is now "a red state", and Oregon is "a blue state". For most of the twentieth century, the phrase "he's a red" was unambiguous. It has no currency in the current vernacular, and one would have to asterisk it (★he's a red) as anomalous, whereas the phrase, "voter turnout in red states" is readily understood. The color shift took hold more quickly than the Russian revolution itself. The phrase "red scare" peaked in usage in 2000 and plummeted radically afterward. The phrase "red states" skyrocketed in usage beginning in 2000 (Michel et al., 2010).

"Liberal" indicates left wing, and "red" indicates right wing. Does the confusion of language reflect or determine the confusion of thought? This is a chicken-or-egg question. The answer is that they act in unison and effect a disempowerment of oppositional language. If you do not have words for something, it is hard to talk about it. Especially if your emotional investment limits what you desire to know and hear.

American English has performed a most curious operation on the understanding of literature. It is called "English".

> Tu connais Tolstoï? Oui, j'ai pris un cours de français
> Kennst du Tolstoi? Ja, ich habe einen Deutschkurs genommen
> Conosci Tolstoj? Sì, ho preso un corso d'Italiano
> Ulisoma Tolstoy? Ndiyo, nilijifunza Kiswahili

What are these sentences attempting to do? Something impossible. They are attempting to transculturate the following dialogue I recently heard while passing by two American undergraduates:

> y'know, like, Tolstoy?
> -yeah, I took English

Why is this utterance intelligible and transparent in American English but absurd in any other language? Indeed, had I interrupted and attempted to qualify the utterance and say, "Excuse me, but that was not an English course; it was a literature course", my interjection would have likely been met with utter befuddlement. The United States is the only nation that uses the name of its majority language as a trope for world literature; other nations do not use the name of the national language in this context. In Italy, *italiano* does not mean the study of all world literature, nor does *français* mean that in France. Faculty who teach in departments of allophone (non-English) literatures and cultures continually have to educate the public, and other academics as well, that the degrees they grant are not "in a language", but in the literature, culture, and linguistics expressed in the given language. They continually encounter resistance to the fact that the courses in their majors are content based, and that the content is not just a vehicle for practicing language skills.

The truth is, that in the United States, English studies are but a subset of literary studies, which include texts from many national traditions, such as French, Italian, Chinese, and so on. These texts are studied in their original languages. French studies French texts in French, German studies German texts in German, and so on. This is a fact that Americans have a very hard time understanding. The operative American formulae are: English = literature: French, German, Italian, Russian, Spanish, etc. = languages as skills. Americans are comfortable perceiving English as a clear window to all the world's information. They do not need to know second languages. Someone will translate the ideas expressed in the foreign language into English for them, and the content will be the same. They resist knowing that content could be language specific, because such knowledge threatens the hegemony of their language. And why does the following idea seem counterintuitive in the United States? An American could learn a second language well enough to perform in that language in a manner not qualitatively dissimilar from the manner in which that person performs in English. Why is this idea met with skepticism, denial, and disbelief? The familiar explanations refer to American monolingualism, American isolation(ism), the globalization of English, etc. These are not really explanations, but descriptions, even tautologies, that do not account for the phenomenon of resistance, which can only be explained by psychoanalytic reflection upon ideology and American ethnocentrism. The idea of effective bilingualism is, as well, resisted, because it threatens the hegemony of English. The term "English" underwent massive semantic extension in order to occupy allophone literatures, again, in unison with American postwar expansionism.

There are numerous examples of the type of linguistic relativity that one sees in the terms: tipping, exceptionalism, liberal, red, and English, where words shift meaning in acts of displacement and condensation involving defense mechanisms of repression, sublimation, inversion, and denial. A linguistic relativizing of the phenomenon is strongly resisted, because it problematizes the configuration of national identity. The important aspect here is the fact that the shifts restrict meaning and cognition. Americans will resist seeing exceptionalism as anomaly, tipping as exploitation, liberalism as conservativism, a degree in Italian as a degree in literary studies (but not English), and so on. These are excellent examples of lexical linguistic relativity, in which meaning becomes culturally fixed and resistant to intercultural understanding. It was Michel Bréal who said that every nation is inclined to believe that its language puts words in the right place (Bréal, 2005, p. 156).

It is the dreamwork of psychoanalytic forces that effects the congealing of language and cognition.

# References

Blow, C.M. (2011, November 19). Decline of American exceptionalism. *The New York Times*, 21.
Bonfiglio, T. (2017). *The psychopathology of American capitalism*. Macmillan.
Bréal, M. (2005). *Essaie de sémantique*. Lambert-Lucas.

De Tocqueville, A. (1840). *De la démocratie en Amérique II* (1re et 2e parties). 1840. Un document produit en version numérique par Jean-Marie Tremblay. Accessed February 15, 2017. [English edition: De Tocqueville, A. (2006). *Democracy in America*. Harper Perennial Modern Classics].

Deutscher, G. (2010). *Through the language glass: Why the world looks different in other languages*. Picador.

*Merriam-Webster Unabridged Dictionary*. http://unabridged.merriam-webster.com/. Accessed February 13, 2017.

Michel et al. (2010). *Quantitative analysis of culture using millions of digitized books*. Science (Published online ahead of print: 12/16/2010).

Popper, K. (1934). *Logik der Forschung*. Springer. [English edition: Popper, K. (1959). *The logic of scientific discovery*. Routledge].

Taylor, C. (2016). *The language animal: The full shape of the human linguistic capacity*. Harvard University Press.

*The Oxford English Dictionary*. www.oed.com. Accessed February 13, 2017.

Whorf, B. (1964). "The relation of habitual thought and language to behavior". In J. Carrel (Ed.), *Language, thought, and reality: Selected writings of Benjamin Lee Whorf* (pp. 134–159). MIT Press.

# CONCLUSION

This study has proposed a linguistic configuration of cognition structured by the fundamental mechanisms of psychoanalytic theory: displacement, condensation, overdetermination, inversion, repression, projection, and secondary revision. It has attempted to show that these mechanisms inform the transition from unconscious, to preconscious, and to conscious modes of thought. The origin, production, and processing of language unfold along this transition, arriving at the articulation of language and consciousness, which emerge gradually, incrementally, in reciprocal codetermination, and also in dialog with the construction and maintenance of identity.

In 1897, Michel Bréal, a contemporary of Freud, carefully explained the illogic of language and warned against a configuration of language based on formal logic (Bréal, 2005). In 1967, Charles Hockett (1973) proposed to take seriously Freud's idea that studying slips of the tongue may shed light on the generation of speech. In 1981, Julia Kristeva hoped that a psychoanalytic perspective

> will invade the field of study of signifying systems in general, the semiology that Saussure dreamed of, and that, from that angle, it will modify the Cartesian conception of language and enable science to grasp the multiplicity of signifying systems elaborated in and from *la langue*.
> *(Kristeva, 1981, pp. 276–277)*

This study has sought to contribute to that vision.

It has been shown in these pages that the model of recursion and merge, downloaded from information science and imposed upon language, has only a minimal application to the genesis, production, and processing of language. Recursive extrapolation, e.g., "thinking about thinking about...", is nowhere

DOI: 10.4324/9781003180197-15

infinite in speech; it is limited to four, perhaps five, levels of reflection. A rhizomic model of associative connections needs to be implemented, one that proceeds according to the principal psychoanalytic mechanisms.

The research of Piaget shows that language is acquired in a state of adualism and of the embodiment of language and thought. The persistence of primary, pre-logical processes in the child's conception of thought and language coincides with the critical period for language acquisition, both for *langage* and *langue*, for the engagement of the faculty of language and for the acquisition of what is popularly termed "native fluency" in a given language. This is a phase dominated by echolalia and the pleasure of repetition of sounds, in which the meaning that infuses the word is multivalent and overdetermined by the associations that crisscross among the syntactic elements in the phrase, with little respect paid to parts of speech. There is a homology here between the child's conception of language and thought and the configuration of language and cognition in (adult) dreamwork (Piaget, 1923a, 1923b, 1945, 1947).

Creativity with language comes naturally to children and engages preoperational (primary process) mechanisms, ones that become suppressed in adult cognition, but that are continually present in unconscious and preconscious modes of the processing of language and thought. For adults, these emerge in the act of dreaming, in which preoperational modes become observable once again. Dreamwork seeks phonetic correspondences in indifference to "formal" rules of syntax and grammar. Constructed by fundamental psychoanalytic mechanisms, ideation and language in dream emerge in rebus form, and sequences of phonemes can resonate and recombine randomly. The solidification of morphemes in formal speech is a secondary process imposed upon the random recombination of phonemes. Syntactic conventions become imposed upon the infrastructure of language and restrict and transform dream thoughts (latent) into dream content (manifest). And in the return of the repressed, the primary processes can transgress surface boundaries and generate parapraxes. Secondary revision is the entry port of grammar, as the utterance moves through the preconscious into consciousness. This problematizes the traditional distinction between competence and performance.

The analysis of "musical grammar" by Jackendoff and Lehrdahl (2006) shows that it is not separable from the function of verbal, i.e., nonmusical grammar. In the interconnective perspective on language, cognition, and embodiment described in this study, the structural similarities between musical and verbal grammar open pathways for the entry of play, repetition, and echolalia into a psychoanalytic configuration of language.

The continual unconscious and preconscious processing of language is also visible in speech errors, which offer insight into the production and processing of language. They show the eruption into the surface structure of language by the battery of psychoanalytic mechanisms: displacement, condensation, overdetermination, inversion, repression, projection, and secondary revision.

Freud's investigation of speech errors shows how these mechanisms construct not only language slips, but also misreadings and miswritings, the forgetting of names and sequences of words, and bodily parapraxes, i.e., physical blunders. It is these blunders that reveal the embodiment of language most clearly; they are nascent examples of conversion disorders, in which psychological issues become redirected to the body. In other words, there is a structural homology between motivated linguistic slips and motivated physical blunders.

It is argued here that the processes constituting speech errors occur at the basis of language, and that they can be motivated by psychological factors. Hockett invoked Freud's idea in *The Psychopathology of Everyday Life* that speech errors may hold the key to the nature of language. Proceeding below the threshold of consciousness, the mechanisms underlying parapraxes are continually present in adult speech processing. The mechanisms of motivated and unmotivated speech errors are the same, the difference being that the motivated speech error will favor some phonetic and morphophonemic correspondences over others. Thus the psychoanalytic perspective recommends a suspicious hearing. The psychological motivation may or may not be present, but one should consider the possibility that it may be so.

This study also accesses research that argues for the primacy of allomorphy over morphology. This aligns with a progressive formulation and concretization of morphology in the emergence of language and consciousness, one in which the end result is subject to interruptions from earlier stages. The correspondence of syllabicity, displacement, and condensation with the recent research on morphology (Carstairs-McCarthy, 2005) shows how allomorphy precedes morphology, i.e., how the perception of syllabic rhyme precedes the formation of discrete morphemes. In the evolution of language, the blending of sounds would have been the rule rather than the exception; this is especially true in the child's mind. The blending of sounds is governed by the principal psychoanalytic mechanisms; the blurring of boundaries between adjacent elements would precede grammar and eventually yield to morphemes in the standardizing process.

The function of play in the generation of language has also been demonstrated here. It is clearly evident in the linguistic play of children, both phylogenetically and ontogenetically. The play element in language is clearly connected to the production of speech errors; a continual morphophonemic process of association is common to both. Ritual is discussed within this model, as well, and a comparison is made between the structures of ritual as play and the structures of the linguistic play of children, as well as adults.

The inclusion of research on the function of the formation of identity in the articulation of language and consciousness is also crucial to this study. This relies upon Freud's characterization of the difference between consciousness and the unconscious as a product of the tension between a coherent ego and the repressed information that has been separated from it (Freud, 1923).

Thus repression results from the activity of maintaining a coherent identity, which then enters into the view of consciousness as a linguistic construct. In this view, thought is completed in the word. Freud holds that a perception first enters into the preconscious by a connection to its word-representations. Thinking in images is seen as a quite incomplete form of consciousness, as is inner speech, which clearly lacks the structure seen in the conscious linguistic production.

This is related to Guiora's research on the "language ego" (Guiora, 1991), especially the function of accent in the formation and perception of identity. Research on the primacy of the auditory sphere is used here to demonstrate the construction of self through communication with authority and/or prestige figures. It places the evolution and production and processing of language in a social and ego-psychological situation. Solms spoke of a process of auditory self-reflection in comparison with one's own speech and the speech of parents, i.e., authority and prestige figures. He sees this as the foundation of the super-ego (Solms, 1996). The superego can thus be understood as a sociolinguistic structure emergent in the interactive dynamics of child and parent, both in ontogeny and phylogeny.

Humans understand symbolic reference interactively with other humans. To develop this skill, children must engage in role reversal imitation, put themselves in the place of the adult, and must use a symbol toward the adult in the same way the adult used the same symbol toward them. Children not only imitate the adult, but they also must see themselves in the eyes of that adult. They become aware of themselves as the object of the symbolic gesture. This is a recognition of self as mediated by the gaze of the other, in which they see themselves being seen and take on the role of the observer of themselves. This clearly coordinates with the theory of the mirror stage, as formulated by Lacan (1966).

The expression of language as fundamentally an act of self-consciousness in the dynamic of identity formation is here situated within the field of neurolinguistic research. The research conducted on language in the field of neuro-psychoanalysis (Kaplan-Solms and Solms, 2000; Solms, 1997) is crucial for the understanding of the tripartite structure of language, consciousness, and identity formation. Consciousness is engaged in and through language and is above all a consciousness of self. The authors have also described cerebral pathways that form the physiological basis for the primary process.

The gradual progression of the matrix of language and thought along the continuum of unconscious–preconscious–consciousness is seen as ultimately processed in the frontal lobe and subject to the sequential nature of frontal syntheses; language ultimately enters into predicative and propositional structures, where cognition organizes it in terms of "first this, then that" and "if this, then that" sequences. This transcription into a system of logico-grammatical rules occurs at the final destination of the production of language and thought.

It is in no way present at the origin of language, neither ontogenetically nor phylogenetically. It is not in the nature of language, but in the instantiation in language of cognitive processes of sequentialization and dependency. This constitutes the function of secondary revision, a process that emerges when one recalls the dream, and that imposes a (more) logical structure on the dream narrative. But these rules of grammar and logic are suspended in dream, where one finds a regression to simultaneous (rhizomic), rather than sequential (and hierarchical) forms of synthesis. Dreamwork (the unconscious and preconscious processing of dream) is the locus of cognitive dissonance, a precognitive process that comfortably expresses simultaneous antitheses, contradictions, nominal realism, rebuses, etc.

Moreover, this study recovers Freud's early work on aphasia (1891) and his observation that "the word" is produced by a complex functional system, with a number of component parts, linked (among other things) with the four primary modalities of language: visual, auditory, kinesthetic, and motor. The word is thus a complex neuropsychological entity.

The unity of gesture and speech—their "equiprimordiality"—constitutes the moment of the embodiment of language and is thus the bridge to conversion and conversion disorder (hysteria).

The meaningfulness of gesture occurs when one views one's own actions as if they were those of someone else. Due to the neural interconnectivity of language and gesture, gesture must be present in language, even when not directly visible: It may even surface in some other part of the body. This observation accesses psychoanalytic work on conversion, the process of displacing the mental to the physical, and this also corresponds to the theory of embodied cognition.

McNeill (2012, 2016) has noted the ineluctability of the process of conversion in the gesture–speech dynamic. If gesture is repressed, it remains nonetheless corporealized and emerges through some other part of the body. The element of repression aligns perfectly with the psychoanalytic account of conversion disorder, where the repression of linguistic articulation causes the idea to become embodied in pathological form. Again, consciousness and language are a unity; the blocking of the word–thought intensifies the corporeal displacement.

Everett (2017) posits that a frightened homo erectus may have screamed out a sequence of phonemes, all the while gesticulating and engaging the entire body to communicate what had been seen. Eventually, the early human intonated and emphasized one morpheme over another. This spread by imitation, the emphasized elements became isolated, and this generated grammar and syntax.

Similarly, Bickerton (2009) proposes that human language began when someone came back from the hunt, having found a large carcass, and imitated the sound of the animal. Thus imitation of something not present would have been the beginning of symbolic language.

This description of the development of intonation corresponds to the motivated word segmentations discussed in Freud's analysis of verbal parapraxes, where one segment is emphasized over another (Freud, 1901). It is relevant to note that in the parapraxis, the emphasis on one segment is overdetermined by homophonic connection to highly charged psychological elements, with little attention to morpho-syllabic integrity. The segment gains meaning post-facto when a motivated emphasis becomes placed upon it via homophonic correspondences.

Networks of symbolic and acoustic reference lie at the basis of language, and these interact at the phonetic, morphemic, and lexical levels: Deacon (1997) has observed that the symbolic basis of a word involves the elicitation of other words, even if we do not consciously experience this elicitation, as is evidenced in word association tests. And he notes that the content words that combine in sentences are almost invariably metonymically related to one another. This understanding of the formation of symbolic language corresponds to the psychoanalytic mechanisms of overdetermination and displacement.

The foundational processes of syllable and morpheme in the generation of language were and are furthered by the mimetic and ludic function of human behavior. The aping capacities of the highest primate became co-opted in the development of language. Play involves repetition of base structures, as is evidenced in any game. This must have been facilitated by the emergence of a behavior that took pleasure in repetition and imitation. That is to say that pleasure in repetition would have been selected for. This is a mimetic function, in which laughter becomes contagious. Hurford (2014) devotes a lengthy discussion to mirror neurons and imitation, noting that laughing can be contagious, as can be yawning. Deacon notes this, as well, and proposes that the connection between laughter and humor may be related to the adaptation for symbol learning. This is an astute observation, as jokes and wit require higher-level symbolic reasoning and comprehension. This is especially the case in punning, and most certainly in the reversals found in ironic expression.

Human children endlessly rehearse and refine their own actions. They engage in a form of intentional representation, where an act is used to represent itself. Here, the child is also developing the capacity for metacognition and representation. This also relates to psychoanalytic accounts of play and repetition, especially the repetition compulsion. This is a *mimetic culture*; it can be argued that one is dealing, fundamentally, with a mimetic instinct, not a language instinct.

The recent research on mirror neurons is most valuable for the development of a psychoanalytic linguistics in the context of the production of language via identity/ego formation, especially as concerns embodied cognition and the psychoanalytic notion that the ego is above all a *bodily* ego. Neurological research has shown that reading or listening to a sentence describing a manual gesture activates the corresponding motor representation; this also occurs in the comprehension of abstract and figurative use of language, as in metaphors. Lieberman has demonstrated the embodiment of language within the basal ganglia used for motor coordination. The subcortical circuits involving basal ganglia are also involved in the functional language system regulating speech and comprehension of syntax. In the brain, a highly plastic organ, there is no input-free module, nor are there autonomous neural subnetworks; each receives neural input from other parts of the brain that perform different operations.

Langacker's theory of cognitive grammar proposes a taxonomy of language that recruits the cognitive processes of association and automatization (Langacker, 2008). Association entails psychological connections, an overdetermined matrix of interconnectivity, where one sees the basic condensation involved in the association of a sound with a meaning. In automatization, things become habitual; this can be connected to the mastering evident in the repetition compulsion, in which language can be seen as the expression of a desire to establish a connection. In the discussion of the repetition compulsion, the child's mastering efforts were responses to a disconnection—the absence of the mother—and a desire to compensate for the absence. The syntactic elements in this mastering process are to be noted, as well; the process of repetition and automatization would necessarily include a sequentialization. Langacker holds that ultimately, language needs only semantic, phonological, and symbolic structures. One sees here a configuration of grammar that consists in symbolic relationships among semantic and phonological structures, where syntax is a product of repetition and, ergo, habit.

Calvin and Bickerton (2000) have attempted to derive linguistic structures, especially syntax, from the phenomenon of reciprocal altruism. They place this within the pressure of collaboration, one that recapitulates the theories of the primal horde as expressed by Darwin and Freud. In prehistoric human culture, the dominant male would have monopolized the females in the group. The other males would have been forced to collaborate in order to dethrone the dominant male and share the females. They would have set up a reciprocal social order, in which the sharing of power—the beginnings of morality and democracy—and the structures of language operate in unison. This coordinates very well with the psychoanalytic account of the band of brothers rebelling against the patriarch, as described by Freud (1913), who adds a psychoanalytic moment to the fraternal rebellion—a continuation, in group form, of the oedipal rebellion against the father. One sees here a *psychoanalytic* moment in the development of the structures of in-group collaboration. Cognition of interdependent relationships would have crystallized in the matrix of a grammar/syntax of *language and behavior*.

Lakoff and Johnson's work on metaphor also aligns well with the psychoanalytic configuration of language (Lakoff & Johnson, 1980). Their work illuminates the primacy of unconscious and preconscious processes involved in metaphorical expression and their persistence into adult language and cognition.

The homology of metaphor/metonymy and condensation/displacement is evident in their research. One views here a continuation of concretism in the use of language, despite Piaget's notion that concretism disappears in full adult operationality in language. One sees concretism in the child's understanding of language, in dreamwork, and also in the construction of metaphor in the operational adult.

It is important to emphasize that non-metaphorical speech (if at all possible) can be seen as pedantic and boring. Not only is metaphorical and metonymic speech necessary, it is also preferred. We appreciate the clever trope in language, as well as the quip. This displays *a priori* the ludic basis of language, manipulated in infancy and appreciated in adulthood. Lakoff and Johnson also situate ritual in a context that corresponds well to psychoanalytic theory. Religious rituals are constructions of condensation, displacement, overdetermination, and especially repetition. Ritualistic repetitions unite the group so as to preserve the cultural structures against loss.

Lakoff and Johnson use the term "embattlement" frequently in analyzing conversations.

A speaker can offer an interpretation of an issue and then find it qualified by an interlocutor, who informs the speaker of exceptions to her/his perspective. The speaker, being curious, can then modify the perspective. One could ask where the battle is here, but that would ignore the sublimating aspect of the interchange. Hostility is diffused, sublimated, and deflected by rules of politeness. This is caused by the mechanism of the suppression of instincts, which is foundational in human culture, as Freud (1930) insisted in his work on malaise in human culture. Lakoff and Johnson hold that all rational arguments cloak irrational tactics that the rational arguments are supposed to transcend. Thus the rational argument is a sublimation of the pathos that motivates the argument; they note that thought and reason are mostly unconscious, and they speak at length of a "cognitive unconscious".

This instantiates the psychoanalytic view that acculturation, the "civilizing" of the individual, is a process of containing, suppressing, sublimating, and diffusing aggressive instincts. These examples can be seen as illuminating the irrational basis of the apparently rational, the sublimation of hostility. And this is one of the main points to be gleaned from this study: that metaphors both express and conceal urges that are suppressed from formal discourse and displaced into more acceptable forms.

It is important to note that metaphorical extension is not caused by the insufficient expressive potential of language. In other words, metaphor does not arise because the speaker is consciously looking for another way to say something. Metaphor (and metonymy) emerge from the cognitive linguistic system of displacement, condensation, and overdetermination, embodied along the ineluctable networks of associations among psyche, body, and language. Kövecses argues well that metaphor is simultaneously linguistic, conceptual, social-cultural, neural, and physical. And Bolognesi and Bichisecchi include ego articulation into this process. They hold that a metaphor's ultimate goal is to integrate and validate the identity of the person who produced it.

The embodiment of metaphor recalls Freud's observation that the ego is above all a bodily ego, and that language is the medium for the expression of identity and the articulation of consciousness. The idea that these mechanisms are fundamental to the articulation of identity aids in the understanding of linguistic relativity, for language can configure the individual, social, and national self. This means that information threatening to the configuration of identity will meet with resistance, a resistance to the linguistic understanding of a "foreign" concept.

The chapter on linguistic relativity has examined some alterations of word-concepts and sees them as acts of dissimulation that resist criticism. And in the alterations, one finds psychoanalytic dreamwork mechanisms—especially condensation, displacement, inversion, and denial—that collude in an act of the preservation of national identity. A linguistic relativizing of the phenomena is strongly resisted, because it would threaten that identity; the linguistic shifts restrict meaning and cognition. In the examples cited, Americans will resist seeing exceptionalism as anomaly, tipping as exploitation, liberalism as conservativism, a degree in, e.g., Italian as a degree in literary studies (but not English), and so on. These are examples of lexical linguistic relativity, in which meaning becomes culturally fixed and resistant to intercultural understanding. It is the dreamwork of psychoanalytic forces that effects the congealing of language and cognition. One may extend this beyond lexica to other peculiarities of language, where attachment to the conventions of one's own language act to resist intercultural and interlanguage communication. This is a resistance that would increase with the perception of the apparent eccentricity of the features of the other language in question.

Language consists of a continual and preconscious processing via perceptions, anticipations, and perseverations involving the principal psychoanalytic mechanisms that associate elements within the semantics and phonology of the language in question. These would be the constructions that "sound right" to the L1 speaker. As stated in Chapter 10, Chomsky's assertions (Chomsky, 2002) in the interview on minimalism—that there are no constructions anyway: no passive, no raising, etc., and that there is just the option of dislocating something somewhere else under certain conditions—offer a casino model of the production of language, akin to dice-throwing, where everything is randomly generated by the mechanisms of recursion and merge. The psychoanalytic model proposed in this study offers a more structured account of language production.

Language is a psychological phenomenon, in the largest sense of the term. Its nature is most succinctly indicated in the etymology of the word "psychology".

## References

Bickerton, D. (2009). *Adam's tongue: How humans made language, how language made humans*. Hill and Wang.
Bréal, M. (2005). *Essaie de sémantique*. Lambert-Lucas.
Calvin, W., & Bickerton, D. (2000). *Lingua ex machina. Reconciling Darwin and Chomsky with the human brain*. MIT Press.
Carstairs-McCarthy, A. (2005). The evolutionary origin of morphology. In M. Tallerman (Ed.), *Language origins: Perspectives on evolution* (pp. 166–184). Oxford University Press.
Chomsky, N. (2002). An interview on minimalism. In N. Chomsky et al. (2002). *On nature and language*. Cambridge University Press.
Deacon, T. (1997). *The symbolic species. The co-evolution of language and the brain*. W.W. Norton & Co.
Everett, D. (2017). *How language began*. Liveright.
Freud, S. (1901). *Zur Psychopathologie des Alltagslebens. Über Vergessen, Versprechen, Vergreifen, Aberglaube und Irrtum*. Gesammelte Werke (Vol. 4, pp. 5–321). Imago. [English edition: Freud, S. (1953–1974). *The Psychopathology of everyday life. The standard edition of the complete psychological works of Sigmund Freud* (Vol. 6, pp. 1–279). Hogarth].
Freud, S. (1913). *Totem und Tabu*. Gesammelte Werke (Vol. 9, pp 1–194). Imago. [English edition: Freud, S. (1953–1974). *Totem and taboo. The standard edition of the complete psychological works of Sigmund Freud* (Vol. 13, pp. 7–161). Hogarth].
Freud, S. (1923). *Das Ich und das Es*. Gesammelte Werke (Vol. 13, pp. 235–289). Imago. [English edition: Freud, S. (1953–1974). *The ego and the id. The standard edition of the complete psychological works of Sigmund Freud* (Vol. 19, pp. 13–66). Hogarth].
Freud, S. (1930). *Das Unbehagen in der Kultur*. Gesammelte Werke (Vol. 14, pp. 419–506). Imago. [English edition: Freud, S. (1953–1974). *Civilization and its discontents. The standard edition of the complete psychological works of Sigmund Freud* (Vol. 21, pp. 57–145). Hogarth].
Guiora, A. (1991). The two faces of language ego. *Toegepaste taalwetenschap in artikelen* 41(3), 5–14.
Hockett, C. (1973). Where the tongue slips, there slip I. In V. Fromkin (Ed.), *Speech errors as linguistic evidence* (pp. 93–119). De Gruyter.
Hurford, J. (2014). *The origins of language: A slim guide*. Oxford University Press.
Jackendoff, R., & Lehrdahl, F. (2006). The capacity for music: What is it, and what's special about it? *Cognition* 100, 33–72.
Kaplan-Solms, K., & Solms, M. (2000). *Clinical studies in neuro-psychoanalysis. Introduction to a depth neuropsychology*. Karnac.
Kristeva, J. (1981). *Le langage, cet inconnu*. Editions du Seuil. [English edition: Kristeva, J. (1989). *Language: The unknown: An initiation into linguistics*. Harvester Wheatsheaf].
Lacan, J. (1966). *Le stade du miroir, comme formateur de la fonction du Je, telle qu'elle nous est révélée dans l'expérience psychanalytique*. Ecrits (vol. 2, pp. 93–100). Editions du Seuil. [English edition: Lacan, J. (2006). *The mirror stage as formative of the I function. Ecrits* (vol. 2, pp. 75–81). W.W. Norton].
Lakoff, G., & Johnson, M. (1980). *Metaphors we live by*. University of Chicago Press.
Langacker, R. (2008). *Cognitive grammar: A basic introduction*. Oxford University Press.
McNeill, D. (2012). *How language began. Gesture and speech in human evolution*. Cambridge University Press.

McNeill, D. (2016). *Why we gesture. The surprising role of hand movements in communication.* Cambridge University Press.
Piaget, J. (1923a). *Le langage et la pensée chez l'enfant.* Delacheux & Niestlé.
Piaget, J. (1923b). La pensée symbolique et la pensée de l'enfant. *Archives de Psychologie* 18, 273–304.
Piaget, J. (1945). *La formation du symbole chez l'enfant.* Delacheux & Niestlé.
Piaget, J. (1947). *La représentation du monde chez l'enfant.* Presses Universitaires de France.
Solms, M. (1996). Towards an anatomy of the unconscious. *Journal of Clinical Psychoanalysis* 5, 331–367.
Solms, M. (1997). What is consciousness? *Journal of the American Psychoanalytic Association* 45(3), 681–703.

# GLOSSARY OF RELEVANT PSYCHOANALYTIC TERMS

Arranged thematically. Compiled by the author, with the aid of the *American Psychological Association Dictionary of Psychology* (American Psychological Association, 2022).

**Condensation (Gm. *Verdichtung*):** The fusion of multiple meanings, concepts, or emotions into one image or symbol. Condensation corresponds to metaphor, and the two terms are coterminous in this study. Condensation is particularly common in dreams, but also in daydreams. Along with displacement, it is fundamental to cognition, and to the production and processing of language.

**Displacement (Gm. *Verschiebung*):** The transfer of feelings or behavior from their original object to another person or thing. In psychoanalytic theory, displacement is considered to be a defense mechanism in which the individual discharges tensions associated with, for example, hostility and fear, by taking them out on a less threatening target. Displacement corresponds to metonymy, and the two terms are coterminous in this study. Along with condensation, it is fundamental to cognition, and to the production and processing of language.

**Overdetermination (Gm. *Überdeterminierung*):** The concept that several unconscious factors may combine to produce one symptom, disorder, or aspect of behavior. Because drives and defenses operate simultaneously and derive from different layers of the personality, a single symptom may serve more than one purpose or fulfill more than one unconscious wish. Overdetermination dominates in the unconscious, operates along neurological networks, and creates a multivalent context for verbal meaning, especially as concerns embodied cognition.

**Secondary revision:** A rearrangement of the seemingly incoherent elements of the dream into a form serviceable for narration. This involves logical and temporal reorganization in obedience to the principles of noncontradiction, temporal sequence, and causality, which characterize the secondary processes of conscious thought. It is instrumental in the articulation of speech, especially conscious, reflective speech. (Modified from source: ecyclopedia.com (Cengage; Gale Research)).

**Dreamwork:** The composite action of condensation, displacement, rebus formation, repetition, overdetermination, and secondary revision that transforms the latent dream content into the manifest content. This is a transformation from infrastructure to superstructure. Dreamwork operates at the basis of the codeterminative matrix of language and thought.

**Repetition compulsion:** An unconscious need to reenact early traumas in the attempt to overcome or master them. Such traumas are repeated in a new situation symbolic of the repressed prototype. Repetition compulsion acts as a resistance to therapeutic change, since the goal of therapy is not to repeat but to remember the trauma and to see its relation to present behavior. Connected to repetition as a fundamental mode of cognition.

**Preconscious:** The level of the psyche that contains thoughts, feelings, and impulses not presently in awareness but that can be more or less readily called into consciousness.

**Unconscious:** The region of the psyche containing memories, emotional conflicts, wishes, and repressed impulses that are not directly accessible to awareness but that have dynamic effects on thought and behavior. These proceed into consciousness via the preconscious, which is a crucial process in the formation of language.

**Repression:** A defense mechanism that excludes painful experiences and unacceptable impulses from consciousness. Repression operates on an unconscious level as a protection against anxiety produced by ego-threatening experiences. It also comes into play in many other forms of defense, as in denial, in which individuals avoid unpleasant realities by first trying to repress them and then negating them when repression fails. Repression is fundamental to the articulation of language. To be distinguished from suppression, which is a conscious effort to inhibit awareness of impulses and experiences.

**Primary process:** The unconscious mental activity in which there is free, uninhibited flow of psychic energy from one idea to another, via condensation, displacement, and overdetermination. This mental process operates without regard for logic or reality. Examples are the dreams, fantasies, and magical thinking of young children. These processes are posited to predominate in the unconscious.

**Secondary process:** Conscious, rational mental activities under the control of the ego and the reality principle. It is fundamental to the conscious formulation of language. It is also the process of imposing a logical structure on the manifest recollection of the dream to the extent that the dream that is recalled is far removed from the original dream thoughts.

**Id:** The component of the personality that contains the instinctual, biological drives that supply the psyche with its basic energy or libido. The most primitive component of the personality, it is located in the unconscious. It is dominated by the desire for immediate gratification of instincts, such as hunger and sex, until the ego begins to develop and operate in accordance with reality. See also primary process.

**Ego:** The component of the personality that deals with the external world and its practical demands. More specifically, the ego enables the individual to perceive, reason, solve problems, test reality, and adjust the instinctual impulses of the id to the demands of the superego.

**Superego:** The moral component of the personality that represents parental and societal standards and determines personal standards of right and wrong, or conscience, as well as aims and aspirations. In the classic tripartite structure of the psyche, the ego controls personal impulses and operates by the rules and principles of the superego, which stem from parental demands and prohibitions. The formation of the superego occurs largely through identification with the parents and later with admired models of behavior.

**Projection:** The process by which one attributes one's own individual positive or negative characteristics, affects, and impulses to another person or group. This is often a defense mechanism in which unacceptable impulses, effects, and ideas are attributed to others. It is a denial and a displacement in the maintenance of identity and ego integrity.

**Parapraxis:** An error that can be unmotivated, but if motivated, it expresses unconscious wishes, attitudes, or impulses. Examples of such errors include slips of the pen, slips of the tongue and other forms of verbal leakage, forgetting significant events, mislaying objects with unpleasant associations, unintentional puns, and motivated accidents. Parapraxes reveal the intrusion of preconscious elements into observable language and behavior. They constitute a key to the understanding, production, and processing of language.

**Libido:** Either the psychic energy of the life instinct in general, or the energy of the sexual instinct in particular. In his first formulation, Sigmund Freud conceived of this energy as narrowly sexual, but subsequently, he broadened the concept to include all expressions of love, pleasure, and self-preservation.

**Conversion disorder (initially called "hysteria", but that term is now outdated):** A disorder, in which patients present with one or more symptoms or deficits affecting voluntary motor and sensory functioning that suggest a physical disorder but for which there is instead evidence of psychological involvement. These conversion symptoms are not intentionally produced or feigned and are not under voluntary control. Symptoms can include paralysis, loss of voice, blindness, seizures, disturbance in coordination and balance, and loss of pain and touch sensations.

**Transference:** An unconscious repetition of earlier behaviors and their projection onto new subjects. In therapy, it involves a patient's displacement or projection onto the analyst of those unconscious feelings and wishes originally directed toward important individuals, such as parents, in the patient's childhood. This process brings repressed material to the surface where it can be reexperienced and studied.

# INDEX

accent 103; acquisition of 106; American 105; anglophone 97; audition of 101; British 105; function of 103; and identity 98; as in-group identity 106; maintenance of local 98; non-native 99, 102; subliminal perception of 105
*Adam's Tongue, How Humans Made Language, How Language Made Humans* (Bickerton) 167–168
adjectival past participles in German 155–156
adualism 40, 198; stages of development in 41–42
affective language ego 99
affective motivation 76, 90
agglutination in inner speech 63
Aitchison, J.: "Lexical Storage and Retrieval: A Developing Skill?" 88
algorithmic models of language 3, 142, 144, 145, 149, 150
allocentric (conventional) speech 63
allomorphy 83, 163, 199
American accents 105
American English 190, 191, 194
American exceptionalism: semantic shift in term 190–192, 195
analog *vs.* digital language models 83–84
Anglo-American analytic philosophy 181, 182
animism 42
anosodiaphoria 116
anosognosia 116, 117

anticipations 7, 56, 68, 71, 83, 86, 96, 157, 159, 160, 205
aphasia 3, 112–114, 122, 201
Arbib, M. 124
arithmetic progression and recursion 23
association in cognitive processes 156
associative learning 143, 144
associative linking function 116
Attardo, Salvatore: *Linguistic Theories of Humor* 76
audioverbal modality: relation to consciousness of 109
auditory perception and ego formation 95, 113
auditory self-reflection 109, 172, 200
autism 25
automatization in cognitive processes 141, 156, 157, 203
"Awareness of Language: Some Evidence from What Children Say and Do" (Clark) 48–49

Baars, Bernard: *A Cognitive Theory of Consciousness* 37
Baldwin effect 137
*Basic Problems of Neurolinguistics* (Vygotsky) 112
Bates, E. 104; "Beyond Phrenology: Brain and Language in the Next Millennium" 143
belladonna: word as condensation in motor parapraxis 74

Bellah, Robert: *Religion in Human Evolution* 154
Berthoud-Papandropoulou, Ioanna: "An Experimental Study of Children's Ideas About Language" 49
Berwick, R.: *Why Only Us. Language and Evolution* 31
"Beyond Phrenology: Brain and Language in the Next Millennium" (Bates and Dick) 143
*Beyond the Pleasure Principle* (Freud) 123
Bichisecchi, Roberto 205; "Metaphors in Dreams: Where Cognitive Linguistics meets Psychoanalysis" 185
Bickerton, D. 170, 172, 201, 203; *Adam's Tongue, How Humans Made Language, How Language Made Humans* 167–168; *Lingua Ex Machina. Reconciling Darwin and Chomsky with the Human Brain* 84
Bierce, Ambrose 21
binary distinction of thought *vs.* language 4, 94
Bingham, Paul M.: "On the Evolution of Language: Implications of a New and General Theory of Human Origins, Properties, and History" 30
blending 78, 79, 84, 199
bodily ego 95, 98, 136, 138, 205
Bolognesi, Marianna 205; "Metaphors in Dreams: Where Cognitive Linguistics meets Psychoanalysis" 185
Boltraffio 69; segmentation of 70
Boomer, D. 80
Bosch, Hieronymus 97
Bréal, Michel 5, 10, 11, 19, 195, 197; *Essaie de sémantique* 10; language and formal logic 13–14; language originates in subjectivity 15; misprisions override lexical categories 12; origin of relative pronoun 12–13
Breuer, Josef 127
British accents 105

Calvin, W. 170, 172, 203; *Lingua Ex Machina. Reconciling Darwin and Chomsky with the Human Brain* 84
"The Capacity for Music: What Is It, and What's Special about It?" (Jackendoff and Lehrdahl) 65
Carruthers, P.: "The Evolution of Consciousness" 30
Carstairs-McCarthy, A.: "The Evolutionary Origin of Morphology" 83

*Cartesian Linguistics* (Chomsky) 132, 149, 184–185
Cartesian school 132
casino model of language 160, 205
Catania, A. Charles 185
categorization: cognitive processes in 156, 157
"Categorization of Action Slips" (Norman) 88–89
causality: misattribution of 11
causation 177–178
child's conception of language 6, 43, 198
Chomsky, Noam 43, 79, 119, 140, 148, 160, 205; *Cartesian Linguistics* 132, 149, 184–185; genesis of human speech 33; "An Interview on Minimalism" 147; language evolution 34; *The Minimalist Program* 153; model of brain 144; native speaker authority 59; "Some Simple Evo Devo Theses: How True Might They Be for Language?" 34; *Why Only Us. Language and Evolution* 31
Clark, Eve V.: "Awareness of Language: Some Evidence from What Children Say and Do" 48–49
classical mathematics as objectivist model for language 182
*Clinical Studies in Neuro-Psychoanalysis. Introduction to a Depth Neuropsychology* (Kaplan-Solms and Solms) 112
closed vowels and gesturing 136
clothing: emergence of 166–167
cognition: flexible 162; of interdependent relationships 203; linguistic configuration of 197; multivalent perspective on 165; restructuring of 166
cognitive dissonance: phenomenon of 87
cognitive functions: and recursion 23; of psychoanalytic mechanisms 88; sociocultural 159; non-insularity of 165
cognitive grammar (CG) 156, 159, 203
*Cognitive Grammar: A Basic Introduction* (Langacker) 156
cognitive language ego 99
cognitive linguistics 9, 108, 177, 183, 204
cognitive metaphor 158, 174
cognitive repression 116–117
cognitive science and metaphor 183, 185
*A Cognitive Theory of Consciousness* (Baars) 37
cognitive unconscious 8, 185, 204
Cohen, A. 59; "Errors of Speech and Their Implication for Understanding the Strategy of Language Users" 83

colorless green ideas sleep furiously 158
communicative model of language 25
competence and performance 58, 79, 159, 198
complex symbolic network 16
computer science: recursion in 22
conceptual metaphors and psychoanalysis 185–186
conceptual metaphor theory (CMT) 185
concretism in use of language 175, 204
concretization 41, 199
condensation 63; and displacement 76; and dystaxia 60; matrix of 168; as metaphor 162; processes of 116; as *Verdichtung* 2
*conscience du moi* 40
conscious memory 123
conscious mind as verbal analog 27
conscious modes of thought and language 44
consciousness 108, 200; cognitive theory of 37; conception of 27; development of 40; discourse of 28–29; in ego 92; emergence of 199; features of 27–28; function of 130; Jaynes's view of 29; fundamental metalinguistic unit of 43; language and 38; literal and overdetermined embodiment of 109; materialist element to 28; nature of 166; *sine qua non* of 27; permeability of 92; subjective experience of 166
conscious–unconscious relationship 93
constructed cognitive unawareness 116
conversion 127; in gesture–speech dynamic 128, 201; of psyche into soma 142, 159; psychoanalytic work on 201
conversion disorder (hysteria) 112, 127, 201; and transference 8
Corballis, Michael 30–31, 33, 36; *The Recursive Mind: The Origins of Human Language, Thought, and Civilization* 21–22
covert language prestige 106
creationism 185
critical period for language acquisition 1, 42, 198
Cuccio, V.: "The Paradigmatic Body: Embodied Simulation, Intersubjectivity, the Bodily Self, and Language" 139
*The Cultural Origins of Human Cognition* (Tomasello) 129
cultural transmission 129; executive function of 131
"Culture and Biology in the Origins of Linguistic Structure" (Kirby) 169–170

*cum hoc ergo propter hoc* 11, 14
Cutler, A.: "The Reliability of Speech Error Data" 85

Dante Alighieri: *De vulgari eloquentia* 33
Darwin, C. 5, 7, 10, 144, 168, 171, 203; *The Descent of Man* 154; *On the Origin of Species* 30, 154; primal horde of 7, 71, 203
*Das Ich und das Es* (Freud) 3
*Das Unbehagen in der Kultur* (Freud) 176
Deacon, Terrence 163–166, 202; *The Symbolic Species. The Co-evolution of Language and the Brain* 163
decentering 45, 46
defense mechanisms 5, 8, 36, 37, 54, 62, 92, 122, 123, 130, 192, 195
*De la démocratie en Amérique* (Tocqueville) 191
Derrida, Jacques 87
Descartes, R. 21, 140, 149
Deutscher, Guy: *Through the Language Glass: Why the World Looks Different in Other Languages* 188–189
*De vulgari eloquentia* (Dante) 33
De Weerd, H.: "Negotiating with Other Minds: The Role of Recursive Theory of Mind in Negotiation with Incomplete Information" 26
Dick, F.: "Beyond Phrenology: Brain and Language in the Next Millennium" 143
*Die Traumdeutung* (Freud) 2, 52–53
diplopia *see* double vision
*Discontinuous Syntax: Hyperbaton in Greek* (Devine and Stephens) 15
displacement: condensation and 76; dreamwork process of 69; errors 58; matrix of 168; processes of 116; as *Verschiebung* 2
distributed network in functional language system 142, 143
ditransitives 131
Donald, Merlin: "Mimesis and the Executive Suite: Missing Links in Language Evolution" 132–134
*Doppelgänger* 55
double vision 88
"Dream of the Botanical Monograph" 53
dreams: basic anxieties of 53; in transition to consciousness 54; language errors in 59; logical relations in 61; narration of 53; presence of nonsense neologisms in 55, 59; speech disturbances in 56; words in 55

dreamwork 201; structural differences between transformational grammar and 58
dreamwork language processing 57
Dunbar, Robin 24, 25; "On the Origin of the Human Mind" 23–24
dystaxia: condensation and 60

Eagleman, David: *Incognito: The Secret Lives of the Brain* 109, 115
*Early Social Interaction* (Forrester) 5, 93
echolalia 43, 66, 103, 198
economic liberalism 192
ego 16, 40; constitution of 95; dynamics of formation of 95; language and consciousness in 92; mediating functions of 110; part of mental apparatus 95; process of formation of 100; secondary process and structuralization of 119; self-contradictory nature of 118; transcendental 30
*The Ego and the Id* (Freud) 18, 92, 93, 100, 110, 113
egocentric language 42–43
egocentric (idiosyncratic) speech 63
egocentrism 42
ego formation: psychoanalytic theories of 36
ego-ideal 95
ego psychology 129
Ellis, Andrew 86; "On the Freudian Theory of Speech Errors" 85
embedding 24, 26; degree of 33; infinite 37; in reading process 25
embodied cognition 201; investigations of 140
embodied ego 95, 97
embodiment: of language 198, 199; of metaphor 186, 205; of thought 198
emotional memory 123–124
encyclopedic semantics and cognitive grammar 157
English 190, 193–195; ideological use of the term 194–195
English translations: problems with 71–72
equiprimordiality 201; and growth point hypothesis 127; of speech and gesture 126, 128
"Errors of Speech and Their Implication for Understanding the Strategy of Language Users" (Cohen) 83
*Essaie de sémantique* (Bréal) 10

Everett, D. 152–153, 201; *How Language Began: The Story of Humanity's Greatest Invention* 22, 161–162
*Ever Since Darwin* (Gould) 5
*Eve Spoke* (Lieberman) 141–143
"Evidence That Accent is a Dimension of Social Categorization, Not a Byproduct of Perceptual Salience, Familiarity, or Ease-of-processing" (Pietraszewski and Schwartz) 103–104
"The Evolutionary Origin of Morphology" (Carstairs-McCarthy) 83
"Evolutionary Psychological Approaches to Dream Content" (Valli and Revonsuo) 62
evolutionary theory 5
"The Evolution of Consciousness" (Carruthers) 30
evolution of eye 169
"Evolution: The Pleasures of Pluralism" (Gould) 168–169
exaptation: of functional sensorimotor processes 139; phenomenon of 35; of syllables for syntax 83
"An Experimental Study of Children's Ideas About Language" (Berthoud-Papandropoulou) 49
externalization in the minimalist model 31, 32

"The Faculty of Language: What Is It, Who Has It, and How Did It Evolve?" (Hauser, Chomsky, and Fitch) 21
falsifiability 86, 189
Ferri, F.: "Schizophrenia, Bodily Selves, and Embodied Simulation" 138
"Finding the Body in the Brain. From Simulation Theory to Embodied Simulation" (Gallese) 140
Fitch, W.: "Three Meanings of 'Recursion': Key Distinctions for Biolinguistics" 22
fixed language identity 97
flexible cognition and symbolization 162
FLS *see* functional language system (FLS)
fluidity of identity 97, 101, 106
forgetting: of foreign words 70; of names 68–72, 199
formal language 17; emergence of 141
formal linguistics 16
Forrester, John: *Language and the Origins of Psychoanalysis* 10, 127
Forrester, Michael: *Early Social Interaction* 5, 93

*fort/da* problem 123
Frank, S.: "How Hierarchical Is Language Use?" 32
French language: ambiguity of *point* 11; pronouns 96; pronunciation 106
"'Freudian Slips' and Semantic Prearticulatory Editing" (Motley) 87–88
Freudian theory and falsifiability 86
Freud, S. 1, 4–7, 17, 27, 37, 40, 54, 58, 59, 61, 62, 64, 75, 81, 106, 108, 112, 127, 138, 143, 197, 200, 203; analysis of verbal parapraxes 162, 202; *Beyond the Pleasure Principle* 123; conflicting tendencies in speech errors 73; *Das Ich und das Es* 3; *Das Unbehagen in der Kultur* 176; *Die Traumdeutung* 2, 52–53; *The Ego and the Id* 18, 92, 93, 100, 110, 113; essay on value of psychoanalysis for science of language 52; imagistic cognition 119; mechanisms for humor 76; notion of primary narcissism 42; *The Outline of Psychoanalysis* 115, 121; on presence of nonsense neologisms in dreams 55; primal horde of 7, 71, 203; *The Psychopathology of Everyday Life* 15–16, 19, 46, 68–70, 87, 199; psychopathology of speech errors 68; "Slips of the Tongue" 77, 80; on symbolism in dreamwork 110; *Totem und Tabu* 171; work on aphasia 201
Fromkin, Victoria 87, 88; "Grammatical Aspects of Speech Errors" 76–77; "The Non-Anomalous Nature of Anomalous Utterances" 84–85; *Speech Errors as Linguistic Evidence* 77
fully operational stage 6
functional language system (FLS) 141–142, 203
Furth, Hans G.: "Symbol formation: Where Freud and Piaget Meet" 50
future tense: metonymy in creation of 132

Gallese, V.: "Finding the Body in the Brain. From Simulation Theory to Embodied Simulation" 140; "The Paradigmatic Body: Embodied Simulation, Intersubjectivity, the Bodily Self, and Language" 139; "Schizophrenia, Bodily Selves, and Embodied Simulation" 138
Galletti, Johann Georg August 57
generative grammar 18
*Genesis* 33
Gentilucci, M. 136

geometric progression and recursion 22
German language 12; passive use of present active participle in 155, 156; syntactic habits of 57; words in dreamwork 55–56
gesture 127; and body language 159; and conversion disorder 201; equiprimordiality with speech 126, 128; imagery component in 128; intonation and 7; meaningfulness of 201; and mimesis 126–128, 134; pronunciation and 137; and speech 128, 136, 163, 201; symbolic 200; and words 136
gesture–speech dynamic: conversion process in 128, 201
gesture–speech equiprimordiality 128
gesture–speech unity 128
Ghazali, L. 118
Gombert, J. 46
Gould, Stephen J. 154; *Ever Since Darwin* 5; "Evolution: The Pleasures of Pluralism" 168–169
grammar 161; baroque intricacies of 183; configuration of 159–160; defined as 148; and dreamwork 58; of language and behavior 172; and morphology 156; minimalist program as safe space for 147
"Grammatical Aspects of Speech Errors" (Fromkin) 76–77
Greatrex, T.: "Projective Identification: How Does It Work?" 122–124
Greek language: study on syntactic variability in 15
group organization and language 103
growth point hypothesis (GP) 127, 128
Guiora, Alexander 99, 101, 105, 130; natural bilinguals 102–103; "A Psychological Theory of Second Language Pronunciation" 100; research on language ego 200; "The Two Faces of Language Ego" 97–98

Hartmann, Ernest: "The Nature and Functions of Dreaming" 62
Hauser, M. 21; "The Faculty of Language: What Is It, Who Has It, and How Did It Evolve?" 21
Heine, Heinrich 81
*Herr* as condensation in parapraxis 69, 70
Heynick, Frank 59; *Language and Its Disturbances in Dreams* 58
hierarchical configuration of language 32–33

Hill, Archibald A.: "A Theory of Speech Errors" 82
Hockett, Charles 15, 79, 80, 84, 85, 197; "Where the Tongue Slips, There Slip I" 77–78
homo erectus 162, 163, 166, 201
Hopi language 188
"How Hierarchical Is Language Use?" (Frank) 32
*How Language Began. Gesture and Speech in Human Evolution* (McNeill) 126
*How Language Began: The Story of Humanity's Greatest Invention* (Everett) 22, 161–162
Huizinga, Johann: *Homo Ludens. A Study of the Play Element in Culture* 81
human oral anatomy 154
Humboldt, Wilhelm von 9
humor: enigmatic connection between laughter and 166; mechanisms for 76; mutual exclusivity in 118; primacy of 81
Hurford, James R. 166, 202; *The Origins of Language: A Slim Guide* 143, 166–167
hyperbaton 15

icon, index, and symbol 163, 166
id 8, 62, 121
identity: construction of 97, 98, 109; establishment of 102; pronunciation and 93, 97–103, 106; role in articulation of language and consciousness 197, 199
identity formation 108; dynamic of 200; function of 199; function of auditory sphere in 110; self-contradictory nature of 118
imitation: as beginning of symbolic language 167, 201
incest taboo 110
*Incognito: The Secret Lives of the Brain* (Eagleman) 109, 115
indexicality 163, 166
Indo-European languages 12, 13
Indo-European roots: semantic extension in 193
inequality and exploitation: repression of awareness of 191
infinite recursion 33, 38
information-processing model of speech production 85
infrastructure 2, 10, 58, 76, 198
in-group identity formation 64
inner speech 60, 119–120; semantic features of 63; transgressive fluidity of 64

innocent jokes 81
"An Interview on Minimalism" (Chomsky) 147
intonation: development of 202; and gesture 7; and morphology 152
intransitive verbs as predating transitives 12
inversion 1, 5, 8, 15, 18, 61, 190, 193, 195, 197, 198, 205
Isakower, O. 110

Jackendoff, R. 21, 23, 64, 76, 150, 154, 198; "The Capacity for Music: What Is It, and What's Special about It?" 65
Jaeger, Jeri: *Kid's Slips: What Children's Slips of the Tongue Reveal About Language Development* 89
Jakobson, Roman 2, 3, 76
James, William: *Psychology. Briefer Course* 29
Jaynes, Julian 28, 36, 186; *The Origins of Consciousness in the Breakdown of the Bicameral Mind* 27, 183–184; view of consciousness 29
*je* and *moi* (pronouns) 96
Jespersen, O. 79
Johnson, M. 8, 116, 132–133, 172, 175, 176, 179, 180, 182, 183, 203, 204; *Metaphors We Live By* 174
jokes: psychoanalytic mechanisms in 18

Kant, I. 30
Kaplan, B. 61; *Symbol Formation: An Organismic-developmental Approach to Language and the Expression of Thought* 59–60
Kaplan-Solms, K. 108, 114, 116, 117, 120, 121; *Clinical Studies in Neuro-Psychoanalysis. Introduction to a Depth Neuropsychology* 112
Karlsson, Fred 37
Karmiloff-Smith, A. 130
Kenneally, C. 65, 158, 168–170, 185
kettle joke: as example of cognitive dissonance in speech 87
*Kid's Slips: What Children's Slips of the Tongue Reveal About Language Development* (Jaeger) 89
kinship systems as language-dependent 151
Kirby, Simon: "Culture and Biology in the Origins of Linguistic Structure" 169–170
Kolinsky, R. 46–47
Kövecses, Z. 163; *Language, Mind, and Culture* 175

Kraeplin, Emil 58; examples of compression and condensation 57; *Über Sprachstörungen im Traume* 56
Kristeva, Julia 17, 19, 197; *Language: The Unknown: An Initiation into Linguistics* 16
Kurvers, J. 46

Labov, W. 98
Lacan, J. 16, 18, 62, 109; concept of mirror stage 98, 138; *Le stade du miroir* 95–96
*La formation du symbole chez l'enfant* (Piaget) 45, 51
Lakoff, G. 8, 116, 132–133, 172, 175, 176, 179, 180, 182, 183, 203, 204; *Metaphors We Live By* 174; *Philosophy in the Flesh. The Embodied Mind and Its Challenge to Western Thought* 184
Lane, C. 145
Langacker, R. 157–159, 203; *Cognitive Grammar: A Basic Introduction* 156
*langage* 16, 18, 42, 198
language 3; abstract knowledge of 46; acquisition of 42; alliterative dynamics of 78; arbitrary elements in 154; articulation of repressions in 5; beginning in subjectivity 15; casino model of 160, 205; and cognition 151; communicative model of 25; comparing music with 65; concretism in use of 175, 204; configuration of 93, 182; conscious modes of thought and 44; and consciousness 38; continual unconscious and preconscious processing of 198; and conversion disorder 127, 142, 199; creativity with 198; development of 1; dynamic nexus of 128; in ego 92; embodiment of 88, 198, 199; emergence of 199; empiricist *vs.* nativist concepts of 150; evolution of 34, 163, 199; expression of as act of self-consciousness 200; faculty of 150; and formal logic 13–14; formation of 93; function of 116; function of play in 199; genesis of 19, 112; grammar and vocabulary of 99; hierarchical configuration of 32–33; influence of computer science on configuration of 22; literal and overdetermined embodiment of 109; meditation on 140–141; and memory 184; metaphoric configuration of 179; mimetic configuration of 37; mimetic foundation for 132; modalities of 201; modular configuration of 60; multivalent perspective on 165; musicality of 76; nucleus of 152; operationality in 40; organic nature of 10; origin and development of 40; overgeneralization of term 158–159, 168; preformal and preconscious generation of 58; processing of 19, 69–70; as product of formal logic 19; progression along matrix of unconscious–preconscious–conscious 200; *prosodic* aspects of 64–65; psychoanalysis and 19; psychoanalytic configuration of 32; in psychoanalytic framework 10; psychoanalytic model of 16; psychoanalytic understanding of 58; psychoanalytic view of 29; rebus (picture puzzle) in, basis of formation 53; relationship between thought and 49; rhizomic configuration of 19, 38; rules of 148; scientific study of 9; in service of psyche 12; study in clinical situation 110; taxonomy of 156–157; teaching of 23; thought *vs.* 94; transmission in mimetic context 129; of the unconscious 52; unconscious and preconscious processing of 66; unconscious workings of 175; underdevelopment of 63; usages of 15; as virus 163, 170
language acquisition 92, 103, 156, 170; atrophying of 104, 106; critical period for 1, 42, 198
*Language and Its Disturbances in Dreams* (Heynick) 58
*Language and the Origins of Psychoanalysis* (Forrester) 10, 127
"Language and the Psychoanalytic Process: Psychoanalysis and Vygotskian Psychology. II" (Wilson and Weinstein) 62
*The Language Animal: The Full Shape of the Human Linguistic Capacity* (Taylor) 189–190
language ego 125, 130; boundaries of 102; research on 200
language gene mutation 34
language gene saltation theory 30
*Language, Mind, and Culture* (Kövecses) 175
language processing 46, 51, 59; modularity in 133; placement of 4
*Language: The Unknown: An Initiation into Linguistics* (Kristeva) 16
"Language, Thought, and Interiorization. A Vygotskian and Psychoanalytic

Perspective" (Wilson and Weinstein) 49–50
*langue* 16, 18, 42, 198
*La nuova scienza* (Vico) 179–180
*La représentation du monde chez l'enfant* (Piaget) 40
Latin: adverbs in 11; nouns and pronouns in 14
Laver, J. 80
LeDoux, Joseph 123
Lehrdahl, F. 76, 198; "The Capacity for Music: What Is It, and What's Special about It?" 65
*Le langage et la pensée chez l'enfant* (Piaget) 42–43
*Le stade du miroir* (Lacan) 95–96
lexical awareness of illiterates 43
"Lexical Storage and Retrieval: A Developing Skill?" (Aitchison and Straf) 88
lexicon and CG 156; and UG 157
liberal: misunderstanding of term 190, 192–195
liberalism: misunderstanding of term 192, 193, 195
libido 8
Lieberman, Philip 203; *Eve Spoke* 141–143; *The Unpredictable Species* 143
*Lingua Ex Machina. Reconciling Darwin and Chomsky with the Human Brain* (Calvin and Bickerton) 84
lingualizing process 122
linguistic habituation 84
linguistic insecurity 98
linguistic relativity 178, 179, 186, 188, 195, 205; and dreamwork 190; as expressed ideologically in lexica 190–195; psychoanalytic perspectives on 190
linguistics 9; analytic philosophy and 181, 182; recursion in 21; relation between psychoanalysis and 16
*Linguistic Theories of Humor* (Attardo) 76
literacy 41, 43, 46, 48, 88, 152, 164
logico-grammatical concepts 116
logico-grammatical rules 110, 121, 200
Luria, A. R. 110, 112

MacKay, D.: "Mental Diplopia: Towards a Model of Speech Perception at the Semantic Level" 88
managerial metaphors 116
"May-Beetle Dream" 54
McGilvray, James 34, 150; "On the History of Universal Grammar" 148

McNeill, David 126–128, 201; *How Language Began. Gesture and Speech in Human Evolution* 126; *Why We Gesture. The Surprising Role of Hand Movements in Communication* 128
McWhorter, John 154
Mead, George Herbert: *Mind, Self, and Society from the Standpoint of a Social Behaviorist* 126
Mead's loop 127, 128
memory confusion paradigm 104–105
"Mental Diplopia: Towards a Model of Speech Perception at the Semantic Level" (MacKay) 88
mental life *(Seelenleben)* 27
merge (as combined with recursion) 148–150, 152, 197, 205
Meringer, R. 68, 72, 74, 80, 81; *Versprechen und Verlesen* 71
*Merriam-Webster Unabridged Dictionary* 192
metacognition 23, 28, 96, 126, 166
metalinguistic knowledge of illiterates 164
metalinguistic language algorithm 150
metaphor 203–204; as an unconscious process 175, 183–185; as basic to cognition 179; as condensation 175, 177, 185, 186; as consolidation of identity 186; contradictory aspects of 183; embodiment of 186, 205; function in dreams 186; ineluctability of 175; and linguistic relativity 178, 179, 186; and literalism 176; and sublimation 177
metaphorical extension 53, 63, 129, 177, 179, 186, 204
metaphoric configuration of language 179
"Metaphors in Dreams: Where Cognitive Linguistics meets Psychoanalysis" (Bolognesi and Bichisecchi) 185
*Metaphors We Live By* (Lakoff and Johnson) 174
metonymy 100; as displacement 57, 75, 80, 100, 175, 204; dominance of 57; homology of 175, 204; identity and 58
Meyer, C. 68, 72, 74, 80, 81; *Versprechen und Verlesen* 71
Mill, John Stuart 114
mimesis: in acquisition of language 134; precedes language 132; and recursivity 126, 130; role in evolution of facial expressions 137
"Mimesis and the Executive Suite: Missing Links in Language Evolution" (Donald) 132–134
mimetic culture 202

mimetic function 166, 202
mind-body dichotomy 112, 140, 179, 184
*Mind, Self, and Society from the Standpoint of a Social Behaviorist* (Mead) 126
minimal consciousness and language acquisition 40
*The Minimalist Program* (Chomsky) 153
mirror neurons 186; investigations of 140; research on 136, 202; self-referential quality of 186
mirror stage 96–98, 109, 117, 130, 138, 200
misreading 73, 74, 199
miswriting 73, 199
Monsieur 13 août 98–99
morphemes 69, 162, 165, 201; bound 69; diminutive 70; foundational processes of 202; free 69, 70; structural and formal processing of 72
morphology 18, 46, 83, 84, 156, 199
Mosher Sex-Guilt Inventory Test 87
motherese 33
mother tongue: ideology of 179
Motley, Michael T.: "Freudian Slips' and Semantic Prearticulatory Editing" 87–88
*Mrs. Dalloway* (Woolf) 26
musical grammar 65, 66, 198
musicality of language 66, 76

narrow language faculty (FLN) 21, 139, 152, 153
native fluency 42, 198
native pronunciation 101
natural bilinguals 102–103
natural science methodology: characterization of 149
"The Nature and Functions of Dreaming" (Hartmann) 62
neglect syndrome 116
"Negotiating with Other Minds: The Role of Recursive Theory of Mind in Negotiation with Incomplete Information" (De Weerd) 26
neo-capitalism 174
neoliberal 193
neuro-biological approach to language 132
"Neurology, Freud, and the Inner Ear" (Ramachandran) 116–117
neuro-psychoanalysis 108, 200; and projective identification 122; research on 125
neuroscience 108; cognitive 132

*New Frontiers in Mirror Neurons Research* (Ferrari and Rizzolatti) 136, 137
*New York Times* 192
"The Non-Anomalous Nature of Anomalous Utterances" (Fromkin) 84–85
nonlinguistic asymbolic signals in animal communication 60
non-localizable physiological disorders 112
nonverbal parapraxes 88
Nootka 61
Norman, Don: "Categorization of Action Slips" 88–89

oedipal stage 63, 171, 203
Ong, Walter 48
"On the Evolution of Language: Implications of a New and General Theory of Human Origins, Properties, and History" (Bingham) 30
"On the Freudian Theory of Speech Errors" (Ellis) 85
"On the History of Universal Grammar" (McGilvray) 148
"On the Origin of the Human Mind" (Dunbar) 23–24
ontological metaphors 175
open vowels and gesturing 136
*The Origins of Consciousness in the Breakdown of the Bicameral Mind* (Jaynes) 27, 183–184
*The Origins of Language: A Slim Guide* (Hurford) 143, 166–167
orthography 11, 33, 41, 43, 46, 52
*An Outline of Psychoanalysis* (Freud) 121
overdetermination 1, 4, 5, 7, 8, 10, 18, 32, 38, 52–55, 58, 59, 62, 78, 84, 88, 113, 141, 145, 156–158, 160, 164, 177, 185, 197, 198, 202, 204
*Oxford English Dictionary* 190

pan-animism 42
parabolic dental arcade 154
"The Paradigmatic Body: Embodied Simulation, Intersubjectivity, the Bodily Self, and Language" (Gallese and Cuccio) 139
parapraxes: and conventional fluid speech 79; gap in theory of 89; physical 68; verbal and nonverbal 88
para-semantic words 60
perception-consciousness system 108
perceptual information: internal and external 121; structuralization of 122

perseveration 7, 56, 68, 71, 83, 157, 159, 160, 205
"A Pessimistic Estimate of the Time Required for an Eye to Evolve" (Nilsson and Pelger) 169
philology: status of in nineteenth century 9
*Philosophy in the Flesh. The Embodied Mind and Its Challenge to Western Thought* (Lakoff and Johnson) 184
phrenology: recent instances of 44
Piaget, Jean 5, 38, 40, 62, 198; on concretism 175, 204; *La formation du symbole chez l'enfant* 45, 51; *La représentation du monde chez l'enfant* 40; *Le langage et la pensée chez l'enfant* 42–43; on persistence of unconscious and preconscious motivation 45; on stages of development 41; on syncretism 42; on transition from assimilation to accommodation 46
Pietraszewski, D.: "Evidence That Accent is a Dimension of Social Categorization, Not a Byproduct of Perceptual Salience, Familiarity, or Ease-of-processing" 103–104
Pinker, S. 21, 23, 64, 143, 150, 154
Pirahã language 161
plasticity of brain 5, 145
polysynthesis 61
polysynthetic language 46, 61–62
Popper, K. 86
*post hoc ergo propter hoc* 12
poverty of stimulus argument 164
preconscious 2, 6–8; fluid continuum from unconscious to 44; generation of language 58; linguistic repertory 80; modes of thought 90; motivation in adult 45; transition to conscious 141
preconscious language processing 57, 66, 198, 205
predicative and propositional structures 111, 200
"Predicting Slips of the Tongue" (Wells) 83
prefrontal brain region 110
prefrontal cortex 165
preoperational stage 45
prescriptivism 168
primal horde of Darwin and Freud 7, 71, 203
primary processes 58, 64, 87, 118, 120, 198
prior affective meaning 63
projection 1, 5, 8, 41, 95, 118, 197, 198; adult 41; in construction of self 122–123; defense mechanism of 122; in infant's neurological propensity 123; mental 109; neuro-psychoanalytic work on 122; and projective identification 122
"Projective Identification: How Does It Work?" (Greatrex) 122–124
pronoun: primacy of 12
pronunciation 93, 97–103, 106; and ego boundaries 101; and gesture 137; of vowels 136–137
prose: relation to verse and memory 163–164
protolanguage 84
psyche 3, 10, 12, 40, 92, 121, 142
psychoanalysis: misunderstanding of 1; and language 19; marginalization of 37; relation between linguistics and 16–19
psychoanalytic linguistics 202; development of 136
psychoanalytic model: of language 16; of repression 115
psychoanalytic theory 44, 182–183; fundamental mechanisms of 197
psychological motivation in slips 71, 74, 81
"A Psychological Theory of Second Language Pronunciation" (Guiora) 100
*Psychology. Briefer Course* (James) 29
*The Psychopathology of Everyday Life* (Freud) 15–16, 19, 46, 68–70, 87, 199
psychosomatic disorders: psychosocial perspective on 118
puns as appreciated by children 49

Ramachandran, V.: "Neurology, Freud, and the Inner Ear" 116–117
rebuses 2, 52, 53, 70, 198
rebus-like writing system 52
reciprocal altruism 171, 172, 203
recursion 21; cognitive function of 23; in computer science 22; configuration of memory and 36; discourse of 28–29; infinite 33, 38; and infinite hierarchy 38; issue of 21; and merge 152; model of 38; in reading process 25
recursion mutation 34
recursive language 151
recursive metacognition 138
*The Recursive Mind: The Origins of Human Language, Thought, and Civilization* (Corballis) 21–22
recursivity 139, 158; function of 130
red as political term 190, 193–195

reflective meta-discourse 130
*The Relation of Habitual Thought and Behavior to Language* (Whorf) 188–189
relative clauses 13, 21–23, 152
relative pronoun: origin of 12–13
"The Reliability of Speech Error Data" (Cutler) 85
*Religion in Human Evolution* (Bellah) 154
REM sleep 62
repetition compulsion 123, 134, 203
representational redescription 130
repression 62, 89, 192, 200; basis of 62–63; and coherent identity 93; psychoanalytic model of 115; and word representations 94
Revonsuo, A.: "Evolutionary Psychological Approaches to Dream Content" 62
rhizomic configuration of language 19, 38
rhyme in language acquisition 163–164
rhyming words: adult and child production of 47
ritual and displacement (metonymy) 182–183
ritual and overdetermination 204
Rizzolatti, G. 124
Rizzuto, Ana Marià 110, 143
role-reversal imitation 7, 130, 200
Rothschild, Baron 81
Rüegg, Walter 9

saltation 30, 34
saltation theory 31
Sanskrit 9
Sapir, Edward 188
Sapir–Whorf hypothesis *see* Whorf hypothesis
Saussure, Ferdinand de 10, 52, 164–165
schematization and cognitive processes 156, 157
"Schizophrenia, Bodily Selves, and Embodied Simulation" (Gallese and Ferri) 138
schizophrenics 138–139
Schwartz, A.: "Evidence That Accent is a Dimension of Social Categorization, Not a Byproduct of Perceptual Salience, Familiarity, or Ease-of-processing" 103–104
secondary process: in articulation of language 141; of ego 119; psychoanalytic concepts of 79
secondary revision 54, 58, 59, 66; function of 201; process of 122

self-consciousness 108, 200; audioverbal modality and 109
self-embedding 22, 23
self-mirroring 97, 125
self: perception and construction of 36
self-presentation 102
self-recognition 28, 96, 133
self-reflection 23, 130, 200; auditory 109, 172, 200; as origin of the symbolic 200
self-representation 98
semantic motivations in speech errors 76
sequentialization 119, 203; cognitive processes of 111, 201
sex-error spoonerisms 87
sexual anxiety: and dreamwork 54; and speech errors 87
sexual object and identity formation 100
*Signor* as condensation in parapraxis 69, 70
slips of the tongue *see* speech errors
social categorization as determined by language 104–105
social cognition 132
Solms, M. 108–112, 114, 116, 117, 120, 121, 162; *Clinical Studies in Neuro-Psychoanalysis. Introduction to a Depth Neuropsychology* 112
"Some Simple Evo Devo Theses: How True Might They Be for Language?" (Chomsky) 34
spandrels 168–169
spatialization metaphors 175
speech 127, 128; as analog rather than digital 83; equiprimordiality with gesture 126, 128; unity with gesture 201
speech acquisition 110
speech disturbances in dreaming 56
speech errors 55–57, 59, 66, 198–199; collection of 89; condensation in 72; mechanisms of 69; psychoanalytic configuration of 84; psychoanalytic framework for 89; psychoanalytic study of 77; psychological motivations in 81; psychopathology of 68; and slips of pen 74; tendency of research on 85
*Speech Errors as Linguistic Evidence* (Fromkin) 77
speech sounds: transcendental properties of 82
spoken language and audioverbal construction of identity 109
Steiner, George 66
Stephens, L.: *Discontinuous Syntax: Hyperbaton in Greek* 15

Straf, M.: "Lexical Storage and Retrieval: A Developing Skill?" 88
structuralization: of ego 119; of perceptual information 122; of thought 119
structural metaphors 174
subjective conscious mind: and language 27
subjectivism 181
sublimation 65, 177, 195, 204
sugar–alcohol group study on pronunciation 101
Sumerian language 38
superego 95, 117, 200
superstructure 2, 10, 58, 76
suppression 71, 106; phenomenon of 116
supralaryngeal vocal tract (SVT) 154
survival of the fittest 154
syllables and the genesis of language 163, 165, 202
syllogisms and relation to literacy 48
symbol 163–167; formation of 45, 50, 51; as context-free referent 130
*Symbol Formation: An Organismic-developmental Approach to Language and the Expression of Thought* (Werner and Kaplan) 59–60
"Symbol formation: Where Freud and Piaget Meet" (Furth) 50
symbolic cognition 35
symbolic communication 163
symbolic gesture 130, 200
symbolic language 127, 201
symbolic play 45, 51
*The Symbolic Species. The Co-evolution of Language and the Brain* (Deacon) 163
symbolism 2, 18, 34, 70, 111
symbolizing: as core of language 162; and prehistoric emergence of clothing 166
symptom pool in psychosomatic illness 118
syncretism 42–44
synecdoche 3
syntactic mechanisms for encoding meaning 154
syntax 148, 156, 158–160; and basal ganglia 141–143, 203; as imposition upon infrastructure of language 58, 198; of language and behavior 172; and matrisomes 141; mutation for 161; and reciprocal altruism 172, 203; as repetition 7

talking bodies 16
Tattersall, Ian 35

Taylor, Charles: *The Language Animal: The Full Shape of the Human Linguistic Capacity* 189–190
tendentious jokes 81
tension and resolution in musical grammar: dynamic of 66; sinusoidal alternation of 65
theory of mind (ToM) 25, 26, 27, 30, 124, 126, 129; social cognition and 132
"Theory of Mind and Experimental Representations of Fictional Consciousness" (Zunshine) 24–25
"A Theory of Speech Errors" (Hill) 82
thought: conscious modes of language and 44; embodiment of 198; formation of 93; *vs.* language 94; progression of matrix of language and 200; rebus (picture puzzle) in formation of 53; relationship between language and 49; structuralization of 120
"Three Meanings of 'Recursion': Key Distinctions for Biolinguistics" (Fitch) 22
*Through the Language Glass: Why the World Looks Different in Other Languages* (Deutscher) 188–189
tipping: ideology of term 190, 191, 195
Tocqueville, Alexis de: *De la démocratie en Amérique* 191
Todorov, Tzvetan 76
Tomasello, Michael 17, 130; *The Cultural Origins of Human Cognition* 129; self/non-self mirroring and reversal 131
totemism 171
*Totem und Tabu* (Freud) 171
transcendental ego 30
transference 5, 8, 136
transformational grammar *vs.* dreamwork 58
transpositions 56, 68, 71, 82, 83, 180
"The Two Faces of Language Ego" (Guiora) 97–98

*Über Sprachstörungen im Traume* (Kraeplin) 56
UG *see* universal grammar (UG)
unconscious 4–5; cognitive theory of 37; of language 66; signifying system of 17; in songs 75; transformational dynamic of 10; transitional phenomenon between conscious and 19
unconscious hostility as motivating parapraxis 74
unconscious internal psychological conflicts 78

unconscious language processing 57
unconscious motivation in parapraxes 74, 85
unconscious–preconscious–conscious processes 2, 200
universal grammar (UG) 147, 148, 157; formulations of 22; nuclear program of 150; proposals for 149; theory of 86, 166
*The Unpredictable Species* (Lieberman) 143

Valli, K.: "Evolutionary Psychological Approaches to Dream Content" 62
verse, rhyme, and meter 163–164
*Versprechen und Verlesen* (Meringer and Mayer) 71
Vico, Giambattista: *La nuova scienza* 179–180
visual cortex 142, 145; and syntactic processing 145
vocalizations of significant others as constitutive of language 109
vowels: pronunciation of with gesture 136–137
Vygotsky, Lev 4, 49, 93, 94; *Basic Problems of Neurolinguistics* 112; visual perception 50

Weinstein, L. 4, 64, 93–95; "Language and the Psychoanalytic Process: Psychoanalysis and Vygotskian Psychology. II" 62; "Language, Thought, and Interiorization. A Vygotskian and Psychoanalytic Perspective" 49–50
Wells, Rulon: "Predicting Slips of the Tongue" 83
Werner, H. 61; *Symbol Formation: An Organismic-developmental Approach to Language and the Expression of Thought* 59–60
wheel: invention of 35
"Where the Tongue Slips, There Slip I" (Hockett) 77–78
Whorf, B. 61, 188; *The Relation of Habitual Thought and Behavior to Language* 188–189
Whorf hypothesis 188
*Why Only Us. Language and Evolution* (Chomsky and Berwick) 31
*Why We Gesture. The Surprising Role of Hand Movements in Communication* (McNeill) 128
Wilson, A. 4, 64, 93–95; "Language and the Psychoanalytic Process: Psychoanalysis and Vygotskian Psychology. II" 62; "Language, Thought, and Interiorization. A Vygotskian and Psychoanalytic Perspective" 49–50
Woolf, Virginia: *Mrs. Dalloway* 26
word-concepts and linguistic relativity 190, 205
word play 44, 106, 128
word-representation 93–95, 115, 122, 200; visualization of 113
words: composite nature of 84; in dreams 55; German language 55–56; gestures and 136; linguistic definition of 46; illiterates' conception of 48; as overdetermined psycho-physical products 112–113; para-semantic 60; perception of 49; *vs.* visual image 49–50

Žižek, Slavoj 62
Zunshine, Lisa 25–26; "Theory of Mind and Experimental Representations of Fictional Consciousness" 24–25

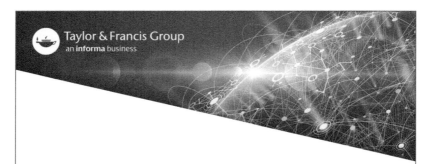